# The Hazards of Nation Building

*Nurturing Competing Visions*

John Gai Yoh

Copyright © John Gai Yoh
Published by Africa World Books, 2018.
ISBN 978-0-6482591-7-6

Cover design, typesetting and layout:
All in One Book Design, Western Australia

All rights reserved. No part of this publication may be reproduced, stored in retrieval system, or transmitted, in any form or by any means without the prior written permission of the author, nor be otherwise circulated in any form of binding or cover other than that in which it is published and without a similar condition being imposed on the subsequent purchaser.

# Table of Contents

| | | |
|---|---|---:|
| Acknowledgements | | 5 |
| Dedication | | 7 |
| Preface | | 9 |
| Introduction | | 12 |
| *Chapter One* | The Epidemic Fear of Change in Sudan | 15 |
| *Chapter Two* | How Sudan Central Governments in Khartoum Underdeveloped Southern Sudan? | 29 |
| *Chapter Three* | Politics of War and Peace in the Sudan | 41 |
| *Chapter Four* | Peace Initiatives in Sudan and Lessons Learned (1984-2002) | 56 |
| *Chapter Five* | Scenarios of Alliances among Sudanese Stakeholders during the interim Period | 108 |
| *Chapter Six* | The CPA is born: What should (not) be done… | 137 |
| *Chapter Seven* | Homecoming of a hero to an enemy's den | 144 |
| *Chapter Eight* | Building the capacity and mobilizing human resources for development | 158 |
| *Chapter Nine* | What lessons the SPLM leadership must learn from the Formation of Governments? | 166 |
| *Chapter Ten* | The CPA: Five Years to go to Referendum | 173 |

| | | |
|---|---|---|
| Chapter Eleven | Prospects of Sustaining the Naivasha consensus in Sudan | 184 |
| Chapter Twelve | Challenges and Opportunities for the Implementation of the CPA: Personal Reflections | 188 |
| Chapter Thirteen | Challenges of service delivery and infrastructure development in Southern Sudan | 206 |
| Chapter Fourteen | Culture, Conflict and Reconciliation in Sudan | 221 |
| Chapter Fifteen | The Cairo Massacre: A Model for Neighborhood Relations? | 227 |
| Chapter Sixteen | "Attractive Unity": A minimum goal towards the establishment of the New Sudan | 237 |
| Chapter Seventeen | The Second SPLM National Convention: Looking beyond the 25th Anniversary | 245 |
| Chapter Eighteen | Managing daunting agenda of unity and peace in Sudan | 254 |
| Chapter Nineteen | Two years to go for referendum | 267 |
| Chapter Twenty | The history of the twin objectives: New United Sudan and Self-Determination | 281 |
| References | | 291 |

# Acknowledgements

WRITING ABOUT PEACE PROCESSES AND SPECULATING ABOUT THE PROSPECTS and challenges of any peace agreements is one of the challenging intellectual exercises, especially if the commentator is not directly involved on day-to -day activities of these processes. I have had the privilege to advise, facilitated behind the scenes and interacted at various occasions with people who were involved with peace making in Sudan. For almost eighteen years I have followed and read about the conflict in the country.

I have written extensively about it, and shared some of my writings with friends, relatives and the general public. Some of my commentaries were presented to and pubished by different fora online and in journals or newspapers.

After attainment of independence of South Sudan on the 9th July 2011 following the successful referendum as stipulated by the Comprehensive Peace Agreement (CPA), several friends encouraged me to publish some of these papers into a book form, to enable a wider readership access them.

These articles were written to address specific issues related to war and peace politics during the period between 1983 and 2011. The contexts in which they were written varied depending on the issues at stake in those particular times. I did not alter the contents of the articles, so that the reader may appreciate the circumstances of the issues discussed.

Several friends and relatives made it possible for me to publish this book. My brother, Farouk Gatkuoth Kam, took the burden of constantly reminding me to publish these papers into a book form.

One of my mentors and friend Prof Korwa Adar was instrumental in convincing me that it is intellectually correct to be generous with one's works with his readers. Many other friends encouraged me to publish the articles. I am indebted to all of them.

# Dedication

John Garang De Mabior,
William Nyuon Bany
Keribino Kwanyin Bol
Arok Thon Arok
John Kulang Puot
Nyachigak Nyachiluk
Galario Modi
Lual Diing Wol

# Preface

ONE OF THE DIFFICULT SITUATIONS THAT COMMENTATORS OFTEN FIND themselves in, is when critizing their own organizations through critical examination of the pros and cons of their national politics. The beauty of this exercise though lies in the nobility of being genuine and the commitment to the type of transformation of the organisation that one is calling for. Being a cadre and active member of the Sudan People's Liberation Movement, mostly dealing with underground activities, I have found myself confronted with three choices in relation to the Movement's political and ideological activism: to submit fully to the hierarchy of the movement, complying with all the regulations without questioning the correctness or lack of them; openly critique some of the policies of the movement constructively, with the view to transform some of these shortcomings even if the leadership feels it is out of the order, or decide to oppose the leadership, if it refuses to accommodate my views. It was natural that I chose the second option to constructively critique the SPLM's views for the wellbeing of the organization.

The Sudan state have been in crisis for too long, and rarely did any of numerous political organizations in the country took the risk and the burden to debate, fight and negotiate for the transformation of the country from a dedicated military coup prone underdeveloped state to a viable democratic country; and from a religious fanatic and racist state to a multi-cultural and multi-religious tolerant state. Since independence, apart from the secessionist leanings of the Anya Anya movement in the south, only the Sudan People's Liberation Movement/Army (SPLM/A) dared to challenge all the shades of Sudanese political spectrum to transform the country into a viable economic and political democratic and secular country, where citizenship is the criteria for belonging to a nation.

It was not an easy task for the SPLM/A to shoulder the burden of the transformation given that it grew up in South Sudan where challenges of political and socio-economic marginalization over weight the flight of the rest of the country in the hands of sectarian and militarist regimes in Khartoum. It was therefore natural that the SPM/A should face ideological and organizational challenges, some of which this author was and continues to be critical of.

The Comprehensive Peace Agreement (CPA), which was signed in Nairobi in January 2005 and the period leading to its signing, became a subject of headed debates among observers and commentators on Sudanese affairs, and for the past twenty six years, this author devoted a significant time to debate some aspects of war and peace in Sudan. In some instances, the author's views reflected frustration either on the manner in which the peace processes were handled, or indeed the pace with which the subsequent peace agreements were implemented. Yes, Sudan crisis has always been complex, and would require a sober mind to figure out some of its delicate dynamics. However, even within that complexity, the history of the conflict itself, there were chances that one can understand the over all framework, through which any opportunity can be grasped to resolve the inter-connected puzzles. The CPA gave an opportunity to do just that.

In the same way that the causes of the North-South conflict were identified through the CPA, it was equally possible to delineate the causes of conflicts in Darfur, Nuba Mountains, Blue Nile, Eastern Sudan and far north, because they all centered on socio-economic deprivation and political marginalization by the riverine elites in the centre, who used Arab culture and Islam as basis for political legitimacy to cling to power in Sudan.

Issues of economic and political development, services delivery, cultural equality and security sector reforms are but some of the issues that any peace agreement should handle. In many ways, the CPA had attempted to address these issues and provided frameworks for the implementation.

What this book has tried to do is to trace the peace processes in Sudan since 1984, which culminated in the signing of the CPA in 2005. It contains commentaries on various aspects of the conflict in Sudan, the peace processes as well as processes of implementing the CPA since January 2005, culminating in the establishment of Government of Southern Sudan (GOSS), the body that run the affairs of South Sudan during the interim period (November 2005-July 2011).

# Introduction

The history of politics in Sudan has always been the history of demands and complains to negotiate the future basis and conditions for the state and nation building and co-existence of various nationalities in the country.

While the Sudanese disagreed on many aspects of the state they inherited from the British, it seems that they all agreed that one of the achievements for which the British could be accredited for was that they left Sudan with efficient administrative system, good education system and professional army and police systems. Indeed the British Government managed to create a functioning state at least in Northern Sudan.

It was up to the Sudanese therefore, to build a state and a nation that is for all the Sudanese people irrespective of their race, religion, ethnicity or cultural background. The demand for dialogue over the future of co-existence had faced fierce resistance from the establishment, particularly the sectarian organizations in Sudan. The resistance manifested itself in terms of military confrontations, imposed cultural and sectarian hegemony, political maneuvering and ethnic chauvinisms. Even when efforts were exerted to discuss serious political and economic issues pertaining to post independent Sudan, the tendency was not to respect the agreements reached upon by all.

The Sudanese psychology was quit often, manifested in form of fear of change and lack of nationalism. The Sudanese endeavor to forge Sudan for all was always frustrated by the tendency to look on religion and culture as forms of national identity. Islam and the Arab culture were equal to being a Sudanese and therefore, anybody who was not affiliated to these two characteristics of Sudan was always projected to be a non-Sudanese.

The disagreements over who is a Sudanese or what does it mean to be a Sudanese, degenerated over time, into lack of agreement on the identity of Sudan. Are Sudanese Africans or they are Arabs? Which one comes first, being a Muslim or a Sudanese? The wrong answer to these pertinent questions often resulted in long civil wars between the center and the peripheries or the marginalized regions of Sudan. The main theatre of the conflict was Southern Sudan where identity conflict was understood to be the center of the Sudanese conflict.

Furthermore, the identity crisis had alienated big segment of Sudanese people from Southern Sudan as well as other regions who were considered, though Muslims, not Arabs culturally. This identity question was detrimental factor in the conflict, particularly in terms of the developmental of programs within the country, where some regions of Sudan particularly in the South, West, East and far North did not benefit from development and resources of the country.

In fact, the economic hegemony by the riverine elites or "Arab Sudanese" manifested itself in various rebellions from peripheral regions of Sudan and continued from 1955 to date. The project of "Sudan nation" was therefore aborted and all the attempts to reach agreement among Sudanese were faced with resistance by the riverine aristocracy whose alternative project was the establishment of an "Islamic Arab State".

The Sudanese national project was therefore, destined to fail because it was limited to difficult choices: an "Arab Islamic nation" or "African nation", neither of which makes the people of Sudan "Sudanese." The inherent hazards of nation building in Sudan seem to have left no room for alternative options to find acceptable blocks and pillars on which a new nation could be built. Moreover, one of the paradoxes of the Sudanese politics was that the national elites have a short memory and do not learn from annals of their history. In fact, all the Sudanese, whether from the north, south or west, have the same psychology: they think the same way on issues and lack organizational commitment. They do not believe in ideology or in a collective national agenda. Instead, they are subjective in their thinking or believe in super natural ideology or external interventions. They think that problems must solve themselves or someone else will.

These kinds of belief systems commit the Sudanese elites to pursuing their personal and not public interests. This might explain why their negotiations on national issues tended to gear towards personal gains than public interests. That is why the period extending from 1955 to 2011, when South Sudan gained its independence, the wars that were fought witnessed splits and counter splits among political and military organizations in the North and in the South because personal interests were more important than the national interests.

The tendency to work against what unite people has degenerated the country into situation where unfairness in distributing services and development, becomes a right of few individuals in the country. This entails that, among the Sudanese elites, very few take time to think beyond their own generations, and have little confidence in the future.

This book therefore, gives samples of political behavior of the leaderships in the country and the lack of accountability and collective responsibility in Sudan.

CHAPTER ONE

# The Epidemic Fear of Change in Sudan

ONE OF THE IRONIES IN SUDAN IS THAT WHENEVER SYMPTOMS OF CHANGE surfaced in the political scene, or the alliances between/among politicians changed, or when the centers of powers shifted or whenever the political tricks and maneuvers reached deadlock; or whenever a major revolution/uprising takes place or when an important peace settlement is worked out; and whenever the hopes of the Sudanese people reached the highest stages for a final true change; the irony remains: nothing really changes!

There are lots of expectations about major changes in the country expected from the ongoing peace process in Kenya, and perhaps another consensual dispensation will emerge from this process sometime soon. The question that every Sudanese seems to be interested to get an answer for is: will things be different this time round, in terms of participatory and people-centered politics and policies? Will a true change come about this time, or once the euphoria is over, things will go back to the 'business as usual' system: the patronage politics and the business of war?

A political conscious visitor to Sudan would not miss to observe how Sudanese politicians, the majority of whom are articulate in expressing and showing off their democratic credentials, tend to do exactly the opposite of what they preach.

As teenager in the 1980s, I was surprised by the Southern Sudanese politicians boasting about their democratic experiment during the Local Autonomy era (1973-1983), especially parliamentary politics in Juba. In fact, Southern Sudanese politicians by 1982, were openly boasting that the South was the cradle of democracy in Sudan, thanks to Addis Ababa Consensus, and that the true democracy was in the South, where opposition groups had to wait patiently for the next round of elections, while the ruling party, or rather 'the ruling group' was constantly checked through parliament by the opposition.

While this political experience was happening in the South, we are told that the North was run by General Jaafar Nimeiri and his associates, exercising a brutal military dictatorship, through patronage alliances between the riverine middle class, religious elite leaders, security operatives and army generals over the rest of the country through Sudan Socialist Union, SSU, the then ruling party.

While the above state of affairs was to some extent expressive of what was happening in the country in 1970s and early 80s, what we had in Southern Sudan could best be described as 'periodic electoral exercise', and not necessarily an exercise of democracy, a necessity which the Addis Ababa Consensus brought about, and one doubts whether Uncle Abel Alier or General Joseph Lagu and other stakeholders in the South, most of whom were members of the SSU, would have done otherwise.

The politics of 'Rumbek old boys' in the South, as some of my colleagues prefer to call them, represented the first ever experience for the Southern Sudan first and second generations to physically run a government in the South, and from those ten years a lot of good lessons would have been learned. Moreover, the experiences of Southern Sudanese exile politics in the 1960s, as pioneered by Sudan African National Union (SANU) factions, and the Southern Sudanese 'liberal age politics' of the Southern Liberal Party, Federal Party and Southern Front had a wealth of experience, which would have made the period of 1970s and early 80s unique in the manner in which Southerners would have exercised 'participatory politics', whose focus should have been indeed the ordinary Southerners in their villages, and not the labor migrants in urban centers, as was the case during the Local Autonomy era and later on in the 1980s and 90s.

Throughout the years of 'Juba power centers alliances' era, politics in the South were conducted through four contradictory political flat forms: General Nimeiri secret agents and his Southern allies in the South; the Southern Front elite group; SANU-inside elite group; and the 'bush guys', the Anya Nya leaders. While political grouping system would have been a healthy political exercise and a means of consolidating alliances among Southern political activists, especially that General Nimeiri banned all the political parties in the country when he came to power in May 1969, the major impediment in that system was that it lacked purpose and had no clear objective as to what the vast majority of Southern Sudan population expected from each of these informal political groupings. The dominant party in the country was SSU, and every leader in the South who had political ambitions had to enroll in that party, and thus the allegiance of active politicians in the South was to SSU and its leader, General Nimeiri. Those who had reservations about how politics were conducted in Juba ended up in Nimeiri's jails.

One obvious weakness of Southern Sudanese politicians in 1970s was that they did not take time to work ways and means to bring up an alternative and politically conscious young leadership. They did not bother to nurture and mentor a generation, which would do and look at things differently.

As a primary school boy in 1970s, and like many of my generation, I was oriented to give my absolute allegiance to President Nimeiri and his May revolution. Sadly enough, and as young as ten year olds, we were forced by our teachers to vote in the referendums, which were held to endorse Nimeiri's Presidency in his one-man presidential elections.

Later, having understood what that exercise meant, one wondered how did the President and his Southern allies, looking back in time, would ethically speaking justify forcing teens to vote in Presidential elections.

We were not taught for example the political history of Southern Sudan and its people. As teens, we were forced by our teachers and SSU operatives in the South to sing for and praise General Numieri, at least three times a year (1st January, 3rd March and 25 May).

We were not in fact taught for example to appreciate that the Local Autonomy was a hard won achievement through which every Southern Sudanese family had paid some high price. Regretfully, we did not hear our leaders emphasising that the Addis Ababa Consensus forced the North to recognize, for the first time, recognition embodied in the 1973 Constitution, that the people of Southern Sudan were a distinct entity.

Another disappointment to those who lived in urban centers in the South during the Local Autonomy era was the lack of printed media, at least in the three Southern provinces capitals, apart from Sudanow, a magazine, which did not reach, on time, other cities outside Juba. Looking back to those days, one wonders, how the regional government could have kept the Southern Sudanese public opinion, especially the literate one, informed about government policies and programs without newspapers.

Even printed media in local Southern Sudanese vernaculars was not encouraged. This situation might have explained, partly, the lack of intellectual activity and why most Southern Sudanese politicians and technocrats in the main Southern cities, used to spend most of their time either taking alcohol or playing cards.

Needless, to mention that both private and public printed media houses, which were mainly located in Khartoum, did not bother to open branch offices in the South, or even in other regions outside Khartoum.

As school boys and girls we were not encouraged to ask questions such as who Southern Sudanese are or indeed who are Sudanese, what make an individual a Sudanese: a history, colour, religion, or ethnic belonging? Or why did the South go to war against the North in the 1950s and 60s? The leaders of the South in 1970s and 80s did not encourage us to discuss the topical issues of unity and secession or whether the South is indeed capable of running its affairs, and what lessons to be learned from the 1960s, 70s and 80s of the liberal and exile experiments? We were not made to appreciate the extent to which the Southern Sudanese educators worked hard in the 1970s to introduce education almost in every Southern Sudanese village. It was after 1981, that secondary school students became involve in discussing politics, it was then that we came to know that indeed, South Sudanese politicians did hve their secret forums where they discuss the future trends of South-north relations.

During the Addis Ababa Agreement era, we expected to learn at schools about our cultural heritages, instead we were taught through "al-tar'biya al-wataniya', or 'national guidance' course, to appreciate Arab culture and Islamic customs. Whose false was it?

Dr Mahieddin Al-Sabber, the minister who was in charge of Arabizing the educational system in the South, whose mission was to consolidate 'National Unity', could not be blamed by Southerners for doing his job well. The majority of leaderships of the South in the 1970s, were not, it seemed, interested in bringing up generations whose loyalty should have been to South Sudan or to Sudan for that matter, and even if some of them were interested, perhaps they did not know how to go about achieving that goal or simply were not organized enough to make a breakthrough. The idea of creating a Sudanese identity would have been a good start if South Sudanese politicians in 1970s opted to pioneer it.

However, the Addis Ababa Consensus era, had also important aspects, which are worth mentioning. Some of the major achievements of 'Juba politics' included the fact that Southern Sudanese of different ethnic and communal backgrounds were introduced to each other in big numbers for the first time.

For example, the regional government introduced the system of diverse transfer of officials, where technocrats from different communal backgrounds were transferred to other parts of the South, where in some instances it was the first time for these communities to meet someone from a different Southern community or area. This was equally true of some South Sudanese being sent to other parts of Sudan where they served and came to know other Sudanese cultures.

That system was effective in bringing Southerners together. Campus and domitory life also brought Southerners together, to the extent that some of these students forged long-term friendships, which, apart from marriages between different communal groups, were later on transformed into political alliances.

Another important contribution made by the Local Autonomy governments was expansion of scope of education throughout the South, with a significance improvement in the quality of education. Southern Sudanese teachers were trained to teach at various levels of education. Schools for girls, at various levels were established and education in general reached places, which in the past were isolated zones of cronic illiteracy. The current leadership of the South, especially those in their 30s, 40s and 50s, owe much of their educational achievements to the Addis Ababa Consensus era. Domitories in Rumbek. Loka, Malakal, Atar, Malek, Ombili secondary schools were instrumental in nurturing the concept of 'Southerness'

The question, which begs for an answer is, if a ten year peace settlement could achieve this much in integrating Southern Sudanese people and in expanding educational system, what more would that peace agreement achieved had it been extended to over twenty or thirty years?

Looking back to the 1970s and early 80s, one wonder sometimes what would have happened to me and thousands of colleagues, had Southern Sudanese leaderships decided to build in us a sense of national belonging to South Sudan. Most of us who went to schools in 1970s and 80s, became leaders of the South, whether inside the country or in the liberation struggle.

There are today tens of commissioners, ministers and governors from Southern Sudan who are in their 30s and 40s, most of who graduated from high schools and from higher education institutions at home and abraod. There is a good number of them who are senior political and militarty officers in SPLA/M, who will be the ones certainly shouldering the rebuilding of the South during the envisaged interim period arrangements as stated in the Machakos and Naivasha Protocols of July 2002 and November 2003 respectively.

What we are trying to drive at is that the majority of the fourth and the fifth generations in the South were not mentored nor were they made ready to take over the reign of power in the South by the three previous Southern generations of politicians and technocrats.

Politics of patronage system which the North introduced in the South in 1970s, 80s, and later on became well established in 1990s, entailed that a Southern politician or technocrat does not need to be loyal to his people or to the Southern national cause nor was he obliged to work for the interests of his people, as long as he/she has a patron in Khartoum, who can transform him/her into an important leader in the South anytime.

This kind of politics was obviously inherited by the SPLA/M and its various factions, where it is observed that loyalty to the leader of the faction is more important than loyalty to the revolution or to the cause. This might explain, partly of course, why the constant shift of political loyalty/allegiance in the South became a semi-accepted phenomenon during the past three decades.

Patronage system in Northern Sudan, as has always been the case in party politics in central governments, is a well documented case, since the mainstream body politics in the North beginning from the 1930s onward was built on loyalty to the leader of the religious party/sect or to the Secretary General of the party, in the case of the right/leftist and some regional-based organisations in the North.

Apparently, a good number of Southern Sudanese politicians and technocrats seem to be comfortable with this system, and copied it without bothering to introduce to it significance alterations.

With such an unorganised political system in place, issues pertaining to popular participation, eradication of poverty, qualitative health, education, transport systems, and debates about the objectives of struggle, developmental matters and participatory politics; freedom of expression, priorities of national interests; nation building; wealth and power distributions; all these important issues became less important as the main focus of national debates. This is because politics in patronage system is often individualized, and always centers on 'prominent' personalities and elite groups.

But there are some small and significant changes taking place in the Sudanese politics. In fact, the themes of the debates these days in Sudan, is whether the post-war Sudan will bring a 'democratic' dispensation both in the South and the North and whether the 'New Sudan' and 'Two Sudans' formulas, if implemented correctly and sincerely, will bring drastic and true changes in the country or not.

I would not very much disagree with anyone who might suggest that a lot of significance changes have already taken place in Sudanese political understanding of what change means.

The SPLAM factions have introduced some elements of participatory structures and various Southern Sudanese groups have been talking about post war Southern Sudan more frequently in the past three years than they have been doing, during the past two decades. The Northern religious parties and secular leftist parties, due to calls for internal reforms, have split, some reunited and introduced some measures of participatory politics within their structures.

There is no doubt that the SPLA/M's repeated calls throughout the 80s and 90s for a new kind of political dispensation in the country, and its emphasis on participatory politics, have had some significant positive impact on the emergence of the changes mentioned above. In fact, the SPLA/M has been instrumental in instigating various political groups in the country to buy into the idea that the 'Old Sudan' is no longer viable to sustain the unity of the country. The SPLA/M also has been calling for a 'New Sudan', which, in many ways is different in substance from the current political system or what the Movement often prefers to call the 'Old Sudan'.

The setback perhaps regarding SPLM factions' new politics (following the split in the movement in August 1991) is that they seem to have difficulty putting into practice what they have been preaching to their supporters during the past twenty years. It is observed for example that the areas which have been under control of the SPLM factions did not necessarily witnessed the existence of the kind of the new structures and developmental dispensation preached in the SPLM Manifesto of July 1983, and as amended in 1994 or in the Nasir Declaration of August 1991.

The question is, considering the partial failure of the SPLM to introduce drastic changes in the areas under its control during the war, will its leadership during the envisaged interim period convince the Northern Sudanese people, the majority of whom are still comfortable with the 'Old Sudan' system, will they convince them that the 'New Sudan' or the 'Two Sudans' formulas as propagated by SPLM power centers are viable options for the new dispensation, which will bring them democracy, development, stability and to consolidate the unity of the country?

Having emphasised the SPLM instrumental role in opening up the spectrum of national politics from center to the peripheries, it is to be stressed that participatory politics is about people. It is not about what the leaders always think their people want nor about what they always think is right, but about what really people need most. Thus lies the importance of a continuous dialogue between the Southern Sudanese leaders and the youth on the one hand, and among themselves on the other.

Contrary to Addis Ababa Agreement era experience of non-dialogue among Southern Sudanese, one would like to see more active and continuous South-South dialogue and particularly between the youth and the current Southern Sudanese leadership on topical and important issues such as the dynamics of the interim period (2004-2011) and for them to try to speculate on the trends which might emerge as a result of the interim period politics.

One can understand some misgivings which the SPLM leaders might have on those SPLM faction leaders who previously forged deals with GoS, and who are currently back in the movement, but will the SPLM leaders and immediate advisors survive the GoS tricks and games without drawing from the experiences of their colleagues who have gained bitter experiences with the National Congress ideologues?

For example, the Southern Sudanese youth are interested to know whether the Southern Sudan leadership during the post war Sudan will be based on ethnic identity, professionalism, historical circumstances, personal integrity or the regional belonging of the leaders.

What would qualify for example, Dr John Garang as a leader: being from Dinka ethnic group or his academic/military qualifications, or having led the liberation movement since its inception or because he hails from Upper Nile region? Similar questions might apply to Cdr Salva Kiir Mayardit, Dr Riek Machar, Cdr Wani Igga, Dr Lam Akol, Nhial Deng, Pagan Amum, Deng Alor, Dr Samson Kwaje etc. But examples in no way negate the leading role during the interim period and beyond of the SPLM and its leadership in running the affairs of the South, but rather implies how the public service employment will be based.

Other relevant questions which the Southern Sudanese youth would like to get some answers for from their leadership include: what if the leadership in Northern Sudan, both in the government and the opposition, decided unanimously, somewhere towards the end of the interim period, out of fear that the South might decide to secede should the referendum takes place as stipulated in Machakos and Naivasha protocols, what if they decided to elect or choose a Southern Sudanese Christian to become a President of a united Sudan?

Or what if a Palace coup takes place within the North (i.e. a civilian brand uprising coalition of all the Northern Sudanese political parties and the army as was the case in April 1985, who might get a mass support from a huge segment of Northern Sudanese citizens), thus create a stalemate/chaos in transitional politics in the country? What would be the reaction of those Southern Sudanese who are determined to see the South separated from the North or indeed what will be the future of the peace agreement between the North and the South?

The second hypothetical question is: what if the current mediators in the Sudanese peace process, USA, UK, Norway, the neighboring countries, plus Egypt, in league with Northern Sudanese, and in order to protect their economic interests in the country, decided during the last two years of the Interim period that the South, for security reasons, perhaps caused by internal power struggle, irrespective who caused it, whether it is the north through its divide and rule tactics or the mediators through material bribery or patronage of some willing Southern leaders, what if these mediators and their allies, all of whom are in principle against self-determination of the Southern Sudan for various reasons, decided to extend or avoid altogether the process of referendum in the South? What will be the reaction of the Southern Sudanese to such a move?

From the above highlights, there seems to exist some gaps in the evolution of participatory politics in the South during the past thirty years. But then, what do Southern Sudanese leaders mean when they talk about democracy? Who should decide whether Sudan or Southern Sudan is a democratic entity or not?

Have Southern Sudanese leaderships learned any valuable structural lessons from the past experiences, within the country and beyond, which they could pass on to the young emerging leadership of the South?

What does participatory politics means to the ordinary South Sudanese? Is democracy a prerequisite to development and who should decide on that? What is development, and do we mean by development building roads, schools, clinics, tall government or business buildings etc. or development is indeed about human beings and meeting their distinct needs, which could only be generated through and by their own will?

Do Southern Sudanese of all walks of life have the right to make participatory politics the norm of the new emerging dispensation? And is indeed a new dispensation at hand? Does the current leadership of the Sudan, and of the South in particular represent the will of the people and their urge for genuine changes, and who should really decide, amidst war and peace dynamics, whether they are or not?

In the 'high politics' of veteran politicians and PhDs' world of Sudan, some would prefer to argue that politics in Sudan should not be treated separately from the developing nations' political evolution. This kind of politics is often characterised by politician's loyalty to his/her community, be it to tribe, regional base, religious or sectarian vote banks, or to one's class, family or business connections. The bottom line in such political structure is 'what is there for me and my affiliates'. While there is nothing terribly wrong with politics of loyalty, the issue at point is how does one measure 'what is good for his power base', vis a vis the rest of the country.

Twenty years of war and destruction in Sudan have revealed that neither the SPLA/M factions' leaderships, the Southern political leaderships inside the country, or the Northern Sudanese sectarian opposition parties and their progressive allies, nor the National Congress competing factions' leaderships could claim that the kind of political activity they were engaged in, have been directly beneficial to or met the urgent needs of the vast majority of the Sudanese, whether in the North or South. The SPLA/M as a revolutionary movement may have reservation in accepting such an assertion.

It is our wish that the post war Southern Sudanese politics will, and indeed should emphasise on 'what is there for the ordinary Southern Sudanese', and not another Addis Ababa consensual accommodation, where 'my car and my group' politics of the 1970s succeeded in marginalizing the majority of the Southern population.

One would still hope that if there is a change to come by through Machakos Consensus process, let it be a change, which will be worth the plight and the suffering underwent by Southerners, especially the martyrs who lost their lives during the long struggle. In fact, it has to be a change, which is worth all the sacrifices paid by all the Sudanese.

It was the Egyptian former head of of state, Anwar Al-Sadat who once told his wife, Jihan, that a leader can not initiate or introduce substantive changes in his people's lives or alter their ways of doing things, unless that leader has decided to introduce such changes in his/her way of thinking or the manner in which he/she looks at things. The change, Sadat emphasised, must start from the leader's mind. Any leader who advocates drastic changes in his/her country's political and socio-economic life, and does not practice what he preaches, is in fact, an unchanged leader, who perhaps fears true changes.

The question then would be are the current Sudanese fundamentalist leaders, who have been waging wars against South Sudanese people on the one hand and the Southern leaders in particular who have been fighting Khartoum dictatorial regimes during the past twenty years on the other, in the name of change, are they ready to introduce real and tangible changes they have been preaching for too long or are we to witness yet another expensive window dressing exercise this time in the name of 'change', whether it is called 'New Sudan', 'Two Sudans' or 'petro-dollar politics'?

CHAPTER TWO

# How Sudan Central Governments in Khartoum Underdeveloped Southern Sudan?

This is one of reflections, which I am hoping to shed light on what I consider to be dehumanizing aspects of underdevelopment policies which Southern Sudanese and other marginalized peoples of Sudan were/are subjected to by various central governments in Khartoum. The approach of this reflection is very simple: using everyday examples of daily experiences of Southern Sudanese in towns during the 1950s, 60s, 70s and 80s.

The Sudan People's Liberation Army/Movement (SPLA/M) have celebrated its 22nd anniversary marking the day when the Southern-based 105 battalion of the Sudanese armed forces under command of late Lt Colonel Kerbino Kwanyin Bol and late Sergeant major Yousef Kier Tang, rebelled in the town of Bor, in Upper Nile region against the central government's orders to transfer the battalion to the North. In his speech to the SPLM/A members, supporters and the people of Southern Sudan in Rumbek on 16 May 2005, Dr John Garang de Mabior mapped out what seems to be a sort of a developmental agenda, which, if implemented, it will represent a reversal of existing policies of underdevelopment of the South by the various Central governments in Khartoum. The SPLM/A leader, in his anniversary speech, which was largely drawn from his previous speech on 18 April 2005 in Nairobi, when he meet with some Southern Sudanese opposition leaders during a three day South-South Dialogue meeting, promised many things to the people of Southern Sudan. On the top of these promises was harmony among Southerners, building infratstructure in the South, creating democratic environment and better days ahead for the peoples of the South.

The sad news of course is that very few in the South, whether those still under government controlled areas or in the SPLM/A areas have no access to media, and therefore, apart from the BBC focus of Africa brief summary of what the SPLA/M Chairman has to say, which those who have radio sets might have listened to, no information will reach the 99.9 per cent of Southerners, who were/are the target of Dr Garang's proposed development policy.

It is however important to emphasis that the document represents the essence of the aspirations and long awaited infra-structural focused policies on delivery which the people of the marginalized areas of Sudan have long been fighting and struggle for, particularly the people of the South. Whether the SPLA/M Chairman and his colleagues will deliver these important services to the people of the South during the interim period and beyond, remains to be seen. Whether the Chairman has shared these brilliant ideas with his colleagues in the Central Committee (Leadership Council), and therefore what he said represents a collective will of the SPLA/M entire leadership, also remains to be seen.

In one of his books, the Sudanese Elites and the Addiction of Failure, Mansour Khalid described how Sudanese elites have excelled over years in disappointing their citizens and how over decades, promises after numerous promises, they ended up serving their personal interests and did nothing to uplift the misery and underdevelopment of the people they suppose to serve. Dr Khalid's description of the Sudanese elites fits very well with the history of the underdevelopment policies, which the people of Southern Sudan was/is subjected to by various elites of central governments in Khartoum.

Therefore, it is my humble view that any developmental policies to be implemented in Southern Sudan by the SPLM interim government must be informed by the fact that the Central Governments in Khartoum, since independence in January 1956 have intentionally underdeveloped Southern Sudan. The South was underdeveloped through its intellectuals; through its bureaucrats and government departments; through economic domination of the local markets by Northern Sudanese merchants (Jalaba), who owned transportation system throughout the south. They owned river transportation, they were the main beneficiaries of government contracts and tenders, they were the main suppliers of government boarding schools and universities in the South; they dominated retailer markets, street selling, and most importantly, they controlled the financial institutions in the South, including the only commercial bank branch in the south, the unity bank.

The underdevelopment policies imposed on the South by the Central governments in Khartoum were so effective that the Southern Sudanese college and university graduates over decades were conditioned to believe that once they graduated they will have a government house (thatch house), a government vehicle and an office job and they will be happy there after for ever. The scale of their personal ambitions was therefore reduced to a government house, a car and a job in a government department. Moreover, these high school, college and university graduates; intellectuals and jobists, were cut off from their family members in the countryside and they hardly visit their villages, except in very rare occasions. Those who opted to work in the central government institutions in Khartoum or in other towns in the north, tended to have very little to do with the South and therefore do not bother to visit their relatives; rather it is their relatives who visited them occasionally. The immediate implication of this separation between those who live in what can be referred to as 'shanty towns' and in villages in the country side, have had great impact on children of the town dwellers, who found themselves in constant identity crises. Southern Sudanese elites and intellectuals were therefore educated and trained to become civil servants. Thus, the underdevelopment policy did not encourage young Southern Sudanese students, and marginalized regions' students for that matter, to become scientists or to dream for higher aspirations in life.

When discussing underdevelopment of any people, most sophisticated readers tend to think in terms of political, cultural and economic domination of one group of people or class by other. In fact, at times describing these concepts can be very sophisticated for the ordinary people to understand. In such instances, politicians and intellectuals talk of concepts such as question of national unity, unity in diversity, identity crises, wealth sharing or political power sharing in order to explain the causes of underdevelopment. In Southern Sudan however, the region was underdeveloped for almost one hundred years in a dehumanizing manner; a situation which would require a different, but simple approach to explain it.

There are many examples one can give, which prove that intentionally or not the Turks, Egyptians, British, and especially Northern Sudanese elites and politicians who took over power from the British-Egyptian colonial authorities fifty years ago, acted irresponsibly to the point that some places, which were marked to be towns in Southern Sudan were reduced into huge villages, where signs of urbanism are only in small segregated-ghetto liked quarters.

From an ordinary person's perspective, the underdevelopment of the South and the rural areas of the Sudan was/is there opened for anybody to see. For example, there were/are no postal services in almost all the districts in Southern Sudan. In towns such as Juba, Malakal and Wau, where these services were/are available, very few people used them. Even some individuals, who were government officials in these towns, were not aware that such services were available. For those of us who studied in schools like Malakal, Rumbek or Loka secondary schools during the 1970s and early 1980s, where Southern Sudanese boys and girls from the three Southern Sudan regions were mixed, it would have been logical that the best form of communication between/among us would have been through postal services. For example, hundreds of us who studied at Malakal Secondary School were drawn from Bhar El Ghazal, Equatoria, and Upper Nile regions. Similarly our sister secondary school for girls, Shaabiya, had students from Bhar El Ghazal and Equatoria.

The sad news for those of us who had girl or boy friends from far away districts such as Kapoeta, Bor, Nasir, Bentiu, Yambio, Juba, Yirol, Torit or Pochalla, had no way of communicating during the holidays with our friends, until we returned to schools, during the new academic year. In the process, due to lack of communication, some of us lost, several times, throughout the high school years, their girl and boy friends to others, who might have come from the neighborhoods! Ironically, its seems that the Southern Sudanese leaders at that time were not bothered by the lack of postal services, because, it seemed they were not in need of postal communication anyway.

If the postal services were not availed to Southern districts, although indeed some districts do have with limited access to public, because they were deemed not necessary, what about telephone services, were they also not necessary, at least for government business purposes? In the South, before Sudantel in 1999, for commercial and security reasons, decided to connect the major towns of Juba, Malakal, and Wau in South with Khartoum, there was no telephone communication between Southern Sudanese towns and districts apart from the three main cities. For example during the 1980s, I did not hear of someone talking through telephone from Malakal with someone in Yirol or Gogrial. I did not know for instance, in Malakal, of existence of telephone services before 1985, when I worked with someone who had telephone in his office. Needless to say that there was/is no telephone lines in any of the Southern districts such as Maiwut, Pangak, Renk, Bentiu, Akobo, Yambio, Rumbek, Tonj, Kajikaji or Numeli. In those days if someone resides in Chicago or Dar es Salaam at that time, there was no way he could communicate with his relatives in Nasir or Kajokeji, because there were no telephone or postal services, not to mention the miracle of telegraph, which was limited to security organs.

In fact, up to 1983 when I completed high school, I did not have access to television programs in Malakal, simply because, although there was limited television transmission in town, very few people owned TV sets then. In any event, the transmission was very poor, and hardly any of the senior officials in town bothered to do anything about it. I later on learned, in late 1980s, local mobile TV and radio services were introduced in Malakal, Juba and Wau. They aired their programs for two to four hours daily and covered the town centers only. Those who lived ten kilometers away from the town centers had no access to them. Yes, in addition to the telegram communication system, there was distance-radio communication system between main towns in the South, monitored by security and military agencies. For example if a commissioner or governor of Malakal wants to speak to his counterpart in Juba or to President office in Khartoum, he has to go to the army headquarters in town to use the distanced radio transmitter.

One sometimes wonder, if there was no postal services, telephone lines and TV transmission to the rest of Southern Sudan country side and districts, how did the central governments communicate with the government structures in the districts and towns, out side the main Southern three towns, Malakal, Wau and Juba? How did the Southern based High Executive Council government in Juba communicate with the provincial and local government officials throughout the South without these important services? The answer to these crucial questions is that the central governments and to limited extent the Southern local autonomy government, had its eyes and ears in every Southern Sudan villages, districts and towns through the presence of its security services, be they Jalaba (merchants) or military intelligence officers.

Another source of underdevelopment to those who lived in urban centers in the South during the Local Autonomy era in the 1970s and early 80s was the lack of printed media, at least in the three Southern provincial capitals, apart from *Sudanow* the only government owned magazine. There was no printed media in local Southern Sudanese vernaculars thus rendering dormant the intellectual activity in Southern Sudan's main cities and districts, where as a result most Southern Sudanese politicians, technocrats, and intellectuals spent most of their leisure time either taking alcohol or playing cards. Both private and public printed media houses, which were mainly located in Khartoum, did not bother to open branch offices in the South, or even in other regions outside Khartoum. Therefore even those who might have passion and desire to write books or articles could not do that because they did not have access to publishing houses or newspapers in Khartoum.

In fact, in those days security operatives would arrest any one who possessed a type writer or thought provoking books in foreign languages or even magazines. Anything that would expose or introduce a Southern Sudanese to information or to outside world, was regarded dangerous and whoever possesses such information was regarded a suspect. While it may be understandable during the 1960s due to the intensity of civil war to prevent people from interacting with some foreigners, the irony was that during the 'peace time' in the 1970s, if a person was seen with a foreigner frequently, that person was deemed a threat. In fact, regional ministers and senior officials who spent most of their time socializing and taking alcohol, were left alone, and the focus was on those who, for whatever reasons, did not take alcohol, or frequent night clubs; traveling to neighboring countries, they were regarded to be behaving strangely!

Reading of any kind was discouraged, and in towns like Malakal, there were no public libraries. Social and cultural clubs where urban residents supposed to expose their talents, especially the talented artists, singers, poets, and writers, were none existent. The culture of reading was regarded to be a strange habit, and those who used to read were referred to as 'bookish', as if it is a kind of a disease, which must be prevented.

What about electricity and energy? Apart from some old generators which were purchased in 1960s that provided electricity for restricted parts of Malakal, Wau, Juba, and a few other districts in Equatoria, the majority of Southern Sudanese were condemned not to use, let alone experiencing how electricity/light feel and look like. Similarly, there was no running water for the town dwellers, and even in places like Juba, Malakal, and Wau, which were supposed to be the main urban centers, 95% of their suburbs did not have access to running water. The majority of the inhabitants of these towns got their fresh water from nearby rivers, mainly through local porters, who used donkeys (Karlo) to transport water for sale. There were no vehicles (tankers) to provide water for the suburbs.

Talking about water, Southern Sudan is blessed with several rivers, some originated from within and others from the neighboring countries. Of these rivers, about five can be navigated. However, due to intentional negligent from central governments in Khartoum, almost most of these rivers are inaccessible due to the fact that most of them are blocked by thick grasses. These sick grasses, especially in and around the sudd zone, can be easily cleared.

During the rainy seasons some of these rivers, with difficulty, can be navigated, however by and large, like land roads, the South is almost inaccessible during the period between May and December every year. All the land roads in the South are seasonal. That means, during the rainy seasons, the South is practically closed to outside world and people from other parts of the South would have no access to travel to the other parts of the region.

From a wider perspective, the implications of lack of transport between Southern regions and provinces meant that some government officials in various Southern Sudan did not have the chance to visit other parts of Southern Sudan, to expose themselves to what was happening in other parts of the region. Some of the government officials in the South died in service without visiting other parts of the South. Not because they did not want to visit them, but they did not have access to some of them. It also meant that government officials in the South were wrongly made to believe, thanks to lack of effective radio service, television transmission, postal and telephone services, that everything was fine and that the few services which their regions or provinces were/are getting were/are indeed the best in the rest of the South.

As far as the roads were concerned, there were/are no tarmac roads in Southern Sudan. A visitor to Juba or Malakal would easily notice that these major towns have no tarmac roads. In Malakal and Juba for example, the tarmac roads in these towns are about 5 kilometers long, from the airport to the provincial government headquarters. The rest of the South has never witnessed tarmac roads. The fact that this situation existed since the independence unchanged, it meant that those who were in charge did not feel the need to tarmac roads, not only in the South, but throughout the country.

During early 1980s in Malakal town for example, there was only one old yellow taxi car in town. I was later told that the only old taxi in town went into permanent retirement in about 1986. I remember when I visited Malakal for the first time in early 1970s; there were over fifty yellow taxi vehicles in town, to the extent that for a small kid like me at that time, who was a stranger in town, I concluded that most of the vehicles in Malakal were small yellow caps. Three years into the Addis Ababa agreement of February 1972, all the taxi vehicles in Malakal were shipped to the north. Even the furniture of the Malakal airport, one of the few beautiful buildings in town, were stolen and taken to the north by the Sudan air ways officials who were stationed in Malakal. The Sudan airways throughout its existence had only one weekly transit flight to Juba, Wau and Malakal in that order.

In most instances, a short visit to some of the main towns such as Malakal, Torit or Wau, would reveal that most of these towns were/are professionally planned or surveyed. In general, town planning in Southern Sudan was/is poor. That is why districts like Nasir, Pipor, Pochalla, Akobo, or Maridi were/are not surveyed professionally. Important spaces such as public parks or zoos are not available. In Malakal for example, the only Zoo in the whole of Upper Nile region, which used to host few animals, like Khartoum Zoo, has been sold out. Most of open spaces, such football stadiums, school yards, and public parks in towns like Malakal were sold to private companies or individuals. Even public/government owned schools, were during the war either converted to Islamic schools or were taken over by private companies.

I do not recall seeing petrol or gas stations in several towns and districts I visited in the South. In Malakal for example, the only petrol garage near the main police station in town in the 1970s, was burned down several years ago, and nobody bothered to rebuild it. Most of the gas or petrol reserves used by government or military personnel in Malakal were/are stored in barrels, a risky act which could lead to disastrous situation should an accident occurs in the petrol storage warehouses.

What about hotels and hostels in Southern Sudan? In terms of tourism potential, Southern Sudan stands out as the first region in Sudan that have all it takes to be a tourism destination. It is beautiful, green year long, and has huge reserve of wild life. Despite these facts, those who lived or visited Southern Sudan during the 1970s and early 80s might have vividly noticed that tourism and hospitality services were very limited. Although the region is one of the most beautiful pieces of land on earth, government policies did not encourage tourism as a means of attracting visitors to the region. For whatever reasons, the Southern main towns had only a couple of government owned guest-houses. In Malakal for example, there were two hostels: the main government guest-house near the provincial headquarters and the second guest-house is located near the airport.

What about sanitation system in Southern Sudanese towns? Perhaps the most dehumanizing underdevelopment aspect, which the central governments in Khartoum subjected the Sudanese and the South in particular to, was in the field of health and sanitation. Until mid 1980s, most town dwellers in Southern Sudan used to build surface-based latrines on their compounds; a system which was introduced to the Sudanese by the 'civilized' Great Britain. Because there was no sewerage system in towns, almost everybody in Southern Sudanese towns used plastic or iron buckets, which were placed underneath the seats of the latrines. These buckets were daily collected, normally during the early hours of the nights by city council workers. To me, this was the most dehumanizing act a government can do, by supporting a system, which employs workers to disposed other human beings' wastes.

The use of latrine pits was adopted during late 1980s, when people who lived in Khartoum or outside Sudan, came back and introduced the latrine pits system to the rest of the town dwellers in the South. The latrine pits system is still limited to the main urban centers, while the rest of the country side, who for health purposes needed it most, have not yet been introduced to this new system.

From the above brief reflections, there is no doubt that the magnitude of underdevelopment that the Southern Sudanese and other marginalized peoples in Sudan were subjected to have had great impact and psychological effects particularly on the intellectuals and politicians who were made to believe that their horizons were/are limited to serve as civil servants, directors and ministers and should not expect more than that. The Southern Sudanese leaders were conditioned to pursue politics and political life as the only source of income and glory. A primary school teacher or a medical assistant was looked at as an insignificant, compared to a director or senior civil servant seated in a government office, practically doing nothing to uplift the misery the underdevelopment policies have created.

As a matter of fact, these policies have hypnotized Southern Sudanese citizens to believe that to have no access to electricity, paved roads and fresh water was something to be accepted as normal. The impact of the underdevelopment policies was/is therefore so great that it will take time and will require huge efforts to first and foremost decolonise the mentality of those who are now going to take over power in the South, to admit that such policies existed/exist and to start to reverse them.

CHAPTER THREE

# Politics of War and Peace in the Sudan

## The Causes of the Conflict

ALTHOUGH IT SEEMS THAT VERY FEW COUNTRIES THESE DAYS ARE SERIOUSLY interested in peace process in Sudan than in its oil, the best approach to resolving the Sudanese conflict would still be to address its root causes. The main causes of the Sudanese conflict, throughout its three phases, 1955-1972; 1975-1982; and 1983 to date, could be summed up as follows:

1 Cultural, religious, historical, ethnic, and political diversity between the North and the South: The south sees itself as African, mainly Christian, and historically separate entity from the North that sees itself as Arabicized Muslim entity, where the majority of the population, although black, affiliate to Arab culture and Muslim religion.

2 Colonial history of the two regions: The Turkish-Egyptian and British successive colonial authorities have treated the two regions of the Sudan differently and did very little to forge any meaningful

sort of political integration of the two regions. The South was administered, politically, as a separate entity from the North. The North was treated as part of the Middle Eastern world, whereas the South was administered to become part of the British East Africa territories.

3 Economic dimensions: For various historical reasons, the South is economically underdeveloped compared to the North where the colonial administration had concentrated the main economic projects of the country. However, with the discovery of oil reserve in the early 1980s, in addition to water and fertile agricultural lands potential in the South; and with these resources nowadays becoming increasingly important factors in war and peace politics in the Sudan, there is no doubt that these resources will continue to become the key contentious issues in the North-South relations.

The modern history of civil wars in the Sudan could be traced back to August 1955 when the first military rebellion, historically referred to as "Torit Mutiny", broke out, sparking the first civil war in the country, a war that only came into an end in February 1972, when the Addis Ababa Agreement was signed between the central government and the Southern Sudanese rebels. Indeed, it was hoped that the Addis Ababa Agreement would erase the "Torit Mutiny" legacy from the minds of Southern Sudanese.

Few years later, it turned out that the legacy was destined to stay on, when a group of soldiers rebelled in the town of Akobo in March 1975 in protest against government's policy of transferring to the North some former AnyaNya units that composed the bulk of the pre-Addis Ababa Agreement rebels who were integrated into the Sudan army in 1972. Those who mutinied in Akobo organized themselves into a guerilla force called AnyaNya Two. Their leader was Commander Vincent Kwany Latjor. Eight years later, another mutiny took place in May 1983, this time led by some former senior AnyaNya officers, Kerubino Kwanyin Bol and William Nyuon Bany in the towns of Bor and Ayod, protesting against the central government violation of the Addis Ababa agreement, and joined the 1975 Akobo mutineers who were already waging war against General Jaafar Nimeiri government from their bases at the Ethiopian border with Sudan.

These Southern groups later on organized themselves between July and October 1983, under umbrella of Sudan People's Liberation Army/ Movement (SPLA/SPLM). Colonel John Garang de Mabior, PhD in economics, became the leader of the SPLA/SPLM, until his leadership was challenged in August 1991, due to ideological differences and power struggle within the movement between what was perceived by some as the unionists, led by Col Garang, and secessionists led by Dr Riek Machar, PhD in industrial engineering, and Dr Lam Akol, PhD in chemical engineering. The outcome was a bitter power struggle between these groups, that resulted in the disintegration of the SPLA into several factions, leading eventually to lost of hundreds of innocent lives and dragged on into complex stalemate.

From historical perspective, President Jaafar Mohamed Nimeiri, who came to power in May 1969 through a military coup, committed three deadly political mistakes that led eventually to his overthrow and the eruption of the third civil war in the country. First, he attempted in 1981 to redraw the North-South boundaries as they stood in January 1956, with the aim of annexing to the North the oil rich Southern province, Bentiu, in Western Upper Nile, and Northern Upper Nile agricultural rich district, Renk. Secondly, he re-divided the South in May 1983 into three small regions with capitals in Juba, Malakal and Wau. And the third political suicidal step that General Nimeiri took was declaring the application of Islamic laws throughout the country on 25 September 1983, including the Christian South.

Nimeiri was overthrown by a popular uprising in April 1985. A joint military-civil government under Gen. Abdel Rahman Sawar al-Dahab took over power. In May 1986, an elected civilian government took over the administration of the country under premiership of Sadig al-Mahdi. Al-Mahdi tried along with allies in the North to reach peace with the SPLA/M of Col Garang. In November 1988, Al-Mahdi's ally, Muhammed Osman al-Miraghani, the leader of Democratic Unionist Party (DUP) signed an understanding agreement with Col Garang that called for a general conference to be held in 1989 between the SPLA/M and the other Sudanese parties. Before that conference could take place, an Islamist coup toppled Al-Mahdi's government led by General Omar Ahmed Al-Bashir and Dr Hassan Abdalla al-Turabi.

What follows is a confused situation that led to the ongoing chaotic situation. The government declared "Jihad" (holy war) on the Southern rebel groups. The launching of uncoordinated secret and open peace talks in 1990s between the SPLA/M factions and the government in Nigeria, Kenya, Ethiopia, and in some European and American cities; other peace initiatives were initiated by Sudanese, non-Sudanese and by the OAU through IGAD; the eventual quarrel between al-Turabi and his students, mainly with his deputy Ali Osman Taha, over power and over what some had leveled as uneven distribution of the oil revenues that is being extracted from the war torn South among the ruling National Congress members; the clash among the Sudanese Islamists led to al-Turabi imprisonment; the emergence of role of the oil industry in the war and peace politics in the country; the splits within the National Democratic Alliance, NDA, the umbrella grouping of the Northern Sudanese oppositions that are allied with SPLA/M; and a host of other developments during the past twelve years, including the controversial issue of abduction of Southerners by Northern militia in Western Bhar El-Ghazal region, an excercise refer to by some as slavery.

## The stalemate in the South

It is to be stressed that as a result of power struggle and ideological differences between the Southern Sudanese secessionists and unionists within the SPLA/M, the movement underwent major dramatic, difficult times and changes. In August 1991, SPLA/M split into two main factions, SPLM main-stream under Col John Garang and the SPLM-Nasir faction under Dr Riek Machar. In March 1993, the defactees, led by Dr Riek Machar formed in Kongor, Southern Sudan, SPLM-United, an organization that brought together some senior commanders who defected from Col Garang's mainstream SPLA/M, in addition to those who were jailed by the SPLA/M leadership between 1986-1990. They included Dr Lam Akol, Cdr Kerubino Kwanyin Bol, Cdr William Nyuon Bany, Joseph H. Oduho (who was killed in a surprised attack by Col Garang's SPLA forces against Dr Machar's faction that was in a meeting in Kongor on 27 March 1993), and Cdr Arok Thon Arok.

Most of these men were top leaders of the SPLA/M military high command before they were either jailed or defected from the SPLA/M by ideological or political difficulties. For example, Cdr Kwanyin Bol was Col Garang's Deputy; Cdr Nyuon Bany was chief of Staff of SPLA, Cdr Arok Thon was the logistic commander, and Oduho was the nominal leader of the political wing of the movement, SPLM.

In October 1994, following mass defaction from SPLM-United, Dr Riek Machar held a convention in the Southern town of Akobo and formed a new organization that he christened "South Sudan Independence Movement/Army" (SSIM/A). Meanwhile, Dr Lam Akol took over the leadership of SPLM-United. After his defaction from Dr Machar's movement Cdr William Nyuon Bany redefacted back to Col Garang's faction in late 1995, and attacked Dr Machar positions in Upper Nile where he was killed in a battle in January 1996 near the village of Ayod. Meanwhile, Cdr Kerubino Bol defacted from

Dr Machar's movement and formed his own SPLA-Bahr El-Ghazal Group in 1996.

In April 1996, Dr Machar signed a political Charter with the Sudan Government of General Omar Al-Bashir, and later on that Charter was transformed into what became known as "Khartoum Peace Agreement (KPA)" in April 1997. The Khartoum Peace Agreement was also signed by Cdr Arok Thon Arok and Cdr Kerubino Kwanyin Bol, both Cdr Bol and Cdr Arok died in separate incidents between 1998 and 1999. Meanwhile, Dr Lam Akol signed in the same year in September Fashoa Peace Agreement. Cdr Machar eventually left Khartoum in January 2000, apparently having realized that the peace agreement he had signed with General Al-Bashir will not work, and that the referendum on the political status of the South, whether to secede or remain part of the North, stipulated in the agreement that was supposed to be held in March 2001, will not be respected.

Among the principle signatories to that peace agreement only Dr Lam Akol and Dr Theophilous Ochieng remained in Khartoum. Cdr Kerubino Bol died mysteriously in Mankien, Bentiu State, a district under control of General Paulino Matip in November 1999; Cdr Thon Arok died in a plane crash in Nasir in January 1998; and Samuel Aru Bol died of illness in Khartoum in November 2000. As mentioned earlier, Dr Machar left Khartoum and went back to Southern Sudan bushes, and renamed his organization, SSIM, as Sudan People's Democratic Front/SPDF in January 2000.

## The oil factor in the conflict

It is to be mentioned that the Sudanese government have been trying since 1998 to add as many countries as it could on its shopping list of investors in Sudanese controversial oil industrt. On its client list of investors so far are Belarus, China, Canada, Sweden, Malaysia, Russia,

Japan, France, and several Arab and Middle Eastern countries. Some African countries such as Ethiopia, Zambia and Kenya are importing oil products from Sudan. The list is growing and so is the conflict in the country. The post September 11, 2001 events seem to be working towards a closer relationship between Washington and Khartoum, it is likely that the US government will ask Khartoum to stuck a deal with Washington as a result of which countries such as China, Indonesia and Malaysia could be dropped from the Sudan's list of oil investors or at least cooperate with Washington in sharing information about terrorist organisations which suspected to be closed to NCP leadership. The latter scenario is very likely to happen in the near future, especially that Washington had been more than ready in September 2001 when it offered its blessing to the UN to lift the sanctions it imposed against Sudan six years ago.

The Sudanese oil was first discovered in Bentiu Province, Western Upper Nile region in Southern Sudan in 1979. The drilling work started in 1982. However, the work did not continue because in April 1984, the Southern Sudan based Sudan People's Liberation Army, SPLA attacked the American oil company, Chevron, in Bentiu area killing three workers. Eventually the American company reallocated to Khartoum, a move that brought to an end its oil investment in Sudan. In 1996, Chevron sold its shares to a Canadian oil company. It is to be emphasized that before Chevron left Sudan it was able to drill about six oil crude wells in the so-called "Unity" complex in Bentiu Province.

In 1994, the government of Sudan embarked to implement an ambitious strategy aiming at operating and producing the already drilled oil wells in Bentiu. The process started with the so-called "peace from within", when some southern rebel commanders who were around the oil fields were secretly contacted by the government agents and promised handsome packages. The whole process became a success when the government managed to convince some senior commanders within the SPLA that the Sudanese government was now ready to allow Southern Sudanese to exercise their long-time demand, the right to self-determination, asking them whether they would like to remain as part of united Sudan or secede. As mentioned earlier, a peace agreement with six rebel groups, led by the then leader of South Sudan Independence Movement, SSIM, Dr Riek Machar, was signed in April 1997. It was that peace agreement that gave the government the opportunity to extract oil from Bentiu and invited in the Canadians, the Chinese, the Malaysians and other European and Middle Eastern oil firms to invest in the Sudanese oil. The Chinese built a pipeline within period of three years to transport the oil from Southern Sudan to Portsudan on Red Sea shores. Thousands of Nuer and Dinka Pariang tribesmen in Bentiu province where the oil fields are located were and are still being dislocated from their areas. Most of them ended up displaced in and around Bentiu town.

The Khartoum government strategy has been to attract as many countries as it could to invest in the Sudan's oil with the hope that, once these countries discover the real potential of the country's oil proven reserve, they themselves will become part of the Southern Sudanese conflict. In other words, by internationalizing the Sudanese controversial oil, the government of Sudan will have excuse to continue the war, because it will argue that the Southern Sudanese rebels are not keen to make peace because they do not want the oil to be extracted or exported.

The internationalization of oil and its politicization by the Sudan government would also mean that countries like United Kingdom, the United States of America and South Africa that are not currently involved will have to decide which party to the conflict to support. By inviting countries to invest in its oil, the Sudan government is trying to legitimize itself as the sole representative of the Sudanese people, and that it knows best what is good for the Sudanese people; and that it is ready to go as far as protecting the oil, even if it means killing its own citizens in the South to get the oil extracted and exported.

Secondly, by supporting Southern Sudanese militias that are opposed to the Southern SPLA and Riek Machar's SPDF, the government is buying time to allow the problem get more complicated. As Southern Sudanese inter-factional wars continue, the government will be able to make money through oil investment, a capital that will finance its war machinery. This stalemate, the government hopes to continue until such time that the current Islamist elite are satisfied that their financial books are in order or until the Southern Sudanese elite are disillusioned to the point of surrender to give peace a chance. But then, it will be too late for the Southern Sudanese who are currently scattered all over the world and particularly for those of them who are displaced inside the country, not to mention about two million of them who are already dead.

## Conditions for peace attainment in Sudan

There are three important factors, if not put into serious consideration by the mediators and the warring parties would make the attainment of a comprehensive and inclusive peace agreement between the North and the South rather remote:

1 The ongoing factional fighting and ideological differences among Southern Sudanese politicians and rebel leaders does certainly makes it difficult for the South to be taken seriously by the North. A fragmented South will have little legitimacy to convince the North with, i.e. that the South as an entity is ready to do peace business with its Northern counterpart.

2 Multiplicity of peace initiatives and competition among mediators is another factor that has complicated the peace efforts in the Sudan. Individual politicians, both from North and South have

tried to bring peace in the country for quite sometime. The IGAD peace initiative; Egypt and Libya; South Africa and Qatar; Eritrean and Ugandan leaders; European IGAD Friends' Forum, former US President Jimmy Carter; Lady Caroline Cox of Britain, and several other stakeholders who tried, and still some are, to persuade the warring parties in the Sudan to come to table to negotiate in good faith, all their efforts had failed to solve the conflict.

3  The current position of some Northern Sudanese groups and some Middle Eastern countries that are against the principle and the possibility of inclusion of self-determination for the people of Southern Sudan as part of an over all solution to the conflict, is an obstacle that ought to be addressed. Although the demand of the majority of Southern Sudanese for the right of self-determination has been, nominally on paper, accepted by both the government of Sudan and the Northern Sudanese opposition groups (both in KPA in April 1997 and Asmaray Declaration in June 1995) that are members of National Democratic Alliance, NDA, in practical terms however, the NDA acceptance of self-determination is conditional in a sense that the parties, SPLA and NDA, fledged to give priority to unity of the country during the interim period. The majority of Southern Sudanese are for unconditional acceptance by the North of the right of the people of the South to exercise self-determination in a free and fair internationally supervised referendum.

Sudanese peace process mechanisms:

1  The most important prerequisite to any peace initiative in Sudan would be working for a unity of the southern rebel groups, the SPLA, SPDF and other forces. It has to be some sort of unity that will clearly state what the people of the South are fighting for. By

so doing, factional warfare between the Southern rebel groups will cease and an acceptable peace agenda for the Southern liberation movements could be then tabled to any peace forum with the North.

2   The Northern dominated National Democratic Alliance (NDA) should start serious talks with the Sudan government with the aim of settling their differences on issues relating to governance, human rights, constitutional reforms, party politics, the role of religion in the state, economic reforms etc. On the other hand, the current alliance between the SPLA/M and NDA ought to be re-evaluated because it seems that the NDA leadership is favouring the Egyptian-Libyan peace initiative that does not address the issue of self-determination for the people of the South. The SPLA/M is understood to be favouring the IGAD peace initiative that deals specifically with the Southern Sudan problem and gives priority to right of Southern Sudanese to self-determination; the SPLA/M also seems to accept the idea of merging the two peace initiatives.

3   The question of power sharing and the distribution of oil and other natural resources' revenues ought to be discussed as part of interim period arrangements, between the South and the central government.

Moreover, any peace process in Sudan should use or incorporate as its bases for achieving a comprehensive settlement the following important documents and agreements, because they thoroughly addressed the interim period and post war arrangements that would regulate North-South relationship:

1   The documents of March 1965 "Khartoum Round Table Conference" that brought together the government of Sudan and

the Southern Sudanese political forces inside and outside the country; the documents of February 1972 "Addis Ababa Agreement" between General Jaafar Nimeiri's government and the Southern Sudan Liberation Movement leadership; and the documents of the "Koka Dam Declaration" of March 1986 between the SPLA/M and the Sudanese National Salvation Democratic Alliance (SNSDA).

2  The "IGAD Declaration of Principles" (DoP) (May 1995) documents. In these documents, the warring parties in Sudan, SPLA/M, SSIM (now SPDF), and the Government of Sudan have accepted in principle the right of the people of the South to self-determination. They also addressed issues relating to interim period arrangements etc.

3  The "Asmara Declaration" by the NDA leadership in June 1995 stipulated, among other things, that the NDA is committed to accept the outcome of referendum that will be held in the South after an agreed upon interim period. They also agreed that priority be given to the unity option during the interim period.

4  The "Khartoum Peace Agreement (KPA)" between the United Democratic Salvation Front (UDSF) and the Sudan government in April 1997 stipulated that the government of Sudan recognizes the right of Southern Sudanese to determine their future political status in the country through a plebiscite after a four-year interim period. Although that agreement has been incorporated into the current constitution of the country in 1998, the government did not respect its terms and its major signatories are either dead or left the country back to the bushes of Southern Sudan.

## The Way Forward

1 The Egyptian-Libyan peace initiative is dealing with the issue of governance, role of religion in politics, human rights, and specifically trying to initiate reconciliation between the government and NDA. This initiative must be encouraged because it will help bring Northern Sudanese opposition groups closer to the government. Such reconciliation among northerners will return the Sudanese conflict into its rightful original format: north versus south. Once the North is reconciled, the south will be forced to put its house in order and its rebel movements, SPLA/M, SPDF and other forces, will have to come to peace process with one agenda. SPLA/M transformation agenda, the creation of 'New Sudan' under new basis will then have the chance to be discussed by two equal partners. Some argue though that the SPLA/M being a national liberation movement fighting for liberation of Sudanese should be reduced to a Southern based movement, while this argument holds ideologically speaking, in reality it may be difficult to implement.

2 The problem of Nuba Mountains and Blue Nile whose members are part of the SPLA/M forces should be addressed and resolved first at the level of SPLA/M before a comprehensive peace is signed between the South and North. The SPLA's insistence that the Southern Sudan borders with the North should include these two regions which are traditionally part of the political north, is one of the contentious issues that the SPLA/M and the Sudan government delegates to IGAD peace process are unwilling to compromise on. It is to be mentioned that the map that the SPLA has been presenting to the IGAD mediators since May 1993, is the same map that was based on the 1920 ordinance outlining the British policy of close districts. At that time a map was issued composing the three Southern provinces, some parts of the Blue Nile province and the

Nuba Mountains (now Southern Kordufan). However, the British government reversed that policy in 1930 when it decided that the country was to be administered as one entity. Unless this issue is settled, it will continue to complicate the Sudanese peace process. The best way out would be for the mediators to ask the SPLA/M leaders from Nuba Mountains and those from Blue Nile to spell out clearly what is their position on this issue. As for the question of Abyei, there seems to be a general consensus that it could be discussed and resolved through direct South-North negotiations. In any event, all the documents and agreements mentioned above had directly addressed the Abyei issue, and the disputants could refer to them should disagreements arise.

3   The factional politics in the South have created animosity between the two major tribes in the South, the Dinka and Nuer. Moreover, some small tribes, especially in Equatoria and some from Upper Nile have felt that the SPLA/M, as a movement, has discriminated against and mistreated them as a result of which fierce inter-factional fightings ensued within SPLA/M forces between 1995 and 1999. Reconciling SPLA/M various factions is therefore a vital prerequisite to any serious South-South peace process.

4   Indigenous peace processes among the Southern tribes is one of the best approaches that should be encouraged to avoid post-war Southern Sudan instability. Already the agreement between Dinka and Nuer that was concluded in March 1999 at Wunlit village in Bhar el Ghazal has successfully brought about relative peace in the border areas of Western Upper Nile with Bhar el Ghazal.

5   There is no doubt that southern Sudanese in Diaspora, could be a source of conflict, if they decide to take sides. On the other hand, they could as well become facilitators for reconciliation among

Southerners, if they are included in the peace process. In fact, they ought to be involved more in the peace process, especially that most of the educated Southern Sudanese live abroad.

6 Southern Sudanese militia groups who are currently cooperating and allying themselves with the government of Sudan should be encouraged to become part of, and if possible be incorporated into any peace process as part of Southern Sudan peace agenda, otherwise, if marginalized, they could cause havoc in the post war Southern Sudan.

CHAPTER FOUR

# Elusive Peace Process in Sudan and Lessons Learned (1984-2002)

The history of peace process in Sudan is full of ironies, challenges, and numerous personal and collective experiences that those who participated in them regard as true journeys of self-actualization. There were good times and bad ones. There were times when negotiators were so optimistic to the point of some of them prematurely announcing breakthroughs, only to retract few hours later. Four regimes were involved in negotiating peace deals with various opposition leaders, including the Sudan People's Liberation Movement/Army (SPLM/A), while open and secret rounds of talks were held in different capitals of the world. The following peace initiatives examples will illustrate how the achievement of Comprehensive Peace Agreement (CPA) in January 2005 was a long journey that went through huddles and deadlocks.

Elusive Peace Process in Sudan and Lessons Learned 57

# Peace initiatives under General Gaafar Mohamed Nimeiri government

The period between 1983 and 85 can be regarded as a chaotic political theatre in Sudanese politics. President Nimeiri did not know what to do about the rebellion that took place in the South in May and June 1983. There were three immediate issues that made Nimeiri and his lieutenants insecure:

1 The relationships between Sudan and Libya and Egypt were at their lowest. Muamar al-Ghadafi decided to put his trust on the 'National Front', which was operating from Tripoli, an umbrella of the Northern Sudanese opposition groups in exile (DUP, UMMA and NIF). In fact, Col John Garang de Mabior of SPLA/M visited Libya in 1984 and was promised by the Libyans logistic as well as financial assistance. That visit led to some kind of coordination between SPLA/M and the 'National Front'.

2 President Nimeiri had some internal problems within his government and the ruling party )Sudan Socialist Union, SSU). The basis of his legitimacy, ending the civil war and achieving national unity was already undermined by his decision to re-divide the South into three regions, and his famous degree of 25 September 1983 by which he declared the application of Islamic laws.

3 In 1984 Southern Sudan was in turmoil, both politically and militarily. Nimeiri lost his grip over the South, and couple with his internal problems, there was no way he could survive without some sort of accommodation with the SPLA/M.

### Sir Al-Khatim inquiry Commission (1984)

Nimeiri's first move was to form an inquiry commission whose mission was to find out what might have been behind the rebellion in the South. He charged a ten-man committee, under chairmanship of former Prime Minister Sir El-Khatim Khalifa to investigate. Unfortunately that commission did not start its work on time and could not continue with it, because in April 1985, Nimeiri's regime was overthrown by popular uprising. The question thereafter was what would Khalifa's Commission of Inquiry have achieved had it continued its mission?

### Tiny Rowland Initiatives (1984)

The second mission that Nimeiri dispatched to bring an end to the war was through his friend, the late Tiny Rowland. Rowland, then well known businessman in East Africa and Middle East, was good friend to both Gadaafi and Nimeiri. He visited Addis Ababa twice in 1984, with the aim of convincing Col John Garang to open some kind of negotiation with Nimeiri's government. Nimeiri offered Col Garang two concessions: That Col Garang was to be given the post of First Vice President and that he will be the sole ruler of the South. After shuttling between Addis, Khartoum and Tripoli for some months, Rowland was convinced that Col Garang was not interested in Nimeiri's offer.

In 1984, similar efforts were made my Adnan Kashukji, the Saudi businessman who was Nimeiri's friend, and who was interested in oil investment in Sudan. His efforts also failed to yield fruits.

Using his relationship with Col Garang, Rowland tried again in 1992/3 to mediate between Col Garang and senior officers who defected from the movement, but his efforts did not materialize.

### AnyaNya (II) initiative (1984-85)

President Nimeiri also tried to use the AnyaNya (II) under William Chuol Deang, whose army was in constant fight with the SPLA/M following their disagreement over the objectives and the leadership structure of the SPLA/M in Itang in July 1983, in order to weaken the movement. Nimeiri's aim was to neutralize AnyaNya II, and then use it to fight against the SPLA/M. This is precisely what his successors did under both Transition Military Council Government of General Abdel Rahaman Sawar al-Dhab and under Sadig al-Mahdi government.

Nimeiri was interested in concluding some kind of formal deal with William Chuol Deng. To the surprise of General Nimeiri the AnyaNya II leadership insisted that any peace agreement must be brokered and concluded outside Sudan, preferably in Europe. When General Nimeiri showed his unwillingness to go that route, William Chuol turned down his offers. It was later on after William Chuol death in 1985, during the transitional government that AnyaNya II, under Gordon Koang Chuol (1985-1988) and Paulino Matip Nhial that the Sudan government managed to neutralized AnyaNya II and used it against the SPLA/M forces. This cooperation and understanding made the AnyaNya II forces to become the so-called 'Friendly forces'.

## Peace initiatives under Transitional Government (1985-1986)

*Libyan-South Yemen joint initiative (1985-86)*
In late 1985, the Libyan and South Yemeni governments tried to mediate between the SPLA/M and the transitional government. The Transitional government then Defence Minister delivered some letters from Transitional Military Council leader, General Abdel Rahman Suwar al-Dahab and his civilian Premier Dr Jazuli Dafallah to the SPLA/M leaderships. Both Libya and South Yemeni leaders were close friends to the SPLA/M leadership. The main objective of the mediation was for the SPLA/M to open dialogue with the Transitional Government and if possible path the way for an open mediation through Libya and South Yemen governments. The SPLA/M in 1980s

was a socialist oriented liberation movement, and as mentioned elsewhere, most of the Northern Sudanese who joined the movement from 1985 onward come from leftist oriented political organizations in Sudan. The success of the initiative was hindered by two factors: at that time the SPLA/M was not ready to deal with the TMC as a peace partner, because it was a transitional government. Secondly, the SPLA/M was in an internal struggle with the secessionists (AnyaNya II) who were not impressed by the SPLA/M's unionist leadership's orientation. Thirdly, Libya and South Yemen were not, from 'Southern Sudanese' prospective the best candidates to mediate in any peaceful settlement of the North-South conflict in Sudan.

*The Kokadam Declaration, 24 March 1986*
Immediately after the April 1985 Uprising against General Nimeiri, the National Democratic Salvation Alliance, a grouping composing political parties, trade unions, and leftist activists, initiated contacts with the Sudan People's Liberation Movement (SPLA/M) in Ethiopia. A letter written by the then interim Prime Minister, Dr Jazuli Daffalah to Dr John Garang, proposing a meeting between the interim Government and the SPLA/M delegates prompted the initiative. The letter was delivered to the SPLA/M leadership in Nasir by a government envoy and was received by Commander William Nyuon Bany and Dr Riek Machar in late 1985. The initiative, which was later on facilitated mostly by leftist groups in exile, in collaboration with Northern Sudanese members of the SPLA/M, culminated in a round of negotiations at the Southern Ethiopian resort of Kokadam in March 1986. Late Kerubno Kwanyin Bol, who was then the second man in the movement, led the SPLA/M delegation.

The main objective of the initiative was to convince the SPLA/M leadership that any peace agreement between the Government of Sudan and the SPLA/M should address the main obstacles that led to the war, and ought to be handled as national issues and not specific to

Southern Sudan. Secondly, the Alliance delegates stressed that any peace settlement should be signed during a civilian administration following general elections.

The Kokadam negotiations focused on the structure of government, power sharing, wealth sharing, federal system, human rights and democracy. The two parties agreed in principle that the SPLA/M was fighting to solve the 'Sudan problem' and not 'Southern Sudan problem'. The Declaration, which the two parties signed in Kokadam on 24 March 1986 stressed on the following: To work for resolving the 'Sudan problem' and not 'Southern Sudan problem'. Secondly, to call for an all-Sudanese political forces constitutional conference. Thirdly, lifting the state of emergency in the country; and finally, cancellation of the Islamic laws.

The Kokadam declaration provisions was not implemented after the general elections because: the leftist groups that were instrumental in the April Uprising and in negotiating that agreement were not represented in Sadig Al-Mahdi government. Secondly, the conservative Islamic parties, Umma party and DUP, which were signatories to the Kokadam Declaration did not show any serious interest or commitment to implement it after the elections.

## Peace initiatives during the Third Democracy Period (1986-1989)

*Prime Minister Sadig al Mahdi Initiative (1986-87)*
In 1987, Prime Minister Sadig al-Mhadi sent envoys to the Ethiopian Capital, Addis Ababa from his ruling Party, the Umma with the aim of establishing direct contacts with the SPLA/M leadership to arrange a meeting between him and the SPLM/A leader, Dr John Garang. Premier al-Mahdi was interested in a settlement that would address all the outstanding issues in the country in an all Sudan national

constitutional conference. He was of the opinion that meeting Col Garang, whose ideas of the 'New Sudan' convinced him that, the SPLA/M leadership was unionist in approaching and finding solutions to the causes of the conflict in the country. When Premier al-Mahdi messengers came back to Khartoum they informed him that Col Garang was not ready to meet him as a Prime Minister, but as the leader of the Umma Party. Al-Mahdi's Party was partner to the Kokadam Declaration and the SPLA/M leadership was interested to meet the Umma Party leader such, since not all the Sudanese parties were signatories to that Declaration.

The two men met for about nine hours in the Ethiopian capital and discussed the problem and the conflict from different perspectives. The two leaders could not agree on the raod map for the resolution of the conflict as presented by Premier al-Mahdi, although they both agreed that the issues they discussed formed the basis of what is charaterised as the "problem of Sudan'.

It is to be recalled that the Sadig al-Mahdi's Government sent to London the deputy Chief of Staff General Abdel Azim al Sadig and General Salah Mustafa, then the military intelligence chief to meet with Commander Arok Thon Arok, who was then the deputy chief of SPLA/M commander for logistics. The aim of the meeting was to try to convince the SPLA/M leadership that peaceful resolution of the conflict was the best option for both the government and the SPLA/M.

*The DUP initiative (November 1988)*

Following the lack of progress in Prime Minister, Sadig Al-Mahdi initiative to convince the SPLA/M leadership to accept his proposal to call for an all-Sudanese constitutional conference, the leader of the Democratic Unionist Party, Mohamed Osman al-Mirghani initiated contacts with the SPLA/M leadership. He visited the Ethiopian Capital in November 1988 and meet in several sessions with the SPLA/M leader Dr John Garang. The focus of their discussions was on how to find a lasting peace in Sudan. On 16 November 1988, the two leaders, Mirghani and Garang signed a document in which they agreed that the problem the two leaders were working to resolved was a national problem and no longer restricted to Southern Sudan. They agreed that all the Sudanese political forces, need to convene a constitutional conference where all the outstanding constitutional problems in the country would be tackled. The date fixed for that conference to take place was 31 December 1988. The issues to be discussed in the proposed conference would include the nature of government, human rights, democracy, wealth and power sharing between the central government and the regions. They also agreed on ceasefire before the conference. The DUP-SPLA/M delegates also agreed that as a good will gesture from the part of the DUP-Umma coalition government, the joint military pacts signed between Sudan and Libya and Egypt and emergency laws be nulified, and that the application of Sharia Laws be suspended.

Apparently the two signatories to the 'Mirghani-Garang' agreement as it was referred to, were genuine in the commitment to the necessity of convening a constitutional conference. However, the Prime Minister of the time, Sadig al-Mahdi of the Umma Party, and the official opposition party in the parliament, the National Islamic Front (NIF) of Dr Hassan Abdallah al-Turabi, were not sympathetic to the agreement. Al-Mahdi was reluctant to submit the agreement to the parliament for discussion and approval. As a result, the DUP pulled out from the coalition government. Al-Mahdi asked the NIF to join his party in the coalition, an opportunity the NIF gladly accepted.

In February 1989, four months after 'Mirghani-Garang' agreement, 150 Sudanese senior army officers, submitted a letter to Premier Al-Mhadi giving an ultimatum to choose between arming the army to fight the war against the SPLA/M or accept the al-Mirghani peace initiative. In essence it was a military coup in waiting. The Premier accepted to table the agreement to the Parliament. As a result, the NIF pulled out from the coalition, and the Premier invited again the

DUP to the coalition. The Umma Party accepted the proposal that an All-Sudanese political parties' constitutional conference be convened in mid or late 1989. However, before any move was taken to make arrangements for the proposed conference, the NIF waged a military coup, and the NIF Secretary General Dr Hassan Abdallah al-Turabi, jointly with Brigdier General Omar Hassan al-Bashir became the new leaders of Sudan on 30 June 1989.

Three issues were behind 'Mirghani-Garang' agreement failure: Sadig al-Mahdi's Umma Party reluctant and jealousy; NIF total rejection of the agreement, and DUP's lack of political activism among other political and social forces, which might have helped the party to sell its agreement with SPLA/M to the Sudanese people.

## Peace initiatives under General Omar Hassan al-Bashir's government (1989-2002)

### National Dialogue Conference, September 1989

As part of its policy towards initiating dialogue among its loyalists with respect to the peace process in the country, the National Salvation Revolutionary (NSR) Government of National Islamic Front (NIF), called in September 1989 for a National Dialogue Conference. The conferees adopted the principle that:

> ... the Southern Problem is an inherited issue with historical, political and economic dimensions and that the peaceful solution is a strategic aim that the Revolution exerts great efforts to realize.

In 1990, The National Dialogue Conference on Peace issues was followed by a series of conferences that aimed at two contradictory, but partially successful approaches for the NIF. These were internal peace process and external dialogue with the opposition parties in exile, which aim at absorbing them into the ruling party structures, completely neutralizing them or divide their ranks.

### Jimmy Carter initiatives (1989-1990)

Through the mediation of the US former President Jimmy Carter, a series of meetings between the Government and the SPLA/M outside the Sudan, between 1989 and 1990 in Nairobi (Kenya), and Addis Ababa were held. In these encounters, through direct discussions preliminary understanding was reached on some issues such as federalism as a basis for resolving the country's problems; resolving the problem of the Sudan through dialogue; distribution of power between the States and the Central Government; and, distribution of national wealth. The difficulty that President Carter faced was how to convince the two parties to reach a solution without international support to his initiative. Even his government was not as yet ready to support his efforts at the time. In final analysis, President Carter team came to conclusion that Khartoum government was more interested in selling its newly found version of federation to the SPLA/M than seriously considering resolving the essential issues underlying the conflict. On the other hand, the SPLA/M was not at that time ready to enter into serious peace process with the military junta that was guising as a national army, when indeed it was led by NIF fundamentalists.

### Juba Convention of 1994

The Juba convention was particularly important because it brought together almost all the Southern Sudanese political forces inside the country for the first time. They were asked to advise the government on issues relating to the peace process. The convention was under the auspices of the Peace Advisory Council. The convention, among other things, confirmed the resolutions of the National Dialogue conference on Peace issues. It called for adherence to the unity of the country; support for the principles guaranteeing the rights of Sudanese citizens;

endorsed the federal system of rule for the Sudan and the efforts of the Government to achieve peace from within. The convention rejected the continuation of war and supported the achievement of peace through dialogue. The Juba Convention was thus the go ahead signal to the government to launch the so-called 'internal peace process' or peace within.

*Frankfurt Declaration, February 1992*

Following the split within the SPLA/M in August 1991, the SPLA/M Nasir Faction decided to initiate contacts with the Sudan government. The agenda for the discussion was whether the government was ready to entertain the idea of self-determination for the people of Southern Sudan as the basis for any peace initiative in the country. In Frankfurt in Germany, in February 1992, the Nasir Faction leadership decided to sent Dr Lam Akol, Telar Deng and Deng Tiel to meet the Government representative Dr Ali Al-Haj Mohamed. The meeting discussed the premises on which any future negotiation could be based. The Nasir group insisted that the right for self-determination for the people of the Southern Sudan, in form of a referendum giving Southerners the choice between unity or secession is the minimum demand they would entertain with the government delegation. The government on the other hand insisted that the priority during an interim period to be agreed upon should be for the maintenance of unity. Eventually the two parties signed and approved the Frankfurt Declaration.

There were two important factors that made the two sides to sign that document. The SPLA/M-Nasir Faction was under pressure from the SPLA/M mainstream both politically and military. If it was to show that it was serious about self-determination, it has to show through deed and not rhetoric. The Nasir faction also wanted some kind of recognition from the government as a faction with whom it can make peace.

On the other hand, the NIF government was under pressure from its power base to either make peace with the SPLA/M or defeat it militarily. Secondly, by talking to the breakaway group, the government was sending a message to the SPLA/M leadership that the Nasir faction can become an alternative leadership to the SPLA/M, especially that the Nasir group was using self-determination slogan, which the government knows had a considerable support from the South.. Thirdly, the government was in difficult diplomatic situation and was almost isolated from the regional and international politics at the time.

*Political Charter, April 1996 and Khartoum Peace Agreement (KPA) April 1997*

The period between 1992 and 1995 had witnessed a lot of shifts within the Nasir faction. In March 1993 the Nasir Faction became the SPLA-United, and in 1994, the group led by Dr Riek Machar formed a new organization, the 'South Sudan Independence Movement, SSIM'. The SSIM since 1992 met with the government of the Sudan in separate meetings and sometimes jointly with the SPLA/M mainstream faction of Dr John Garang. It met with the government delegations in Frankfurt in February 1992, in Abuja in May 1993, and in Nairobi in July 1993.

In all these meetings the Nasir grouped tabled self-determination as the basis of its negotiation with the Government. It was along those lines that the SSIM leadership decided to open direct discussions with the Government of Sudan in early 1996 as represented by Cdr Taban Deng Gai and others. The premises of these discussions were based on the agreement between the two parties that the people of Southern Sudan has the right to determine their political status through an internationally supervised referendum and that the two parties will give unity the priority during the interim period. The border of the South will be as it were in January 1956.

In April 1997, the two sides elaborated on the Charter and decided to include other factions in a final agreement. For rhe **Sudan Government** the agreement as signed by Lt General EL Zuber Mohammed Saleh, First Vice President. For United Democratic Salvation Front (**UDSF**) and South Sudan Independence Movement/Army (**SSIM/A**) Dr Riek Macher Teny, Chairman and C-in-C (**SSIM/A**). For Sudan People's Liberation Movement (**SPLM/A**)/Bhar El-Ghazal Group, Cdr Karubino Kawanyn Bol, Chairman C-in-C (**SPLM/A**); South Sudan Independents Group (**SSIG**) Cdr Kawac Makwei, Chairman C-in-C (**SSIG**); for Equatoria Defence Force (**EDF**) Dr Theophilus Ochang Loti, Chairman C-in-C (**EDF**); for the Union of Sudanese African Parties (**USAP**) Samuel Aru Bol, Chairman (**USAP**) and for SPLA/M **Bor Group** Cdr Arok Thon Arok

The agreement, which was signed in the Presidential Palace in Khartoum on 21 April 1997, contained of several components.

On religion and state, the two parties agreed that Sudan is a multi-racial, multi-ethnic, multi-cultural and multi-religious society. Islam is the religion of the majority of the population and Christianity and the African creeds are followed by a considerable number of citizens. Nevertheless the basis of rights and duties in the Sudan shall be citizenship, and all Sudanese shall equally share in all aspects of life and political responsibilities on the basis of citizenship. They also agreed that there shall be no legislation which would adversely affect the religious rights of any citizen. Regarding legislation they agreed that Sharia and Custom shall be the sources of legislation.

On the issue of Sharia, the parties agreed on a formula under which Laws of a general nature that are based on general principles common to the States shall apply at the national level, provided that the States shall have the right to enact any complementary legislation to Federal legislation on matters that are peculiar to them. This power shall be exercised in addition to the powers the States exercise on matters designated as falling within their jurisdiction, including the development of customary law.

On the interim period arrangements, the UDSF and the government of Sudan agreed that the length of the interim period shall be four years. However, it may be shortened or extended if need arises by recommendation from the Coordinating Council to the President of the Republic. The interim period shall commence as from the date of the formation of the Coordinating Council and shall end as soon as the referendum is accomplished and the results are declared.

On the security arrangements during the interim period, they agreed that he South Sudan Defence Force (SSDF) shall remain separate from the National Army and be stationed in their locations under their command. Moreover, it was agreed that the Police, Prisons, Wild Life, Civil Defence, Fire Brigade and Public Security in the Southern States shall be drawn from the people of Southern Sudan. The size of the Sudanese Armed Forces in South Sudan shall be reduced to peacetime level once peace is established.

On the Self-determination the agreement recognized the right of the people of Southern Sudan to determine their political aspirations and to pursue their economic, social and cultural development. The agreement also stipulated that the people of Southern Sudan shall exercise this right in a referendum before the end of the interim period. The options in the referendum shall be Unity and Secession.

The referendum shall be free, fair and be conducted by a Special Referendum Commission (SRC) to be formed by a presidential decree in consultation with the Coordinating Council. Eligible voters for the referendum shall be Southern Sudanese people who have attained the age of eighteen years and above and who are residing inside and outside of South Sudan.

The agreement was incorporated into the July 1998 constitution.

The Southern Sudanese factions that signed the agreement were in short time neutralized, apart from the leader of their coalition, Dr

Machar who, when he realized that the agreement was not going to be implemented, left the country in December 1999. The UDSF was registered as a political party in 1998 and as such became an independent political party from the ruling National Congress, until it split in 2001 when differences erupted between the party's Deputy Chairman Peter Abdel Rahman Sule and Joseph Malwal, one of its leaders, over whether the party should cooperate with the ruling party or it should opt to be an opposition party.

*The Nuba Mountains Peace Agreement, April 1997*
It is to be recalled that the differences and the discussions that took place among the military and political leaders of the Nuba Mountains who are members of the SPLA/M led to the emergence of two main groups. A group led by Commander Mohammed Haroun Kafi Aburass was of the opinion that the SPLA/M was under strong influence of a separatist group from within and thus the people of Nuba Mountains should try to explore the possibilities of finding a separate solution with the government of Sudan. The other group, led by the late Commander Yousef Kuwa Makki felt that the future of the people of Nuba Mountains will have to be decided as part of an over all solution to the marginalized people's problem. Some members of his group saw in the demand for the self-determination for the people of the Nuba Mountains and the possibility of annexing them to the South in any final solution a possibility that worth exploring.

After heated debates between the two groups and as a result of a deadlock, Commander Aburass's group decided to open negotiations with the Sudan government. These negotiations led to the "Declaration of Principles" agreed upon by the two parties on 31.7.1996 in Nairobi, Kenya. On 21 April 1997, a comprehensive Nuba Mountains Peace Agreement was signed between the government of Sudan and Aburass group. The then Secretary-General of the Supreme Council for Peace, Republic of the Sudan Mr. Mohammed

El-Amin Khalifa signed the agreement on behalf of the Government, while Commander Mohammed Haroun Kafi Aburass chairman of SPLA/M Nuba Mountains Central Committee signed on behalf of Nuba Mountains United SPLM/A.

The most outstanding significance of this agreement according to Aburass group was that it recognised for the first time since Sudan independence in 1956, the fact that there has been a long-standing problem in the Nuba mountains area. The agreement acknowledged the following items. The parties recognized that there has been a long-standing problem in the Nuba Mountains state, which has led to the armed struggle since 1984. The two parties also acknowledged their abiding and observing the unity of the Sudan with its geographical and political borders of 1956. Moreover, the parties have acknowledged the importance and necessity of taking stand and a vision of the problems from regional perspective and within the frame of a united Sudan as the ideal means for solving the Nuba Mountains state question far from that of the SPLM/A of Dr John Garang's faction. The sharia and the customary laws shall both be equally the legislative sources of the Nuba Mountains state; in addition the region has the right to legislate complementary laws to those federal ones on questions and problems peculiar to the Nuba Mountains state. Citizenship shall be the basis for the rights and duties that include freedom, equality, justice and human rights.

The parties acknowledge the federal system as a vehicle of governance that can provide the region's citizens with their rights to participate in the administration of their regions affairs and its development, together with their balanced and full participation in the federal power. Powers and resources are shared on equal and just basis between the Nuba Mountains state and the federal government, details shall be worked out by the two parties in separate protocol. They also agreed on the eradication of any and all kinds of socio-economic, cultural injustice and grievances. That includes any agricultural, none agricultural and other lands which have been unfairly distributed or owned, headed by agricultural schemes reforms and redistribution in a way that preserves respect of the natives and avail greater opportunity and priorities for the indigenous people of the area to invest and develop their land. To join efforts for eradication of all kinds of backwardness, illiteracy and ignorance which have caused such situation of injustice and grievances? This alongside with the designing, implementation and execution of a special development programme for the Nuba Mountains state in a such a way that achieves equitable development between the Nuba Mountains state and other regions in the country for a purpose of achieving the region's welfare

The agreement also acknowledged the local cultures and their development as well as to support equal opportunities to reflect them and be expressed within other cultures of the people of the Sudan in all fora mass of expression accredited by both the Nuba Mountains state and federal government. Parties also agreed that the war has badly and effectively led to the destruction of the natural resources, environment and gross violation of human rights in the Nuba Mountains state. The two parties therefore, undertake to deal with these negative effects resulted during the twelve-year war.

The Nuba Mountains agreement could not hold because both the Government and Aburass group new all along that the main SPLA/M faction, led by Cdr Yousef Kuwa Makki and his colleagues represented the true aspirations of the Nuba people, hence until a comprehensive agreement was reached with this group there can be no sustainable peace in the Nuba Mountains. Aburass-NCP agreement did however raise fundamental issues that are at the heart of the Nuba Mountains peoople's grievances.

*Fashoda Peace Agreement 20 September 1997*

The SPLA-United, following elaborate discussions in Fashoda between its leadership and the Government of Sudan delegation signed a peace agreement in September 1997. The negotiation between the two parties centered on issues relating to governance, federalism and self-determination. As was the case with the Khartoum Peace agreement five months earlier, the two parties were the Sudan Government and the SPLM - United Faction, led by Dr Lam Akol Ajawin.

The delegations of Sudan government and the Sudan People's Liberation Movement (SPLM-United) met in Fashoda on 18-20 September 1997 under the mediation and chairmanship of His Majesty Reth Kwongo Dak Padiet, the Reth of the Shiluk. The two parties discussed the Sudan Peace Agreement of April 21, 1997 and agreed on the following amendments:

The SPLM-United shall be guaranteed full legality of status and participation in the political and constitutional processes in the Sudan during the interim period.

The parties to the agreement shall have the right to freely propagate their respective opinion in the referendum among the people. The 14th Constitutional Decree may not be amended except by (2/3) two-thirds majority of the coordinating Council and confirmed by a joint session of the Advisory Council and the ten Southern States Assemblies in a meeting to be held for that purpose at the seat of the Coordinating Council.

As part of the deal, Dr Akol was appointed a Federal Minister of Transport as well as a member of the ruling National Congress Party. He held these positions until September/October 2002 when he resigned from the ruling party and was dismissed as a result from ministerial post. He is a co-founder of Justice Party.

The failure of the Fashoda Peace Agreement could be attributed to many factors. Firstly, there were no regional or international witnesses to the Fashoda Agreement, only the Shilluk King acted as the guarantor of the Agreement. The government was not keen to implement the agreement especially that, unlike Khartoum Peace Agreement, a Federal minister signed it. The agreement was part of the so-called 'Internal Peace process' that aimed at neutralizing the factions that defacted from the SPLA/M mainstream in August 1991.

### Al-Turabi-al- Mahdi initiative

As part of north-north dialogue, the then Speaker of Sudanese Parliament Dr Hassan Al-Turabi met in Geneva on 2 May 1999 with former Prime Minister Sadig al-Mahdi. The objective of their discussion was how to convince the opposition parties, mainly from the north to open dialogue with the NIF government. The two leaders agreed that it was important to open up the political base of the government. Open up media and political participation. They also agreed on the principle of calling for a broad base conference that would discuss all the outstanding issues relating to governance and Southern Sudan problem. That meeting resulted later on in the government negotiating directly with al-Mahdi party even after Turabi and El-Bashir parted ways.

### The Homeland Call

In response to an initiative by President Ismail Omar Gule of the Republic of Djibouti, President Omar Hassan Ahmed Al-Bashir met with Sayed Alsadig Al-Mahdi in Djibouti on 25th November 1999 to discuss means of enhancing national reconciliation in the Sudan. Under the auspices and presence of H.E President Ismail Omar Gule both parties agreed on a declaration of principles for realizing a comprehensive political solution in the Sudan.

*Parties to the conflict adopt and commit themselves to end the civil war and conclude a just Peace agreement based on the following:*
a) Citizenship shall be the basis for constitutional rights and duties.

b) No particular national group of citizens shall be privileged because of ethnic, culture or religious affiliation.
c) Adherence and commitment to the international human rights charters and covenants.
d) Recognition of the religious, cultural and ethnic diversity of the Sudan.
e) The country shall be ruled on federal basis with equitable devolution of powers between the center and the states.
f) Qualifications and professionalism shall be the basis of assuming offices in the national institutions. Special consideration shall be given to the least developed states.
g) Just participation in power at all levels and wealth sharing.
h) Elimination of effects of the civil war and building of confidence among Sudanese people for realization of voluntary unity
i) These procedures shall be completed within an interim period of four years, at the end of which a referendum shall be held for the Southern Sudan according to 1956 borders, to choose either voluntary unity with decentralized powers to be agreed upon or secession.
j) Resolving Nuba Mountains and Ingassana Hills questions in a manner that meets their respective demands for power and wealth sharing within the framework of the united Sudan.

*On the system of Governance the two parties agreed that:*
a) Sudanese political forces shall be committed to the pluralistic democratic system that guarantees human rights and fundamental freedoms.
b) The democratic system that suits Sudan is the federal presidential system that defines federal and state powers and separates between constitutional jurisdictions.
c) Religious and cultural multiplicity in the Sudan shall be considered for coexistence and shall be embodied in the guiding principles of the constitution.

d) Commitment to realize sustainable development as a national goal for building infrastructure, social development and free market mechanism to attain social justice.

*On the mechanisms of political solution the two parties agreed that:*
a) The national initiative constitutes the axis of the Sudanese-Sudanese dialogue and understanding as it works for boosting efforts for a comprehensive political solution through IGAD and the joint Egyptian-Libyan initiatives.
b) Efforts shall be exerted for making the Libyan-Egyptian initiative a success and speeding up the convening of the all-party conference as soon as possible.
c) Affirming the support for IGAD initiative, being one by neighboring countries concerned about the Sudanese affairs, and their role for realizing peace in the Sudan.
d) Underlining the importance of coordination between the two initiatives through a Sudanese-Sudanese dialogue and the agreed upon declaration of principles.

*Blue Nile Peace Agreement, Khartoum 22 December 1999*
This agreement was negotiated and signed in Khartoum between the Sudan Government and former rebel faction namely "BLUE NILE CITIZENS FRONT".

The "Blue Nile Agreement" was signed in a ceremony that took place in the Republican Palace in Khartoum on 22 December 1999. The First-Vice President Sayed Ali Osman Mohamed Taha attended the signing ceremony. The agreement was signed by Dr Nafie Ali Nafie, the Presidential Adviser for Peace Affairs on behalf of the Government of Sudan, and by the tribal Chief Obaid Mohamed Abou-Shutal on behalf of (Blue Nile Citizens Front). Sayed Abou-Shutal was the former Rebel Movement Deputy Governor of (Blue Nile Region).

The 12-point Agreement has called for the democratic rule in the Sudan and for working seriously to preserve the unity of the Sudanese people and territories and to distribute the Sudanese national wealth in a just manner while working for the development of the less developed regions of the country.

It underlined the two parties' commitment to the Federal system of government, a system that allowed the citizens of every state to govern their own region on both the executive and the legislative levels, saying there should be a continued effort to develop it.

The Agreement said the two sides would work seriously to resolve all tribal conflicts in the region and to boost the coexistence between the ethnic groups there with the view to realize stability and to serve the national interests away from fissures and splits.

The agreement called for giving a special consideration to the citizens of the Blue Nile state in representation into the various federal posts so that they would work for serving the homeland. Qualifications and labour law should be taken into account.

It urged the improvement of basic services in the region with particular emphasis given to the health and education services and that they should be expanded and improved in the rural areas. It said voluntary organizations should be encouraged to work for the development of the Blue Nile area and to rehabilitate what was destroyed by the war in the region.

The Agreement called for the establishment of a specialized organization to operate in the Blue Nile area and whose objective would be the development of the region and attracting state, federal and voluntary contributions to the area.

The Agreement called for giving a special consideration to the local administration in the region so that these local administrations would contribute in propagating the culture of peace in collaboration with the other concerned state and federal organs.

The Agreement stipulated a general amnesty for all those who were carrying arms and returned to the homeland and that the returnees be accommodated and be employed in the various society organizations.

Like the rest of the agreements signed between NIF and the northern Sudanese political organisations, the NIF was more interested to divide these organisations rather than entering with then into comprehensive agreement that would address all the issues concerning war and peace politics in Sudan.

Joint Press Statement on Omer Hassan Al Bashir meeting with Mohammed Osman Al Mirghani, in Asmara on 26 September 2000

At the invitation of Isaias Afwerki President of the State of Eritrea, Omer Hassan Al Bashir President of Republic of the Sudan and Mowalana Al Sayed Mohammed Osman Al Mirghani, Chairman of the National Democratic Alliance (NDA) of Sudan met in exploratory talks in Asmara on 26 September 2000.

In these exploratory talks the Government of the Sudan (GOS) and the National Democratic Alliance (NDA) re-affirmed:

- Their Conviction that peace and stability in the Sudan can only be achieved through a comprehensive peaceful settlement and not by military means.
- Their Determination to bring the war to a quick end and create the requisite conditions for voluntary unity and the rebuilding of the country.
- Taking into account the present peace initiatives, the GOS and the NDA agreed to enter into direct negotiations with the aim of arriving at a comprehensive peaceful settlement.

## National Democratic Alliance (NDA) initiatives (1990-2002)

### Asmara Declaration, June 1995

It is to be recalled that the National Democratic Alliance, NDA was first established as national democratic forum in Addis Ababa, Ethiopia in 1990. It became the forum that brought together all the Northern Sudanese political parties that were opposing the NIF regime. In late 1990, the SPLA/M became a full member of the NDA. The SPLA/M's membership to the NDA was negotiated by Dr Lam Akol, who was then responsible for the Movement's external affairs.

On 15-23 June 1995, the NDA and the SPLA/M convened an important conference on the fundamental issues facing Sudan in the Eritrean capital Asmara in which the two opposition agreed on the following:

*Firstly*, the two parties affirmed that their preferred option is unity based on diversity, and the recognition that the Sudan is multi-ethnic, multi-religious, multi-cultural and multi-linguistic country. And that this unity shall also be based on the right of citizenship and equality in rights and responsibilities in accordance with the norms and standards enshrined in international conventions on human rights.

*Secondly*, that true peace in the Sudan cannot be viewed within the framework of the problem of the South but rather from the standpoint that the root causes of our problem have a national character.

*Thirdly*, affirmed that the national problems cannot be solved except through frank, serious and continuous dialogue among all Sudanese national groups. And the nature and history of the Sudanese conflict have proven that permanent peace and stability in the country cannot be achieved through a military solution.

*Fourthly*, reaffirms its commitment to a just peace, democracy and unity based on the free will of the people of the Sudan, and to resolving the present conflict by peaceful means through a just and lasting settlement. To this end the NDA endorses the IGADD Declaration of Principles (DOP) as a viable basis for such a just and lasting settlement.

*Fifthly*, affirms that the right of self-determination is a basic human, democratic and people's right, which may be exercised by any people. And that this right shall be exercised in an atmosphere of democracy and legitimacy and under regional and international supervision.

*Sixthly*, recognizes that the exercise of the right of self-determination constitutes a solution to the on-going civil war, and facilitates the restoration and enhancement of democracy in the Sudan. It also represents a unique historic opportunity to build a new Sudan based on justice, democracy and the free will of its citizens. And Affirms that the areas afflicted by war are Southern Sudan, Abyei District, the Nuba Mountains and Ingessena Hills.

*Seventhly*, declares that the people of Southern Sudan (within its borders as they stood on 1.1.1956 shall exercise the right of self-determination before the expiration of the transitional period. And resolves that the views of the people of Abyei District as regards their wish to either remain within the administrative set up of Southern Kordofan region or join Bahr El Ghazal region shall be ascertained in a referendum to be held during the transitional period but before the exercise of the right of self-determination for the South. If the outcome of the referendum establishes that the majority of the people of this district wish to join Bahr El Ghazal, the people of Abyei shall accordingly exercise the right of self-determination as part of the people of Southern Sudan.

*Eighthly*, resolves that with respect to the Nuba Mountains and Ingessena Hills, a political solution to redress the injustices suffered by the people of these areas shall be sought by the transitional government and that a referendum to ascertain their views on their political and administrative future shall be organized and carried out during the transitional period.

The NDA Declares that its constituent members shall adopt a

common stand on the options to be presented in the referendum in the South, which options shall be:
a) Unity (confederation or federation) and
b) Independent statehood.

And affirms that the Central Authority shall, during the transitional period, devise and implement the necessary confidence-building measures and the appropriate restructuring of the state and socio-economic institutions and processes; so that the exercise of the right of self-determination could have the best chance of upholding the unity option.

The NDA reiterates its determination to lead the Sudanese people in successfully meeting this historic challenge.

On religion and state, the NDA resolves that all laws shall guarantee full equality of citizens on the basis of citizenship respect for religious beliefs and traditions and without discrimination on grounds or religion, race, gender or culture. Any law contrary to the foregoing stipulation shall be considered null and void and unconstitutional. No political party shall be established on religious basis. The state shall acknowledge and respect religious pluralism in the Sudan and shall undertake to promote and bring about peaceful interaction and coexistence, equality and tolerance among religious and noble spiritual beliefs, and shall permit peaceful religious proselytisation and prohibit coercion in religion, or the perpetration in any place, forum or location in the Sudan of any act or measure intended to arouse religious sedition or racial hatred.

On the structures on the government, the NDA resolves that the Sudan shall be ruled during the transitional period as a decentralized state. The powers and functions of the central authority and decentralized entities shall be provided for in the constitution.

The NDA shall give due consideration, in promulgating decentralization laws, to the role of local government and native administration within the new set-up. Moreover, due regard shall be given in the regional administrative divisions to:

a) The wishes of the people in accordance with democratic processes,
b) The fact that the division of power between the Centre and the Entities at this critical juncture of our history is meant to end historical injustices that have led to war and marginalization, restore confidence and consolidate peace, stability and a unity based on the people's free will. In view of the difficult economic conditions of the country, administrative costs of decentralization shall be reduced to the minimum necessary.

The NDA Asmara Declaration was very important document in terms of search for peace in Sudan. The SPLA/M was able to sell fully the principle of self-determination for the people of South Sudan and Abyei to the Northern Sudanese political parties. By and large the Asmara Declaration became the basis, along with the DOP, of the CPA as shall be seen later.

## Inter-Northern Sudanese Dialogue and initiatives (2000-2002)

### 1 – Egyptian-Libyan initiative, 4 July 2001

The Egyptian-Libyan initiative was based on the 'The Tripoli Declaration' of August 1999, which called for the resolution of the Sudanese conflict through bringing together the two parties to the conflict, NDA and the NIF government, with the aim of achieving 'national reconciliation'. This was to be attained through 'All National Conference'. The nine-point document, which was released on 4 July 2001, contained issues pertaining to reconciliation of NDA and the ruling National Congress party in Khartoum. It dealt with democracy, human rights, power and wealth sharing etc. It did not address the problem as a historical conflict mostly between the North and South. Rather it considered NDA as an umbrella of all the opposition groups including the SPLA/M. The initiative did for example address the issue of self-determination, but leaned more on the unity of the country.

The government accepted without reservation the nine-point document, the NDA leadership accepted it in principle, and the SPLA/M rejected them.

The main reasons that led to the sidelining of the Egyptian-Libyan initiative were its open support to the Sudan government positions. The initiators did not trust SPLM/A leadership's stand on the unity of the country. The initiative was generally perceived as an Arab initiative, whereas the IGAD peace process was seen as an African initiative. Moreover, the American and European diplomats where were part of the IGAD process, felt that the Egyptian-Libyan move was aiming at derailing their initiative.

### 2 – Zein Abdin al-Hindi's initiative

Al-Hindi's initaitve between 1998 and 1999 was an attempt from the part of the DUP's Secretary General to fine a formula by which the Northern opposition parties could directly talk with the NIF government.

Al-Hindi's initiative had three main objectives:
a) direct dialogue with the Government;
b) North-North dialogue over issues relating to human rights, democracy and national dialogue.
c) The Government was expected to open up its ranks to the opposition groups through a government of national reconciliation.

Al-Hindi returned to Sudan in 1999, and his group, the so-called 'registered DUP' became a partner in the government of General Omar al-Bashir.

### 3 – Abu al-Ghasim Haj Hamad Initiative, 1999

Haj Hamad was an independent politician and intellectual. He was a political advisor to the Eritrean President Asiyas Aforwerki for many years. His peace efforts were exerted towards bringing together the northern political parties into a national dialogue forum where all the problems facing the country could be resolved.

His ultimate objective was to persuade the Sudan government to accept the principle of dialogue with the NDA as the main opposition group in the country.

Haj Hamad returned to Sudan from his self-imposed exile in 1999. His support based composed of intellectuals and independents. He and his group were instrumental in persuading some government influential centers to open up free media access to the opposition.

*4 – UNESCO and CSI initaitives, September-November 1995*
In September 1995, UNESCO general secretariat decided to convene a conference in Barcelona, which brought together some Southern and Northern personalities. The objective of the conference was to allow the parties to explore the points of disagreement.

A couple of months later, Baroness Caroline Cox of Christian Solidarity International convened in London, on 29 November 1995 a workshop, which was attended by the NDA members, the SPLA/M, and other Southern Suudanese factions. The government of Sudan obtained from attending. The aim of the workshop was to try to outline the outstanding issues in the conflict. The fact that the government delegation obtained, claiming that it did not trust the Baroness intentions prevented any possibility of creating proper atmosphere for discussions between the parties.

## African Peace Initiatives

*1 – Nigerian Abuja peace process (May 1992 and July 1993)*
The Nigerian government peace process in Sudan was prompted by the good offices that the Sudanese government used with former Nigerian Military leader General Obrahim Babangida. The initiative was based

on the principle of peaceful settlement to the problem. The Nigerians were convinced that since they had similar challenges in terms of religious diversity, it was possible for them to mediate in the Sudan problem.

Their governance formula for the resolution of the Sudan conflict was a federal one. The first meeting mediated between the Sudanese government and the SPLA/M took place in May 1992 in the Nigerian capital Abuja. Commander William Nyuon Bany of the SPLA-Torit faction and Dr Lam Akol of the SPLA Nasir faction led the two factions of the SPLA who attended the peace talks. The government in those talks offered the SPLA/M factions a federal type of government where the South would be offered a special status. The SPLA/M main faction demanded a confederal arrangement between the South, Nuba Mountains and Southern Blue Nile and the North.

The SPLA/M-Nasir Faction demanded self-determination for the people of the South. When the government delegation, which was led by Dr Ali Haj Mohamed refused these presentations, the two factions, in a surprise move united their delegations and demanded that the South demand self-determination to be exercised through a referendum in the South with an interim period of two years.

The government delegation could not accept this proposal and thus the talks collapsed.

In May 1993, the SPLA/M main faction and the government delegation met again in Abuja. However they failed to reach any agreement because the SPLA/M this time round demanded a confederal arrangement during the interim period between the North and South (including the marginalized areas) secular state and self-determination for the people of those areas under the SPLA/M. On the other hand the government in the same month met in Nairobi with the SPLA/M-United group (successor of Nasir group). They discussed the same items that the SPLA/M was discussing with them in Nigeria, however neither the Abuja nor the Nairobi talks between the SPLA/M factions and the government delegations reached any concrete results.

The importance of the Abuja talks was based on the fact that they brought closer the SPLA/M factions' views on issues of federalism, confederalism, unity and self-determination, hence paved the way for clearer view on the question of self-determination as discussed during the NDA meeting in Asamara in June 1995.

*2 – IGAD peace initiatives (May 1994-August 1998)*
It is to be recalled that in September 1993 the IGAD council of ministers formed a committee to deal with Sudan peace process, it composed of Kenya, Ethiopia, Eritrea and Uganda, with Kenya as the chair of the committee.

The first round of negotiations between the Sudanese warring parties under the IGAD auspices was held in Nairobi in May 1994, to be followed in July the same year by another round in which the parties agreed on Declaration of principles. The most important points of the DoP included the agreement that the two parties will give priority to the unity of the country during the interim period and that self-determination for the people of Southern Sudan was recognized.

In May 1994 another round was held, but no progress was recorded since both the government and the SPLA/M interpreted the declaration differently. After long break due to the government of Sudan reservations on DoP, the IGAD peace process restarted again and a fifth round was convened in Nairobi on 5-8 May 1998.

The main break through was that the SPLA/M hinted to it giving up insisting in withdrawing the 'New Sudan' map it was presenting to the negotiations which included the Nuba Mountains and Ingassana Hills.

In August 1998, a sixth round under IGAD auspices was convened in Addis Ababa. In these talks, the SPLM asked its two senior military commanders from the Nuba Mountains Yousef Kuwa Makki and

Malek Agar of Ingassana Hills to attend the Addis Ababa talks. There the government delegation insisted that these areas are not part of the Southern Sudan.

The peace talks did not witness any break through except that they two parties accepted the IGAD suggestion that a secretariat within the iGAD Peace and security desk would be created to deal with Sudan peace talks. President Daniel Arap Moi appointed one of his diplomats, Daniel Mbiya to facilitate the Sudanese peace talks. Ambassador Mbiya was later on replaced by Lt Gen. Lazaro K. Sumbeiywo.

## Inter-South Dialogue and initiatives, 1992-2002

*1 – Adare Declaration (September 1992)*
Following the split in the SPLA/m ranks in August 1991, a group of Southern Sudanese intellectuals in Europe and North America met in the Scottish town of Adare. The objective of that meeting was to evaluate the situation within the SPLA/M after the split. It was also an opportunity for those present to evaluate the entire course of the revolution and give suggestions to the leaders of the SPLA/M factions what could be done to resolve their differences.

The significance of the Adare meeting was that the declaration that was issued by Southern intellectuals who called upon Dr John Garang and the leaders of the break away group, Drs Riek Machar and Lam Akol to try to resolve their differences peacefully. They also recommended that the SPLA/M leadership should consider in any future negotiations the following options as the basis for resolving Southern Sudan problem: self-determination for the people of Southern Sudan and marginalized people, to be exercised through internationally supervised referendum and to choose between: unity, federation, confederation or secession.

## 2 – Torit Declaration, September 1992

As a result of the split within the SPLA/M, the leader of the SPLA/M main faction, Dr John Garang called for a meeting of nine military commanders who were members of the High Politico-Military Council in Torit in September 1992. The meeting was to reevaluate the course of the movement and to take some decisions about those senior commanders who defected.

The meeting resolved, in a communiqué dubbed as 'Torit Declaration' among other things, that the breakaway group is welcome back to the ranks of the movement and that the SPLA/M will put into consideration in any peace talks the options of secession, confederation, federation and unity.

The significance of that declaration lies in that it was the first time that the SPLA/M entertained the idea of self-determination for the people of the South. Its official objective has always been the introduction of a new Sudan of unity, democracy, and secularism.

## 3 – Washington Declaration (October 1993)

In October 1993, the US Congressman, Harry Johnson, invited Sudanese opposition groups to meet in Washington DC with the aim of bringing them together to discuss issues relating to war and peace politics in Sudan. On the sidelines of these discussions, Senator Johnson invited Dr John Garang de Mabior and Dr Riek Machar Teny and asked them to sort out their differences. He specifically asked the two leaders to try to sign a document, which would commit both of them to fight for self-determination for the people of Southern Sudan.

The two leaders, after bitter arguments, each trying to stick to his principles, signed separately a document committing them to work for unity of their ranks and to the right of the people of Southern Sudan to self-determination. The document became known as 'Washington' Declaration'.

Although Senator Johnson tried is utmost to persuade the two leaders to reconcile, the fact remained that the two SPLA/M leaders were not convince as yet of reunion, and since both were in the midst of inter-factional fighting, it was difficult for both of them to accept compromising solutions.

Moreover, in the early 1990s, it was the US Congress that was interested in uniting the Sudanese opposition groups; both Bush Sr. and Clinton administration were not at that time enthusiastic of dealing directly with the NDA or the SPLA/M factions.

## New Sudan Council of Churches (NSCC) Peace Initiatives (1993-2002)

The NSCC facilitated South-South dialogue between various factions of the SPLA/M as well as indeginous peace initiatives among Southern Sudanese tribal groups.

### 1 – Wunlit Nuer-Dinka Covenant, March 1999

The Dinka-Nuer West Bank Peace and Reconciliation Conference was held in Wunlit, Bahr el Ghazal, from 27th February until 8th March 1999. The delegates signed the Covenant on 10 March 1999. Among other pertinent issues, the delegates agreed that:

- All hostile acts shall cease between Dinka and Nuer whether between their respective military forces or armed civilians.
- A permanent cease-fire was declared between the Dinka and Nuer people with immediate effect.
- Amnesty was declared for all offences against people and property committed prior to 1/1/1999 involving Dinka and Nuer on the West Bank of the Nile River.
- Freedom of movement was affirmed and inter-communal commerce, trade, development and services are encouraged.
- Local cross-border agreements and arrangements are encouraged and shall be respected.

- It is hereby declared that border grazing lands and fishing grounds shall be available immediately as shared resources.
- Displaced communities are encouraged to return to their original homes and rebuild relationships with their neighbours.
- The spirit of peace and reconciliation this Covenant represents must be extended to all of South Sudan.

Wunlit Covenant became a corner stone for later reunification processes between various SPLA/M factions, particularly those under Dr John Garang and Dr Riek Machar three years later.

*2 – The Waat Lou Nuer Covenant*

On 12 November 1999, after six months of intensive work facilitated by the New Sudan Council of Churches, the Lou Nuer of Upper Nile has reconciled in a seven-day Peace and Governance Conference in Waat, Southern Sudan. The Lou area, including the towns of Waat, Akobo, Yuai, and Langkein, has been wracked by conflict as military forces under three commands (SPLA/M factions) have battled each other. Frequently, the White Army youth militia groups, which number in the thousands, joined various armed groups and entered the conflict. As a result, almost all UN and NGO humanitarian groups had withdrawn from the area and near anarchy had reigned. All forms of civil governance had collapsed. The Covenant brought to halt hostile activites and eventually when the SPLA/M factions were united in the area in 2002, peace was restored.

*3 – Liliir Covenant between the Anyuak, Dinka, Jie, Kachipo, Murle and Nuer: East Bank people-to-people peace and reconciliation conference in Liliir, Bor county Upper Nile, Sudan (May 9th to the 15th, 2000)*

Like Wunlit Nuer-Dinka Covenant, Lillir Covenent was an important forum that provided the East bank communities of Upper Nile Region with the opportunity to meet and discuss all issues related to factional

conflicts as a result of split that took place in SPLA/M in 1991 and its subsequent dynamics. The conferees unanimously agreed that:
- All traditional hostilities will cease among us, and that all military (and militia) groups are to respect the civilian population and abide by, and protect, this covenant;
- The conditions necessary to foster local peace and development are brought about by our communities and leaders, and the provision of basic essential services for the people are made available and improved;
- An amnesty will be upheld for all offences against our people and their property prior to the conference, in the spirit of reconciliation and unity. The amnesty takes effect from this date;
- All abducted women and children are freely returned to their places of origin, and where necessary, marriage customs are fulfilled;
- Freedom of movement across our common borders is upheld, and trade and communication is encouraged and supported;
- All cross border agreements are respected and the authority of the border chiefs and police patrols are justly observed;
- Access to common areas for grazing, fishing and water points will be regulated and shared peacefully among us;
- We will demand good governance from our leaders for the achievement of unity and the observance of human rights.
- We will advocate on behalf of our sisters and brothers who have been scattered and displaced, especially those from the Bor area, for their return to their homeland with the encouragement and co-operation of their communities, leaders and civil authorities of origin.
- This Covenant became important as the South-South Dialogue initiative, a year later was initiated by the NSCC and Lillir Covenant was cited as one of the major achievements of South-South Dialogue, a step forward to unity of the South as they negotiate with the north.

*4 – Strategic Linkages II, Kisumu, Kenya, June 16 - 22, 2001*
This conference, held in Kisumu, Kenya from 16th to 22nd June 2001 at the request of Sudanese traditional leaders, was part of the people-to-people peace and reconciliation process facilitated by the New Sudan Council of Churches (NSCC). It brought traditional leaders, elders and women from Sudan together with representatives of civil society, politicians from the diaspora and members of southern political movements (SPLA/M and SPDF).

The participants of the Kisumu Conference affirmed that:
- The liberation is the common and prime agenda for people of southern Sudan (including Abyei), Nuba Mountains, and South Blue Nile and that it is the people who are at the centre of the liberation struggle.
- Self-determination is the central objective of the people's liberation struggle. This inalienable right of self-determination should be exercised through internationally supervised referendums for all marginalized areas struggling for liberation as mentioned above.
- There should be an extensive program of civic education in preparation for the referendum.
- Common commitment to self-determination should be a unifying factor for everyone involved in the struggle for liberation.
- The conferees also agreed that that all movements should immediately cease hostilities amongst themselves and commit to open dialogue to resolve political differences.
- Establish peace desks in collaboration with civil society organizations coordinate and share information amongst themselves, and maintain close contact with the NSCC.

*5 – Steering Committee of South Sudan Civic Forum and Nigerian inter-South dialogue initiative (2000-2001)*
In May 2000, a group of Southern Sudanese intellectuals and politicians, in Diaspora and inside the country, took an initiative to

bring together the Southern Sudanese military factions, especially the SPLA/M and the SPDF. Prominent politicians and academics pioneered these efforts; prominent among them were Francis Deng, Josepgh Lagu, Abel Alier, Bona Malwal, Daniel Koat Matthews, Michael Wal Duany and several others.

The first meeting was held in London, and later the Nigerian President Olusego Obasanjo got interested in trying to reconcile the Southern Sudanese different factions. The group was trying to persuade the Southern military leaders to struggle on the basis on self-determination for the people of Southern Sudan.

Those efforts were weaken when one of the main engineers of the Forum, Dr Francis Mading Deng resigned from the Steering Committee in October 2000. His resignation has something to do with his disagreement with his colleagues on their insistent that the sole objective of the struggle should be self-determination. Dr.Deng was of the opinion that while this was the major objective of the Southern people, his reading of the international opinion and the US in particular, is less enthusiastic of supporting a secessionist approach in Sudan.

Later on in the same year, Bona Malwal and Dr John Garang went into personal conflict, partly political and partly personal. The Nigerian leadership intervened to solve Garang-Malwal differences and at the same time invited all the Southern Sudanese leaders in exile and inside Sudan to meet in Abuja in November 2001.

The NDA and the Umma Party, while openly accepting the Nigerian mediation worked behind the scenes to abort this process. The Government of Sudan also sent some signals suggesting that it will not allow the Southern Sudanese politicians residing inside Sudan to attend the proposed meeting of the Steering Committee of South Sudan Civic Forum, which was supposed to be held on 12-17 November 2001 in Abuja. Moreover the government and the NDA, Libya and Egypt regarded the Nigerian move as counter to the Egyptian-Libyan initiative that the two countries launched a year earlier.

Moreover, the SPLA/M was reluctant to give a go ahead to the Nigerian initiative partly because most of the politicians who were to attend the proposed meeting besides the SPLA/M were not in agreement with the Movement's understanding of transformation of Sudan through unity in diversity. Thus the Nigerian initiative was aborted.

### 6 – Nairobi Declaration on Unity between the SPLA/M and SPDF, 6 January 2002

As a follow up to their efforts to reunite the two factions of the SPLA/M, Dr John Garang de Mabior and Dr Riek Machar Teny met several times between January 2000 and January 2002 in Nairobi. The main objectives of their meetings were how to work out a formula that would make the SPLA/M and the SPDF formidable force both politically and military and how to stop the factional wars that have exhausted the two factions since August 1991.

Efforts where made by the NSCC, Kenyan and the Ugandan leaders to facilitate the meetings of the two leaders. At one point in June 2001, the two leaders formed a joint committee to work out the merging of the two movements.

After intensive series of meetings between the two leaders, on 6 January 2002, SPLA/M and SPDF leaderships approved and signed the Nairobi Declaration. The following points of agreement, in the opinion of some observers were the most important.

The immediate merger of the two Movements under the historical name of SPLM/SPLA, and on the basis of the following principles:

*Firstly*, that the administration of the Sudan as a Confederal/ Federal United Secular Democratic New Sudan during an Interim Period, as a form of an Interim Unity.

*Secondly*, that Self-determination for the people of Southern Sudan including Abyei, Southern Kordofan, Southern Blue Nile and other marginalized areas, which has been accepted by all the political forces in the country.

*Thirdly*, reaffirmation of the IGAD peace process and the Declaration of Principles (DOP) upon which it is based, as the most credible peace process that will bring about a just and lasting negotiated political settlement in the Sudan.

*Fourthly*, the unity of the people and their struggle.

*Fifthly*, the mobilization of all the human and material resources in the liberated areas and the Diaspora to step up the liberation struggle.

*Sixthly*, recommend to the next SPLM National Convention the issue of electing democratically political leaders (local Councils, Commissioners, Governors, etc.) to run the affairs of the people in a framework of democratic governance.

*Seventhly*, the two sides also agreed on the freedom of delivery of relief and humanitarian assistance to the needy.

*Eighthly*, reorganization of the army into national formations and local defence forces.

*Finally*, the army shall be part of and subordinate to the political organ of the Movement;

As a result of the Nairobi Declaration, Dr Riek Machar Teny became the third Deputy of the Chairman of the SPLA/M and his forces were integrated into the SPLA. With the two main SPLA/M factions reunited, it was possible for the SPLA/M and the Sudan Government to continue negotiations, each representing its constituency without fear of being denied the right of representation.

## Dinka-Nuer Washington Declaration, 13 January, 2002

Representatives of the Dinka and Nuer communities within the Sudanese Diaspora living in the United States of America met from 11-13 January 2002 in Washington, D.C.

The conferees emphasised that this reconciliation process will not rest or be complete until all Dinka and all Nuer are freely incorporated into this peace process and it is extended to all Sudanese who long for peace.

*Firstly*, the conferees agreed that they appreciate and recognize the resolutions of previous People-to-People peace conferences as their resolutions. This includes the conferences at Loki (1998), Wunlit (1999), Waat (1999), Liliir (2000), and Kisumu (2001) in addition to other councils and meetings facilitated by the NSCC.

*Secondly*, that the Dinka and Nuer communities living in the USA declare that we are now One People and that our traditional name of Jieng and Naath in our own languages have a common meaning of being "The People".

*Thirdly*, that we confess on behalf of all of our people and on behalf of our leaders that grave mistakes have been made and wrongs have been committed in the past years and we seek forgiveness from all who have suffered, those who have died and those who live on with deep bitterness and open wounds.

*Fourthly*, that we commit ourselves to a reconciliation process that is much greater than Dinka and Nuer, one that includes all southern Sudanese of all peoples, all movements and factions who seek a just peace for Sudan, all traditional leaders, religious leaders, women and men, youth and adults, the children of today and those yet to be born.

*Fifthly*, that we commit to organize the Sudanese community in the USA for a full engagement in the process of peace in Sudan. We stand ready to work in collaboration with the Sudanese Diaspora communities around the world and all of our sisters and brothers in southern Sudan.

*Finally*, that we call on the international community to commit the necessary resources, both diplomatic and materials, to bring the Sudan conflict to an end in a manner that achieves a just peace for all and includes the right of self-determination.

## United States and the European Peace Initiatives

*1. Center for Strategic and International Studies (CSIS) Initiative*
One of the initiatives that perhaps prompted the US foreign policy makers to seriously consider launching a peace initiative in Sudan was a study of Task Force on Sudan that was released on 20 February 2001. The Study was released by J. Stephen Morrison, head of the Africa Program at Center for Strategic and International Studies (CSIS), and Francis Mading Deng, a southern Sudanese scholar entitled "U.S. Policy to End Sudan's War."

The CSIS report calls upon the Bush administration to "explicitly concentrate U.S. policy toward Sudan on the single, overriding objective of ending the war." For too long, stated Deng, who is also co-chair of CSIS' task force, "the United States has focused on human rights abuses, slavery, terrorism, and other problems in Sudan. But the task force, he said has been forced to recognize that the problems all stem from the war and cannot be solved unless the war is ended". He pointedly noted that "all parties believe that there can be no peace unless the United States plays a leading role." The U.S. policy of pursuing the war against the NIF government in Khartoum is the foundation stone for an overall policy toward Africa that has favored warlords and violence.

The CSIS task force report recommends that the Bush administration take the following eight policy measures to achieve peace:
- Create an international nucleus of Sudan's neighboring states - along with Norway and Britain - to build a peace process.
- Take the Declaration of Principles of the Inter-Governmental Development Authority (IGAD) the basis of negotiations.
- Propose an interim arrangement of one-state, two-systems for Sudan during the peace process.
- Devise multilateral inducements and pressures that move both sides to participate in peace negotiations in good faith.

- Lay the basis for self-government in the south
- Implement confidence-building measures among all sides
- Restore full diplomatic relations with the Sudan government; and
- Complete ongoing U.S.-Sudan negotiations on the issue of terrorism.

It is to be pointed out that the CSIS policy proposal became the basis on which the Bush administration, through its envoy to Sudan framed their involvement in the Sudanese peace process. The essence of the policy was based on power and wealth sharing; one state two systems and self-government for the South during the interim period.

*2. The United States Peace initiative, April 2002*

It is to be recalled that the United States Assistant Secretary of State for Africa Affairs Herman Cohen, initiative a peace process on behalf of his country in 1992. The proposal was for an international force to be deployed between the SPLA and the Government of Sudan forces, prior to any negotiations.

On 28 August 1999, President Bill Clinton named Harry Johnson of Florida special envoy to Sudan. Johnston, a Democrat, was a chairman of the House Foreign Affairs Committee's subcommittee on Africa when he was in Congress. As envoy, Johnson was specifically asked to press Sudan to improve its human rights record as well as explore the possibility of the role that the US administration could play in the Sudan peace process.

It is to be recalled that the US Congress passed on 30 June 1999, Resolution 'S.1234', in which it called for increase of the US humanitarian assistance to the people of the Southern Sudan. It also called for the prevention of Sudan airplanes to go to the South if it refuses to allow food to be transported to the affected areas in the South. On 29 November 1999, President Bill Clinton signed into law two bills, which were passed on 1 July 1999 by the Congress (H.Com.Res.75 and S.Res. 109'. These resolutions became the basis on what became known later as "Sudan Peace Act, tabled to the Congress by the Right Wing Conservative Congress men with support of Evangelical Christian churches. President George W. Bush signed the 'Sudan Peace Act' into law in October 2002. It calls for tough sanctions against the Sudan government if it failed to reach peace agreement with the SPLA/M.

It is worth mentioning that on 23 December 1997, the US Secretary of State Madeline Albright met with Col John Garang and other NDA members in Kampala. She also met Col Garang in October 1999 in Nairobi. Col Garang and Dr Machar also met Collin Powel in March 2002 when they visited the United States.

It is to be recalled that President George W. Bush appointed John C. Danforth, an Episcopal priest who also served 18 years in the Senate, as his envoy to Sudan on 6 September 2001 amid surging public interest in Sudan's war.

Danforth's first visit to the region was delayed for weeks by the terrorist attacks of Sept. 11, 2001. Through his tour November 2001 in Sudan, Danforth emphasized that he carried no U.S. plan to end the war. However he suggested an action on four proposals that he regarded as a test of the two sides' willingness to pursue peace:

- Humanitarian access to the Nuba Mountains, an isolated rebel territory surrounded by government forces, which until November 2001 had never allowed in the U.N. relief planes that have routinely served other rebel areas since 1989.
- Cease-fires to allow humanitarian access to other "zones of tranquillity," especially for immunization campaigns.
- An end to the bombardment of civilians, by shelling, aircraft or helicopter gunship.
- An end to the abduction and enslavement of civilians. He gave the two parties a deadline of mid-January 2002 for positive action on all four points.

The American peace initiative in Sudan was thus based on the CSIS report of February 2001 and Rev. John Danforth's report to

President Bush on 26 April 2002. . The basis, on which the Bush administration policy on peace process in Sudan was formulated, had four main features:

According to Danforth report:

*Firstly*, there cannot be an enduring settlement to Sudan's war unless the oil dimension is effectively addressed. Any peace process should address the oil issue in order to resolve a major cause of conflict and to serve as the basis for a just peace. The fair allocation of oil resources could be the key to working out broader political issues if it were possible to find a monetary formula for sharing oil revenue between the central government and the people of the south.

International oil companies and foreign investors capable of making the investment needed to realize Sudan's oil potential are more likely to venture into Sudan if there is peace and political stability than in current circumstances.

Realizing that the distribution of the oil revenue is an important element in peace process in Sudan, the US administration called upon experts in various departments to develop US best thinking on how the distribution of oil revenues might further the cause of peace in Sudan. Indeed non-governmental organizations have already assembled a profile of Sudan's oil sector and explore revenue-sharing options.

*Secondly*, the US recognized that Southern Sudanese have consistently experienced mistreatment at the hands of governments in the north, including racial, cultural and religious intolerance and restricted access to the nation's resources. And thus, any peace agreement must address the injustices suffered by the southern Sudanese people.

The US administration also recognized that Southern Sudanese have claimed the right of self-determination as a means of protecting themselves against persecution; however, the US administration, for reason best known to it, believes that there are different views of what self-determination means in Sudan's future. The view that self-determination includes the guaranteed option of secession is contained in the IGAD Declaration of Principles, and is supported by many Sudanese. However according to Danforth, secession would be strongly resisted by the Government of Sudan, and would be exceedingly difficult to achieve.

In the view of the US decision makers on Sudan, a more feasible and preferable view of self-determination would ensure the right of the people of southern Sudan to live under a government that respects their religion and culture. Such a system would require robust internal and external guarantees so that any promises made by the Government in peace negotiations could not be ignored in practice.

*Thirdly*, on the role of the religion in the Sudanese politics, the US administration believes that the key will be to create guarantees of religious freedom, which could be either internal or external. Internal guarantees would entail a judicial means of enforcing religious rights, which may be unrealistic in the short-term. External guarantees would include international monitoring of religious freedom with a system of "carrots and sticks" for enforcing religious rights.

*Finally*, on the governance, the Bush administration suggested that the issues that must be considered include the division of power between central and regional governments, the method of selecting government leaders at all levels, and ways of enforcing individual rights. The administration also suggested that any peace process should include the dozen different influential, politico-tribal factions, politico-religious parties, ethnic, regional and civil society groups and a politically powerful army as well as the existing government in in northern Sudan. It will be important to ensure that these various groupings have the ability to make their views known and to participate in decisions relating to peace and the political future of Sudan.

The US peace plan was officially adopted by the IGAD Secretariat although it took different phases in May 2002.

*1 – Nuba Mountains Cease-Fire Agreement 19 January 2002*
The US main interest in the Nuba Mountains cease-fire agreement was to test the two parties' willingness to respect any agreement they would work to achieve. Secondly the Nuba Mountains ceasefire was in a way a blessing in disguise for both the SPLA/M and the Sudan government.

For the SPLA, since the agreement was signed by the leader of the SPLA/M Nuba Mountains sector, it meant that the SPLA/M, a Southern Sudanese dominated movement, would not be blamed if at later stage the movement decides to deal specifically with the Southern aspects of the war.

It would also make things easy for the SPLA/M leadership to ask the Europeans and the Americans to safeguard the Nuba people rights should it become necessary that the Nuba Mountains problem be treated separately.

It would mean that the government of Sudan, by approving to the cease-fire in Nuba Mountains, it succeeded in part to separate the Nuba Mountains problem from the Southern Sudan problem. In final analysis, the cease-fire was a blessing in disguise for all the parties to the conflict, and as the Machakos process has shown, it was easy to separate the Nuba Mountains issue from the Southern Sudan peace tract.

*2 – Garang and El-Bashir Meeting in Kampala on 27 July 2002*
The meeting between the two Sudanese leaders camea week after a ground breaking agreement on a general framework agreement, alas, Machakos Protocol, where the two warring parties of Sudan endorsed the IGAD's DOP of May 1994. The following are excerpts from press communiqué issued highlighting the outcomes Garang-El-Bashir meeting in Kampala.
1. At the invitation of President Yoweri Kaguta Museveni of the Republic of Uganda, President Omar Hassan Ahmen El-Bashir of the Republic of the Sudan paid a two day official visit to

Uganda from 26 to 27 July 2002. President Omar Hassan Ahmed El-Bashir was accompanied by Minister for Presidential Affairs, the Presidential Peace Advisor, the State Minister for Foreign Affairs and other high ranking officials.

2. President Yoweri Kaguta Museveni had also invited Dr John Garang de Mabior, Chairman and Commander in Chief of the SPLM/SPLA, to discus matters pertaining to the Sudan peace process. This visit provided the opportunity for a meeting, which had for some times been outstanding between President Omar Hassan Ahmed EL-Bashir and the SPLA/SPLM leader. Dr John Garang de Mabior was a complained by the Chairman of the SPLM Commission for External Relations, Information and Humanitarian Affairs, the Commissioner for Information and Officials Spokesman of the SPLA, and other high -ranking Officials of the Movement.

3. President Yoweri Kaguta Museveni re-iterated his government's continued support to the IGAD Peace Initiative aimed at resolving the conflict between the Sudanese Government and the SPLA/SPLM.

    In this regard, President Yoweri Kaguta Museveni will continue exerting his personal efforts toward encouraging the Sudanese parties to make more progress for the success of the IGAD initiative.

4. The meeting between President EL-Bashir and Dr. Garang had been arranged by President Moseveni before the Machakos talks as supplementary efforts to the IGAD Peace process. They acknowledged the progress achieved at Machakos particularly on the fundamental issues of "State and Religion" as well as the "Right to Self-determination".

    President EL-Bashir and Chairman Dr Garang applauded the break-through in Machakos and paid tribute to President Daniel Arap Moi, Chairman of the IGAD Sub-Committee on peace in the Sudan, for all his tireless efforts. They undertook to ensure that all

efforts are deployed to resolve the outstanding issues, which will be discussed in the next phase of peace talks. They underscored the need to reinforce the peace process by rallying popular support behind it and building national consensus on comprehensive political settlement.
5. On regional matters, the two Presidents re-iterated their governments' resolve to continue supporting all measures aimed at bringing about peace and security so that steady development can be realized.

*3 – Machakos Protocol 20 July 2002 and the Nairobi MOU, 18 November 2002*
Through the adoption of the Danforth Report of April 2002 and some aspects of CSIS Report of February 2001 by the IGAD Sudan peace process Secretariat in May 2002, it was possible to put into motion the IGAD peace process in Sudan. Moreover, the events of 11 September 2001 and the commitment that Bush administration has shown in trying to push the Sudanese parties to negotiate a peaceful settlement to the problem made it possible for the IGAD secretariat to go ahead with the peace process. There was however some domestic and external important factors that made the Government of Sudan and the SPLA/M leadership to accept the American and European led IGAD peace process. The government of Sudan was under pressure to bring peace in country, especially that its promises to crash the SPLA had failed.

Secondly, the development projects that the government of Sudanhas been trying to carry out, with which it can convince both opposition and the general public that it is a development-oriented government are hindered by war.

On the other hand, after the split within the ruling party government, the number of voluntary recruits in the National Defense Forces has declined and the national army is less enthusiastic to pursue the war without guarantees that a political solution is viable. The Opposition parties do not offer solutions that would make them an alternative to the ruling party. In the South the ordinary people are fed up with the war, and thus have put the SPLA/M under enormous pressure to either find a settlement that would bring an end to the war or fight to the finish. The death toll of the war during the past 20 years has reached alarming stages, and many Southerners seem to have concluded that a just peace means self-determination, which should give them the right to choose either unity of secession. The international community is under pressure to help solve the problem; otherwise it will continue indefinitely to feed millions of Southern Sudanese in liberated areas, internally displaced and refugees in the neighboring countries.

The significance of both Machakos Protocol of 20 July and Nairobi Memorandum of Understanding of 18 November 2002 lies in that the two parties agreed in principle on negotiation on main outstanding issues: self-determination specifically for the people of Southern Sudan, separation of religion from politics, interim period arrangements, power and wealth sharing dynamics, drafting a new constitution, bicameral parliament, general elections and government of national unity. The other two important factors that facilitated the IGAD peace process were the Temporary Cease-Fire signed on 14 October 2002 between the SPLA/M and the GoS, the second serious cease fire ever to be signed by the two parties under IGAD and international supervision. Then there was the October 2002 agreement on aid accesses throughout Southern Sudan between the government and the SPLA/M.

The Machakos Porcess if implemented, will have far reaching effects on the SPLA/M main project, namely the New Sudan Project.:

First of all, it will sideline the marginalized areas that originally gave the SPLA/M the legitimacy of being a Sudanesenational liberation movement. Machakos process separated their cases from that of Southern Sudan thus repositioned the SPLA/M to becoming a Southern based movement.

Secondly, the idea of a secular united state was dropped from the SPLA/M list of demands. Secular state was part of the New Sudan project, which rallied the secularists and leftist groups from the North to support the SPLA/M project.

Thirdly the Protocol will weaken the alliance between the SPLA/M and the NDA. The NDA has been gradually incorporated into the process through Egyptian-Libyan pressures on the US.

During the Machakos process the NDA managed to win two important key demands: general elections and a government of national unity during the interim period. Another key demand of the SPLA/M, which was dropped, is confederation between the Southern and northern entities. What the SPLA/M seems to be left with is self-determination for the people of the South and the idea of making unity attractive during the interim period.

Another observation worth mentioning is the composition of the two delegates. The government team in the negotiations is drawn from different professionals and university lecturers from various fields, including army generals. The government team also has three level backup teams, one in Khartoum, Nairobi and the third in Machakos. The SPLA/M negotiating team seems to rely initially on the drafts of mediators papers, and compared them with the policy papers that the leadership has drafted, The Machakos SPLA/M team was composed of technocrats, academics and politicians. When the negotiations progressed later on, the Movement called in all its cadres of different capacities to become part of the negotiation team in Naivasha.

One of the significant observations regarding Machakos consensus is that several countries and internal organizations have developed interest in following up the process. The US appointed John Danforth in September 2001 to Sudan. Britain appointed one of its diplomats, Alan Goulty on 14 February 2002 to become its envoy to Sudan. The Arab League appointed in October 2002 Dr Nadia Makram Obeid as its envoy to the Sudan peace process. Canada appointed Senator

Mobina Jaffer as its special envoy to the Sudanese peace process. Like the United Nations, the African Union appointed in October 2002 the Nigerian Diplomat Baba Gana Kingibe as its special envoy to the Sudanese peace process.

The appointment of these diplomats seems to suggest that the international community by November 2002 has become seriously involved in the Sudanese peace process.

The subsequent signing of various protocols on wealth and power sharing, Security arrangements, the three disputed areas (Abyei, Nuba Mountains and Blue Nile), which culminated in the signing of the Comprehensive Peace Agreement (CPA), on 9 January 2002, was an expected outcome, given that the two parties at conflict in Sudan and the international community were now ready to bring peace to Sudan.

CHAPTER FIVE

# Scenarios of Alliances among Sudanese Stakeholders during the interim Period

## Introduction

THE SUSPICION AND THE LACK OF CONFIDENCE BETWEEN THE NORTHERN and Southern Sudanese politicians is considered to be the main setback, which could lead to further conflicts during the envisaged interim period (2005-2011). This distrust is manifested in two parallel levels. There is the North-South scepticism on the one hand, and the mistrust between the Sudanese elites/politicians and their constituencies on the other. Ordinary Sudanese citizens for example, regard some of the Sudanese elites as self-centred, and power oriented, as opposed to being people centred. The following statements may explain this situation.

Immediately after the signing of the Machakos Protocol Framework in July 2002, a Southern Sudanese chief residing in Khartoum was asked for his stance on the matter, as to whether he was for the unity of the Sudan, or in favour of secession of the South from the rest of the country after the interim period. Instead of answering the question in a direct manner, he offered the following analogy:

There was a blind man who was invited by some men to enter a house where a new bride was made ready for him to receive. The man stopped at the door and did not move and said to his friends: I will not enter the house until I am certain of what you are inviting me for. Either the bride touches me or takes me personally into the house, because I am afraid that you will force me inside and find it a prison or a door, which will lead to my death.
*Rayaam,* 20 February 2004

As regards the feelings of mistrust between Sudanese elites and their constituencies, a Southern Sudan Paramount Chief was quoted as saying, to a professional Southern Sudanese politician:

I know very well that for you the Southern politicians, we are like spoons for eating fresh hot meals. We endure the heat so that the food reaches your mouths fresh and cold.
*Rayaam,* 20 February 2004

Despite mutual suspicions and a lack of confidence, there exists some consensus among the Sudanese communities and international observers concerning the form of settlement agreed upon by the warring parties in Sudan, through the Inter-Governmental Authority for Development (IGAD) process. The apprehension centres around the form in which the political alliances will take, both between the Sudan People's Liberation mMvement (SPLM) and the ruling National Congress (NC) party on the one hand, and between them and the other political forces in the country during the interim period, as this will determine the direction the implementation process of that peace agreement will take.

The ongoing peace process in Sudan has introduced into the Sudanese political arena new ideological realities, which ought to be recognised, not only by the Sudanese population, but also by the international community peace brokers in the Sudan. Traditionally, the problem was regarded as a conflict of identity, religious intolerance, and economic and power imbalances, between the centre and the peripheries or the marginalised regions. In the past twenty years, new ideological realities have forced themselves into the rules of the game, with the South becoming the centre and driving force behind the transformation-oriented new ideology in the country.

Moreover, one cannot appreciate the basis on which the Machakos and Naivasha peace processes are being conducted, unless one recognises that these peace road maps were informed by three historical and ideological realities, which engendered the problem in Southern Sudan, specifically throughout the past fifty years. These ideological realities may be categorised into three paradigms, two of which were introduced into the Sudanese politics by the SPLM/A.

The Southern based paradigms are 'the New Sudan' and 'the Two Sudans' conflict resolution mechanisms. Traditionally, the Northern Sudanese political elites and the central governments power brokers, who continued to control the state institutions subsequent to independence, were always in charge of the dynamics of war and peace in the Sudan.

These Northern elites determined who should represent the South; they dictated the content of the agenda of peace talks; they interpreted the causes of the problem and prescribed solutions to the dilemma as it suited them; and they decided on the modalities of the entire process and the outcomes of the peace negotiations. They also reserved the right to implement the entire agreements or only parts of them. This was the case in the Round Table Conference in March 1965, the Addis Ababa Agreement in February 1972, and the Khartoum and Fashoda Peace Agreements in April and September 1997.

Perhaps, the difference this time with the Machakos and Naivasha peace processes is that it is the South, which has assumed the role of driving force in furthering the peace initiative. For the first time, the

Scenarios of Alliances among Sudanese Stakeholders 111

South has introduced into the Sudanese political scene two paradigms, which are intended to provide a final, and hopefully, just solution, to the Sudanese conflict. It is also the first time in the Sudanese history that the main Northern Sudanese political parties and their allies in North Africa seem to have had little impact, and a somewhat disillusioned disposition in the wake of new realities, not only surrounding the dynamics of the highly significant transformation process taking place in the country, but also on the current peace process, while the South appears to be driving the transformation process in the country. The question is thus: Are the leaders of the SPLM/A aware of this historical process?

In the following section of this chapter, the three paradigms, which informed the Naivasha peace process, shall be discussed.

# The Three Paradigms

## 1 – The 'Old Sudan' Paradigm

The 'Old Sudan' refers to the existing state structures of the Sudanese central government, as inherited from the Anglo-Egyptian colonial state in January 1956. The supporters of the 'Old Sudan' paradigm, while acknowledging the existence of several inherent structural problems in power and wealth sharing dynamics in the current system of the government, call for symbolic reforms within these structures, which would not necessarily do away with the current quota arrangement between the riverine Northern elite and the so-called marginalised regions.

The collective packaging of the reforms, which were on offer to the South and the marginalised regions, involved partial reforms in the federal structures of the state, without altering the central role of the riverine elite in dominating the executive, legislative, judiciary and economic power vis-à-vis the regions. Any call for comprehensive reforms and the restructuring of political power and economic sectors within the country, or any demand by the regions to secularise the political and religious relationships within the country, was regarded by the power brokers of the 'Old Sudan' as a call for the destruction of Arab and Islamic dominant culture in the country. The regions' demands for constructive and comprehensive transformation was therefore regarded by the Arabicised North as 'racist' attempts, by 'non-Arabs,' to play according to 'racial' rules, and not by 'religious' rules, meaning the majority of the population are Muslims. The adherents of the 'Old Sudan' often offer a window dressing reform package to maintain the status quo.

*2 – The 'Two Sudans' Paradigm*

This forms the dominant ideology in Southern Sudan. The 'Two Sudans' paradigm originally came into being as a result of Southern Sudanese attempts to convince both the Anglo-Egyptian colonial powers and various Sudanese central governments that the South was in possession of distinct historical, political and socio-economic realities, which were not necessarily similar to those prevailing in the rest of the country. This paradigm was initially a modest call in the 1940s and 1950s, for an autonomous status for the South. The initiative was specifically aimed at creating arrangements for safeguards and guarantees for the South from the central government. At a later stage, the venture was developed into a demand for federal arrangements between the South and the North. By the 1960s, it evolved into an overt demand for total independence, through a self-determination process, in which the people of the South were to be asked whether to stay within a united Sudan or establish a state of their own.

The premise of this secessionist paradigm is that the dispensation, which created the independent united Sudan in January 1956, was based on the understanding that upon achieving its independence, the country would consider the concerns and suggestions put forward by the Southern representatives during pre-independence negotiations. These negotiations culminated in the North accepting, in principle, that a federal arrangement would be put into place immediately after becoming an autonomous state. However, the refusal of the North to fulfil its promise soon after independence resulted in successive violent conflicts between the central governments and the Southern based liberation movements. The consecutive governments, whether military or civilian, could not address the issue of Southern Sudan as a national concern, and rather perceived Southern Sudanese transformation-oriented demands as secessionist in character. The relationship between the North and the South was, subsequently, characterised by suspicions and a lack of allegiance by the South to the very essence of a united Sudan. Consequently, a considerable number of Southern Sudanese groups chose not to cooperate with the united Sudanese central governments, mainly because these equated any call for a federal arrangement between the two halves of the country with secession. According to the 'Two Sudans' paradigm adherents, it was the North that was secessionist and not the South, because the North refused to accept the federalist approach to unity, thus pushing the South towards secessionist leanings.

### 3 – The 'New Sudan' Paradigm

This paradigm is another Southern Sudanese proposal aimed at a final, viable solution to the war and peace issues in the Sudan. Its adherents, among other aspects, perceive the South as the base of political mobilisation for the marginalised regions of Sudan. The package of reforms, which this paradigm advocates, involves establishing a new political contract between the centre and the peripheries – a deal that should accommodate a new basis for restructuring power and wealth distribution in the country. The paradigm also proposes that such a restructuring process should favour the regions, and not the centre. It also advocates the substitution of Arab-Muslim cultural domination by a 'New Sudanese' cultural affiliation, to which the majority of the Sudanese are historically and culturally linked, and that this new identity should be governed by a secular system of governance. The proposal shifts power relations in the country, and calls for a redefinition of what Sudan represents to ordinary Sudanese citizens, in terms of its historical, cultural, economic and political evolution, and the ideological affiliation, as well as loyalty to the nation. The ultimate objective for the 'New Sudan' paradigm would be to separate religion from politics and to do away with cultural chauvinism as the base of acquisition of power by the elite in Khartoum.

One should recognise that the founders of the Southern based 'New Sudan' paradigm had, for the past twenty decades, entered into alliances with the coalition of the marginalised populace from Western, Central and Eastern Sudan. The composition of the marginalised coalition is diverse in terms of ethnic backgrounds, social and interest scope, as well as in terms of political and economic objectives. It is a historical oriented school of thought, deriving its arguments from the historical evolutionary experiences of the Sudanese people, although its supporters seem to find some difficulty in linking the historical experiences of the Southern population to those from Northern Sudan proper. This school of thought comprises of social and political Sudanese groups, located in Central Sudan (Nuba Mountains), Western Sudan, especially Darfur (Fur, Masalit, Zagawa), the Southern Blue Nile, the Funj in Eastern Sudan, all of who pay their allegiance to the 'New Sudan' dispensation.

From the above brief background, one can appreciate that the Machakos road map for the Sudanese peace process of 20 July 2002, which forms the basis of the current conflict resolution process in Sudan, has encouraged the relevant parties to the conflict to identify three important issues. The ultimate aim of these three issues is to rectify the shortcomings, which the 'Old Sudan' paradigm has consistently resisted, and to introduce and implement the transformation packages, which the 'Two Sudans' and the 'New Sudan' paradigms are calling for. Indeed, the Machakos road map has explicitly spelled out a number of these issues, while its drafters have chosen to be vague on others. This vagueness has introduced, unintentionally perhaps, contradictory framework that may hinder the implementation of the peace agreement.

The first issue is whether the SPLM/A and the NCP will be committed to democracy and the secularism of national politics as viable options for the post-interim period's political, economic and judiciary permanent arrangements between the South and the North. What is expected from both the NCP and the SPLM/A is the creation of a democratic Sudan. Equipped with the knowledge that the NCP represents the 'Old Sudan' system and the SPLM/A claims to represent the 'New Sudan' school of thought, one wonders whether the vagueness of the issue of democracy in the Machakos Protocol was not intentional, due mainly to the compromises enforced on the two parties during the negotiations.

The Machakos Protocol in particular, is unclear on issues of democracy, a multi-party system, and on secularity of national politics, during the interim period. This may be interpreted, as a partnership between the SPLM/A and the NCP, with the South being taken for granted, as a SPLM/A power base. It must be understood that both the Sudan People's Liberation Movement (SPLM) and the National Congress Party (NCP) military oriented parties, and are not known to be adherents of free democratic opposition. Most observers seem to be advancing tow scenraios: the worse case scenario one foresees the establishment of an internationally recognised dictatorship rules by the SPLM/A administration in the South, and a superimposed, one-party system in the North, under the NCP. The second worse case scenario envisages the establishment of both dictatorships in the name of peaceful implementation of the peace agreement.

The second contentious issue is that of the unity of the country, and what this means, in terms of post-interim period permanent arrangements, especially in relation to power and wealth sharing between the centre and peripheries, including the South. Definitely, the SPLM/A is in favour of a new dispensation. As discussed previously, the movement demands the abolition of the current political system in the Sudan, to be replaced by a 'New Sudan'. However, the current peace process, specifically the Machakos Protocol Framework, seems to have followed the 'reform based approach' and does not favour the dismantlement of the 'Old Sudan' system, which the SPLM/A calls for. This situation will inevitably prove to be a dilemma for the SPLM/A and its allies, because while it espoused the idea of a new dispensation, the requirements for the peaceful implementation of the agreement may force the SPLM/A to forge a partnership with the NCP. If this happens, the foregone conclusion of the whole process would be the implementation of the item of the agreement concerning the right of self-determination for the people of the South. The SPLM/A and the NCP may not be equipped with the right tools to stop the people of the South from voting for secession, and even if they are, these tools may not be effective and attractive to the people in the South during the interim period.

Then there is the issue of self-determination, and the impact it will have on national politics, especially during the post-interim period permanent arrangements (constitutionally and politically) should the South opt to secede from the rest of the country. One must recognise that the SPLM/A is a coalition of two Southern political groups, each advocating contradictory solutions to the power and wealth sharing politics in Sudan. The unionists within the SPLM/A favour, as discussed previously, the 'New Sudan' formula as outlined in the SPLM/A Manifesto of 31 July 1983. The separatists advocate the 'Two Sudans' formula, as detailed in the Nasir Declaration of 28 August 1991, which advocates for the creation of an independent state in Southern Sudan.

Moreover, the unionists are in close alliance with the traditional political parties – the Democratic Unionist Party (DUP), the UMMA party, and other left wing and nationalist parties. The SPLM/A has also established a coalition with the political and military groups from marginalised areas of Central, Eastern and Western Sudan. All these groups are united against the current structure of the Sudanese state, but remain divided over how and by whom the state should be governed. A pertinent question in this regard, would be to what extent these alliances would affect the implementation of any final agreement reached between the SPLM/A and the NCP.

On the other hand, the long-term repercussions of some these bilateral closed-door negotiations between two leaders may prove perilous in the future. This is because certain issues, which they might have agreed upon, and vaguely recorded in the final text of the agreement, may never be implemented. This is exactly what happened to the Israelis and the Palestinians during the Oslo closed-door peace negotiations. Once either of the leaders is no longer in power, during the interim period, for whatever reason, the implementation of the agreement may not proceed smoothly because of these undisclosed personal undertakings.

In summary, the IGAD Peace Process provided an interesting outline of an evolutionary process in the Sudanese conflict, which culminated in three contradictory paradigms, all of which aspired to introduce some form of new social contract among the Sudanese people. The question, however, remains in limbo: Did the Machakos and Naivasha processes concretise these transformation packages and provide genuine solutions to the Sudanese problem, or has the whole process simply identified the issues under discussion, postponing the provision of the solutions to the Sudanese conflict for another round of civil war after 2011?

Other main questions that would require some answers, are whether the Southern Sudanese leadership would handle their part of the bargain appropriately during the interim period; whether the Machakos and Naivasha peace process implementation would succeed without the involvement of the Southern and Northern Sudanese political and military organisations which, although technically in alliance with either the SPLM/A or the NCP, have not directly been involved during the negotiations for the final peace agreement.

## Northern Sudanese Political and Military Organisations

The political map of Northern Sudan, like that of the South is very complex and diverse. Unlike the South, however, the political forces of the North, while they differ on the 'type' and the levels of reforms to be introduced in post-war Sudan, are in total agreement on the necessity to maintain the unity of the country. They would do everything in their power to ensure that the country remains united. There are obviously some ideological and political differences among these political forces; among them are socialists, communists, Arab nationalists, Islamists, religious sectarian loyalists and secularists. It should be recalled that due to internal differences within these political parties during the 1990s, the majority of these split into opposing factions. The dominant reason for the defections was the call by several members within these parties for internal reforms and democracy.

For example, the National Democratic Alliance (NDA), which was formed in 1990 to oppose the then National Islamic Front (NIF) regime, consists of (in addition to the Southern based Union of Sudan African Parties (USAP) and the (SPLM/A), political parties and organisations, which have a different understanding of how the country should be governed. Ideologically and politically, within the NDA, there exist sectarian and religious parties, such as the DUP and UMMA National Party. There are also the Sudan Communist Party,

Sudan Trade Unions Association, Independent National Personalities, and the Ba'ath Party. There are also Northern Sudan based military organisations, which were formed in the 1990s to pioneer the military campaign against the NCP regime. These include the Free Lions (Rashaida), the Legitimate Command, and the Sudanese Allied Forces.

Among these political and military organisations, are the marginalised forces, which are based in the Eastern, Western and Central Sudan. The importance of these forces is centred on their stance on issues such as democracy, unity and self-determination during the interim, which may affect the balance of power and the nature of power alliances within the North. This is because these marginalised political groups, like the SPLM/A, are in favour of the creation of a new Sudan, which must not be based on race, religion or colour, but rather on democratic and secular arrangements.

The marginalised political groups comprise the following forces: The two armed groups in Darfur, namely the Sudan Liberation Movement (SLM) and the Justice and Equality Movement (JEM). These groups are likely to part ways once peace prevails in the country, both generally speaking and more specifically within Darfur itself. The SLM, which joined the NDA in February 2004, could form an alliance with SPLM/A, while JEM may ally itself with the Popular National Congress (PNC) of Hassan al-Turabi. Both factions of the UMMA National Party will face a stiff challenge from Darfur-based organisations. Given that Darfur provided the UMMA National Party with more than a third of its MPs during the 1980s, this could seriously undermine the UMMA parliamentary representation during the interim period.

The Nuba-based parties are likely to seek an alliance with the SPLM/A. This is especially the case for some factions of the Sudan National Party (currently split) and the General Union of the Nuba Mountains.

The Southern Blue Nile based military division of the SPLM/A and associations will be inclined to ally with the SPLM/A. They could either merge or form a loose alliance with the SPLM/A. Divisions among these community-based organisations should not be ruled out, even to the point of splits. Certain parties would clearly like to maintain their historical links with both the DUP and the NCP.

The Beja Congress is now split into a faction with the NCP government, led by Sheikh Omer. The other group, which is also a member of the NDA, is led by newly elected Secretary-General Musa Mohamed Ahmed, depending on the nature of the peace agreement they will reach with the NCP, the options may be limited.

There are also political parties and splinter groups, which are currently in alliance with NCP. The nature of these alliances will certainly affect the balance of power during the interim period, both in the North and the South. It is most likely that during the interim period, the following scenario may occur – the ruling National Congress (Ali Osman Taha and Omar al-Bashir faction) may ally itself with the following parties: Umma Party (wing of Mubarak el Fadil el Mahdi), DUP wing of Sharif El Hindi, The Muslim Brotherhood of (Sadiq Abdalla Abdel Magid) and the UDSF of Joseph Malwal.

On the other hand, the Popular National Congress of Hassan al-Turabi may ally itself with the UMMA National Party of Sadiq el Mahdi and the DUP of Mohamed Osman el Mirghani. Moreover, the DUP of Mohamed Osman al Mirghani, currently an ally of the SPLM/A, faces the challenge of uniting its various splinter groups. Currently, there are three main DUP factions: the Mirghani and Zein Abdin el Hindi wings and the Reform Group with collective leadership of Mirghani Abdel Rahman Sulieman, Amin Akasha and others. Within the Mirghani group, there are five distinct voices: Sid Ahmed el Hussein, Mohamed Ismail Azhari, Ali Mohamoud Hassanien, Haj Mudawi Mohamed Ahmed, and Muhamed Osman Mirghani, himself represented inside Sudan by his brother Ahmed Mirghani.

These in addition to the Sudan Allied Forces of Brigadier Abdel Aziz Khalid; this is a 'nationalist' military group, which supports the SPLM/A leadership's call for the creation of a New Sudan. The long-heralded merger with the SPLM/A may proceed during the first half of the interim period. Should this merger proceed, it might have political implications within the SPLM/A.

What are the implications of the above scenarios and alliances to the implementation of the peace agreement? Certain Sudanese sceptics of the Machakos and Naivasha peace process believe that the Northern Sudanese political forces, despite differing in the details of a settlement to the Sudan conflict, are all, for political and strategic reasons, against self-determination for the people of the South. The implication being that these parties may not necessarily be in favour of peaceful transitional period which may lead to the implementation of the referendum item in the peace agreement.

There are three scenarios suggested by these critics, which the National Congress Party Government and other Northern Sudanese political parties may opt to use in order to frustrate attempts by Southern Sudanese to exercise their right of self-determination.

*Firstly*, adoption of Jafar Nimeiri's policies of 'containment and divide and rule'.

*Secondly*, adopting a calculated program by the Northern Sudanese opposition parties, which are not currently party to the Machakos and Naivasha peace process, to forge alliance with the government in power, with the aim of dismantling the peace agreement between the South and the North.

*Thirdly*, using Omar El-Bashir and Hassan al-Turabi's strategy of 'arming Southerners against Southerners' or 'buying their loyalty through financial or positions' bribery'.

This is further elaborated in the statements below.

In February 1972, the government of Sudan, under the presidency of General Jaafar Nimeiri, decided to resolve the Southern Sudanese problem through a one country, two-systems formula. It signed an agreement with the leader of the Southern Sudan Liberation Movement (SSLM) General Joseph Lagu. The agreement offered the South a local autonomy. As part of the agreement, an understanding was reached to the effect that after five years the agreement would be evaluated to ascertain whether both sides had adhered to it or not. What Nimeiri opted to do during the interim period was forcefully retire all military officers of AnyaNya (SSLM military wing) who were suspected of posing a potential threats to the smooth implementation of the agreement.

Secondly, in April 1972, Nimeiri handed over the administration of the South to his Southern allies, under the leadership of Abel Alier. These Southerners were inside the country, and largely considered by the AnyaNya leaders to be Nimeiri's loyalists. President Nimeiri made it a point that those who were members of SSLM or from its military wing did not hold important positions in Southern Sudan High Executive Council government in Juba. The result was an open-ended agreement, which Numieri finally did away with in May 1983, when he divided the South into three regions. From 1975 onwards, a number of Southern military garrisons started to rebel against the government throughout the South, forming the AnyaNya II liberation movement at the border between Sudan and Ethiopia. Thus, Nimeiri managed to divide Southerners into groups of enemies, and succeeded in doing that over little more than a four-year period (1974-1977).

On the other hand, the Northern Sudanese opposition parties of the time, namely the UMMA, DUP, and NIF, who were against the Addis Ababa Agreement of 1972, persuaded Jafar Nimeiri to give up his alliance with the Southern Sudanese and instead incorporate these parties into his government structures under the National Reconciliation Pact of 1977. The result was that Nimeiri undid all his promises to the South. In fact, three years later, he attempted to annex some of the richest parts of the South to the North in 1980, when he declared the decentralisation policy. This policy was to do away with the special status that the Southern Sudanese region had enjoyed. By 1981, the Southern region became one of the many regions in the country. Subsequently, the relationship between Nimeiri and the Southerners deteriorated to the point of mass rebellion in the South against his regime from May 1983 onwards.

As discussed previously, the Northern Sudanese political forces, whether in the government or in opposition, particularly the riverine Northern elites, consider it their national duty to gain the upper hand in running the country, since they form the religious majority. It is this 'duty' and obligation that would make it natural for them to try, during the interim period, to work towards achieving unity in the country. For this group of Northerners, unity means status quo, where Sudanese who trace the origins of their forefathers to the Arab world, will continue to control the central government institutions. In other words, the opposition Northern political parties, together with their Middle Eastern allies, mainly Egypt and Libya, will do everything in their power to ensure that the South remains part of a united Sudan, even if it means using the three strategies mentioned above.

This will probably be the case, especially if a general election is held during the interim period, where the Northern opposition parties will aim to secure the majority vote. Should this situation prevail, it might create a new reality, threatening the implementation of the peace agreement, particularly since these parties will not be signatories to the envisaged peace agreement.

In April 1997, General Omar Hassan al-Bashir and his former ally, Dr Hassan Abdallah al-Turabi, signed an agreement with South Sudan Independence Movement (SSIM) and five of its allies. Dr Riek Machar, then leader of SSIM, led the coalition and formed a government (Southern Sudan Coordinating Council) in August 1998, which was intended to administer the ten Southern states during a four-year interim period. The interim period, which should have preceded the referendum, would have allowed Southerners to determine the future of their political status in the country. What the NCP government did, was to see to it that its allies from the South, inside the country, would have the upper hand in the affairs of the government, within the ten Southern states and in the central government positions allocated to the South. Secondly, a systematic plan was carried out whereby senior commanders, who were led technically or directly by Dr Machar, were alienated from him. Commander Kerubino Kawanyin Bol and Commander Arok Thon Arok (both were originally part of the Sudan armed forces before they rebelled and became senior officers in the SPLA in 1983) were re-commissioned into the Sudanese army with senior ranks. The two men were thus removed from Machar's chain of command.

Thirdly, Machar's power-based SSIM was divided by the government into small bands of militias who were loyal, not to their leader, but to individual commanders, who had secret understandings with the Government of Sudan. Those politicians, who were loyal to Dr Machar, were either bribed with positions of power or simply developed their own personal differences with him.

Commander Paulino Matip Nhial, in Western Upper Nile, Commander Gordon Koang Chuol, in Eastern Upper Nile, Gabriel Tang Ginya from Central Upper Nile, plus Machar's top political advisors from his own tribe, Taban Deng Gai, Dr Riek Gai Kok, Dr Michael Wal Duany, and several other military commanders and politicians, were persuaded directly or indirectly by the government to desert him.

By 1999, three years after the famous Khartoum Peace Agreement, Dr Riek Machar found himself practically engaged in constant military engagements against his lieutenants, who were, at this point, openly backed by General al-Bashir's government. Dr Machar remained in office in Khartoum for about three years, because the NCP government did everything it could to prevent him from moving to the capital of the South, Juba, where his government was supposed to be based. When Dr Machar left the country in December 1999, to return to the South, his successor, a Southern Sudanese senior military officer and a loyalist to General al-Bashir's government, was permitted to move his government to Juba.

Moreover, and despite the clear stipulation in the Security Arrangements Framework agreement of September 2003, which stated that all the Southern Sudanese militia groups, currently in alliance with the NCP, would be absolved into the SPLM/A structures during the interim period, the NCP government will continue to try, during the interim period, to maintain its alliances with these militias. It must be noted that the South Sudan Defence Forces (SSDF) comprises all forces under the leadership of Dr Riek Machar, upon signing the Khartoum Peace Agreement with NCP in April 1997. This force later fragmented and each group allied itself with the Government of Sudan. The government will carry out this policy, in order to destabilise the SPLM/A power base in the South. However, as time passes, these militias too, will eventually become marginalised – the government, at least during the first two to three years, will focus on the SPLM/A leadership, with particular focus on the wing within the SPLA, which has separatist tendencies, and will try to fully neutralize it.

## Southern Sudanese Political and Military Organisations

When addressing the Machakos and Naivasha peace process dynamics in Southern Sudan, and the manner in which the peace agreement will be implemented, the following questions may be posed: Will the SPLM/A leadership try to isolate the other Southern political forces, or will it opt to appease some and antagonise others? What will be the nature of the current alliances between the SPLM/A and Northern

Sudanese opposition parties, especially those in the NDA, during the interim period? Will the Southern Sudanese military organisations, currently involved in love-hate relationships with the SPLM/A, opt to unite against SPLM/A leadership during post-war Southern Sudan administration? On the other hand, two parallel, opposing ideological trends exist within the SPLM/A – those who prefer a united secular democratic Sudan, in alliance with marginalised areas, and those who envisage the path of self-determination leading to secession of the South, as the best option to solve the Sudanese conflict. What will happen during the interim period if the SPLM/A leader, Dr John Garang, decides to ally with one trend, thereby sidelining the other? The SPLM/A leadership, as a representative of the people of Southern Sudan, is expected by a number of Southerners to open channels of communication with all the Southern Sudanese groups, especially due to the fact that almost all the Southern Sudanese political groups openly support the Machakos and Naivash processes. Will the SPLM leadership wholeheartedly support South-South dialogue, to involve all the militia groups that are currently allying themselves with the government of Sudan?

As discussed earlier, the SPLM/A leadership openly expresses its willingness to assign the unity of the country full priority during the interim period. It is equally true that the current administration in Khartoum is in favour of unifying the country, and has worked hard, on numerous occasions, to neutralise the Southern forces, which had secessionist tendencies in the 1990s. Moreover, the US administration, the main guarantor of the peace process, in addition to its own strategic and economic agenda, has expressed its opposition to self-determination for the people of Southern Sudan, as reported by Senator John Danforth in his famous report on the Sudanese peace process to President George W. Bush in April 2002.

On the other hand, supposing that the SPLM/A leadership, the NCP government, the Northern Sudanese opposition parties and the

US administration, entered into an alliance during the interim period, and opted to skip the process leading to a referendum, ultimately deciding that a referendum is not necessary in the South – what would be the reaction of the other Southern Sudanese forces be

While it may seem easy to speculate on how the North and its strategic allies would handle the Southern secessionist tendencies during the interim period, Southern Sudanese leaders should learn from Nimeiri and El-Bashir's attitudes towards the agreements, which they previously signed with the South, and should invest this knowledge and practical experience during the upcoming six years towards cementing South-South dialogue. One manner in which to promote the South-South dialogue would be to empower Southern Sudanese civil society organisations, and equally render power to the youth in Southern military and political organisations. This would provide these groups with more influence, thereby mobilising the people of the South during the interim period to support the peace agreement.

Based on its national ideology, the SPLM/A qualifies for the categorisation of being a national revolutionary movement, both in Southern and Northern Sudanese power sharing politics. In Southern Sudan, although in a broad sense, the SPLM/A embodies all the Southern Sudanese political shades, it is hoped that it will act as such.

Comparable to the Northern Sudan, the political map of the Southern Sudan is complex and volatile at best. The structures of the political and military alliances among these groups are based on power, ethnicity and ideological considerations. Most of the Southern Sudan pre-1989 political parties were ethnically based and had no specific economic or political policies for the South.

The other political grouping in the South, whose position on unity and self-determination may affect the balance of power within the South during the interim period, is the Union of Sudan African Parties, USAP. This is a coalition of Southern parties in the former democratic parliament, which was dissolved by General Omar Beshir's coup d'état in 1989. These parties include the Southern Sudanese Political Association (SSPA), the People's Progressive Party (PPP), the Sudan African Congress (SAC), the Sudan African People Congress Organisation (SAPCO), and the Sudan Federal Party (SANU), which used be led by Gabriel Yoal Dock's before he joined one of Dr Machar's organisations.

USAP is currently formed of external and internal components. USAP outside Sudan is presently led by Eliaba James Surur, a member of the NDA Leadership Council. The USAP inside is led by Joseph Ukel, the Chairman of NDA secretariat inside Sudan. The union is also recognised as being closer to the SPLM/A than other Southern political parties. Both wings are currently members of the NDA. One cannot disregard the possibility of an alliance or merger forming between the SPLM/A and USAP during the interim period.

It should be mentioned that the Nuba Mountains-based Sudan National Party of Rev. Abbas Ghaboush was a member of the USAP until 1989. However, it joined the NDA separately in 1992. Rev. Ghaboush took exile in Sudan, where his party joined the ruling party (National Congress). He subsequently withdrew yet again, and together with three other Nuba political organisations, established the New Sudan National Party in February 2003 (and in the same year, Rev. Ghabous, living in exile, became officially a member of the SPLM/A).

There is a likelihood that a few of these political groups will resurface again, perhaps even accompanied by new ones on the political scene, once the peace agreement is signed. Should this happen, the political map of the South will be overcrowded and more confusion may ensue.

The second Southern Sudanese political group operating inside the country is the United Salvation Democratic Front (UDSF). The UDSF was formerly under the leadership of Dr Riek Machar, until December 1999, when he returned to SPLM/A following the failure of the Khartoum Peace Agreement in April 1997.

There are currently two wings of the UDSF: the main faction is chaired by Joseph Malwal, Minister of Civil Aviation in the current NCP government. The second faction is chaired by Peter Abdel Rahaman Sule. Sule's faction represents the opposition in the Sudanese parliament. Its chairman is MP for the Juba town Constituency. It is difficult to predict the future alliance of USDF factions once the peace agreement is signed, as the ranks of the UDSF are presently unhappy with the National Congress Party policies.

According to the Khartoum Peace Agreement of April 1997, the UDSF military wing was called the South Sudan Defence Forces/ SSDF. Similar to the UDSF, its leader was Dr Riek Machar. Following the collapse of the agreement, the SSDF officially became a government-backed coalition of Southern based militias. Currently, the SSDF is led by Major General Paulino Matiep Nhial and Major-General Clement Wani, the current Deputy President of Coordination Council of South Sudan. One must emphasise that according to the security arrangements agreement between the Government of Sudan and the SPLM/A of September 2003, the SSDF members are entitled to be absolved into the SPLM/A structures. It remains to be seen what the SSDF and the SPLA leadership will decide, as the dialogue between them progresses. If the entire SSDF force were to become part of the SPLM/A government structures, then the balance of power, militarily speaking, may be in favour of the South during the interim period.

The SSDF is an alliance of the following Southern-armed groups: Mundari Militia, led by Major General Clement Wani; Equatoria Defence Force, led by Dr Theopolous Ochieng and Cdr Martin Kenyi; Murle Militia, led by Major-General Ismail Kony; Fertit Militia, led by Major-General Tom el Nur; Western Nuer Militia (oil fields), led by Major-General Paulino Matip Nhial; Central Nuer Militia (Pangak area), led by Brigadier Gabriel Tang-ginya; Eastern Upper Nile Militia (Nasir area), led by Major-General Gordon Koang Chol.

The third group of Southern Sudanese politicians, which is currently in alliance with the NCP are Southern Sudanese members of the Coordinating Council for Southern States (CCSS). The CCSS is composed mainly of Southern Sudanese politicians who are members of the ruling National Congress. In addition to the current governors of the ten Southern states, regional and federal ministers, the prominent Southern members of the National Congress Party include Dr Riek Gai Kok, Major-General (Retired) Alison Manana Magaya, Dr Lual Lual, Angelo Beda and others. It is probable that a large number of them will remain in the NCP – but at risk of facing tremendous competition during the first general elections in Southern Sudan.

The fourth political group in Southern Sudan, which may affect the balance of power during the interim period, is the London based South Sudan Democratic Forum. It mainly consists of Southern Sudanese politicians and intellectuals in the Diaspora. Its membership includes the South Sudan Liberation Movement/Army (SSLM/SSLA) of Dr Michael Wal Duany and numerous, former SPDF faction defactees led by Commander Chol Gaka. The prominent leaders within the forum are Dr Martin Lemi Elia-Lomurö, Bona Malwal Ring, Joseph Lagu and Daniel Koat Matthews. The forum may cooperate with the SPLM/A during the interim period within the South-South dialogue process. However, it will most likely opt to become the official Southern political opposition.

The fifth Southern group, which may have an impact on the dynamics of political alliances during the interim period, is the civil society organisations, comprising churches, indigenous organisations and intellectual forums. While recognising the importance of the role of the civil society organisations in the post-war democratisation process in the South, the SPLM's established agencies to coordinate the relationship between the movement and the civil society, have not functioned well in this regard.

In the final analysis, if the SPLM/A leadership decided to open channels of communication, cooperation and integration with all the

Southern Sudanese military, political and civil society organisations, such an attitude would definitely encourage the emergence of strong cooperation among Southerners. This would mean that, the SPLM would be required to focus less on who acquires what positions in the Government of Southern Sudan during the interim period, and adopt a more inclusive approach. Indeed, for such a scenario to succeed, it requires hard work, patience and long vision. Most importantly, it requires the use of 'quite diplomacy'.

However, if the SPLM/A leadership opts to suppress and isolate the proponents of self-determination, then it will be difficult to avoid internal conflicts within the SPLM/A administration, and between its leadership and the other Southern organisations. Some observers seem to argue that any peace agreement to be signed as a result of Machakos and Naivasha peace process will be considered by certain SPLM/A leaders as their booty.

In other words, if the SPLM/A leadership and its supporters, choose to adopt an isolationist approach to concentrate power on its leadership, then it is most likely that it will make it a point that anyone, who is not in line with its policies and thus not its ally, is kept away from the administration of the South. Therefore, all the important or sensitive political and senior positions will have to be allocated to those who are loyal to the SPLM/A and its allies.

Alternatively, should the SPLM/A leadership face fierce opposition in the South, its leadership will perhaps be better off if it chose to strengthen its alliance with the NDA, thereby maintaining national unity. Its alliance with NDA would represent the best guarantee for its survival during the interim period. In fact, certain sceptics went so far as to say that the SPLM/A would be correct if it considered its potential alliance with Southern military or political organisations as a threat to its existence. Yet, others argue that the six-year interim period is a long time, and therefore, for an organisation that has had many alliances outside Southern Sudan mainstream politics for over fifteen years, the potentiality to change these alliances during the interim period may prove perilous to the SPLM/A as a political movement.

Moreover the essence of the Machakos framework entails that the SPLM/A leadership should work to consolidate its alliance with the NCP as its partner in forging peace. Equally true would be the assertion that the SPLM/A should keep an eye on whoever opposes the agreement. Naturally, in such a situation, the SPLM/A leadership will have the obligation, in order to preserve the peace agreement, to sideline those Southern Sudanese factions, which might choose to oppose the movement. However, should this be the policy of the SPLM/A, it would have opted to use an isolationist approach, which would complicate matters further in the South.

## External Alliances

When discussing external alliances, the neighbouring countries to Sudan come to mind. The current IGAD member states (Ethiopia, Eritrea, Kenya, Djibouti and Uganda) have their own internal problems. Some of them, such as Uganda and Ethiopia, have already signed security and economic cooperation agreements with the National Congress Party government, while maintaining good relations with the SPLM/A.

At this stage Eritrea is not in a good relationship with both Khartoum and Addis Ababa, although it has close ties with the SPLM/A. Uganda perceives the prospect of peace in Sudan, as an opportunity for it to uproot the Acholi-led Lord's Resistance Army (LRA) from Southern Sudan.

Egypt and Libya have signed controversial integration pacts with the Sudanese government, which may lead to serious misunderstandings with the SPLM/A during the interim period. For example, the NC and the Egyptian governments singed an integration agreement in January 2004, dubbed the 'four freedoms' pact. The pact, if implemented, will allow millions of Egyptians to move, live, work and possess property in any part of Sudan. The direct implications of this agreement and its timing would involve immigration of Egyptians into Sudan – a situation, which will, inevitably, create even more problems between the South and the North.

Moreover, the vagueness of the Machakos Protocol on democracy and secularity of the national federal government, will certainly force thousands of Northern Sudanese who do not want to be ruled under Islamic laws, to migrate in their multitudes, into the South: a situation which, like the potential Egyptians' en mass influx into the Sudan, will create unemployment and tensions during the interim period in the South. The irony of the Machakos process is that it succeeded in creating one state with two systems, and polarised the country into two confederate states with two currencies, two banking systems, two constitutions, two armies and two governments. Moreover, it created three government structures in the South (Government of Southern Sudan, regional and county governments). In the North, the Machakos process created a federal central government and regional governments.

According to some observers, it is an open secret that the US, in particular, had placed intensive pressure on both the NCP and the SPLM/A leaderships, especially the latter to accept the consensus on this illusive interim period. The US administration candidly stated, as expressed in John Danforth's report, that it is not in favour of the right of self-determination for the people of the South. The first reason being that the US's strategic interests in the oil of the Middle East and the Horn of Africa will be best served if the South remains part of a united Sudan. Secondly, as declared by the US administration, the North and its allies would not accept such a right to be exercised by the South.

There are other countries, whose economic interests and political sympathy with either side of the Sudanese conflict, during the interim period, will inevitably determine the course, which the implementation of the peace agreement will take. These countries and organisations include Norway, UK, Italy, Netherlands, China, South Africa, Nigeria, India, Canada, Indonesia, Malaysia, UN, EU, AU, League of Arab States, the World Bank, and the IMF.

## Conclusion

To conclude, it should be emphasised that for any agreement to succeed and eventually be implemented in Sudan, both the NCP and the SPLM/A would be required to institute transparent structures, in collaboration with other Sudanese political forces and international allies. This would mean, in practical terms, that power and wealth sharing institutions should be established. In the case of the SPLM/A and NCP, this would amount to political and economic empowerment of their supporters.

It has also been observed that most liberation movements in the world undergo three critical stages of internal struggle before assuming control, and it appears that the Sudan People's Liberation Movement (SPLM) has not been and may not be the exception to this rule.

The first stage involves each leader, military general or civilian attempting to impose himself/herself as the main nationalist leader of the revolution. At this stage leaders forge internal alliances and one of them emerges as the sole leader of the movement.

The second phase occurs when ethnic or regional and even religious affiliations of the revolutionary leadership take precedent over loyalty to the principles and objectives of the revolution. At this stage, each leader begins to play the card of ethnic majority-minority politics against his opponents with the aim of maintaining power within the movement.

The third stage of power struggle among the liberation movements' leaders commences when the revolution is victorious against the colonial powers or the regime, which they fought against and defeated. As soon as the revolutionaries assume control, another phase of power struggle begins. At this stage, the age factor becomes very important, especially towards the late forties and mid-fifties. Each liberation movement leader or his relatives and/or supporters alert him/her that it is time to think about the welfare of his family, clan or ethnic group. The struggle over state resources among revolutionaries ensues. Moreover, the power struggle proceeds between those who were in exile, who believe that they were the vanguards of the revolution, and those who remained inside, who believe that without them remaining inside the country to serve the interests of the vast majority of the population, the enemy would have annihilated everything in the territory concerned. At this juncture, blackmailing, manipulation, and the questioning of nationalistic credentials of each group overshadow the revolution ethos and principles.

Moreover, certain leaders, who immediately after the victory or the settlement of the conflict, realise that the objectives for which they fought have been abandoned, would try to correct the situation. They may do so by calling all the leaders to abide by the revolution objectives. However, by so doing, they may find themselves confronted by those who think otherwise. Thus, a new kind of power struggle ensues between the 'revolutionaries' and the so-called 'counter-revolutionaries'. The power struggle at this stage, may reach serious and dangerous proportions, including defections, grave misunderstandings, sabotage of government functions, personal enmity among leaders, insults, exposure of revolution secrets and scandals.

It is also an open secret that most African liberation movements, once the war is over, tend to adopt the politics of rhetoric. The name of the liberation movement itself becomes a licence used by the leaders to sideline and oppress others. They use statements such as 'we in the SPLM/A', or 'we in the leadership of the ANC' or 'when we were in the struggle'. These statements become intimidating tools for others who might wish to correct policies of the ruling party.

The question that one should pose, with the above revolutionary power struggle cycle in mind is the following: Has the SPLM/A been the exception to this cycle? Or rather, will it not find itself trapped in certain phases of this cycle, once the implementation of the Machakos and Naivasha peace processes commences? More importantly still, one should ask how these scenarios might be avoided in the Sudanese context.

CHAPTER SIX

# The CPA is born: What should (not) be done...?

While the war in the Southern part of the Sudan has been declared over with the signing of the final Comprehensive Peace Agreement on Sunday, January 9, 2005 in Nairobi, Kenya, the bitter reality is that the real peace will gradually come to the country when the agreement is implemented during the next six years and half. There is no doubt that with the signing of the peace agreement, the Sudanese, especially Southerners will have a lot to cry, laugh and thank God for during the next few years. One thing though is certain, for the Sudanese the long road to peace has begun. It is also the right time for the Sudanese leaders to look east and westward, to resolve the conflicts in Darfur, Kordufan, Eastern and Northern Sudan regions. Indeed until the problems in these regions of Sudan are solved, there will be no real peace in Sudan. It is therefore incumbent upon the Naivasha peace partners, Dr John Garang de Mabior and General Omar El-Bashir to speed the reconciliation with the Drafurians and Beja in the west and the east as well as with the National Democratic Alliance (NDA) opposition groups in Egypt.

Like millions of Sudanese who were following up the celebrations of the signing of the comprehensive peace agreement between the South and North on the Sudan national TV and Radio and on El-Gezira satellite TV, what caught my attention was the number of international community delegates who witnessed and signed the relevant documents containing the agreement. I noticed that the UN, USA, EU, UK, Norway, the African Union, the IGAD, the Arab League and other representatives were keen to affix their signatures to the agreement.

I think that the people of Southern Sudan, who have been consistently deceived by successive Northern Sudanese leaders, should take the international community seriously, and should the North opt to dishonor this agreement again, the South will have witnesses beyond its borders. Similarly, the Southern Sudanese leaders also have moral obligation to respect and implement those provisions in the agreement, which they are responsible for.

While watching that historic event, perhaps the fourth since January 1956, February 1972 and April 1997 in Sudan history, I was also thinking about issues which I think will soon form the bulk of the Sudanese body politics and may pose themselves as impediments to the implementation of the agreement. I also had in mind some observations, which I thought worth sharing:

Firstly, I noticed that the main traditional northern Sudanese top leaderships did not attend the celebrations, notably Sadig Al- Sadiq Al-Mahdi, Mohamed Osman El-Mirghani, Dr Hassan Abdallah Al-Turabi, and Mohamed Ibrahim Nugud; trather hey sent their representatives. Although some former prime ministers and presidents and a huge number of current and former Sudanese ministers attended the event, the absence of the main Northern Sudanese parties' leaders, reminded me of the same picture in February 1972 in Addis Ababa. The same leaders boycotted that historic agreement, and four years later managed to convince General Jaafar Nimeiri to abrogate that agreement, which he did in 1977, when he singed the so-called National Pact with these northern Sudanese parties. It seems that the same leaders are repeating the same scenario by showing the world that, like General Nimeiri, General El-Bashir and colleagues in the

National Congress Party are not representatives of the North, and therefore this agreement in their logic of looking at things is doom to fail. These are the same northern party leaders who are going to contest the 2008/9 general elections according the agreement, which they believe will be won by them. What does this situation entails, as far as the South is concerned?

Secondly, I observed that, while National Congress Party (NCP) and Northern Sudan in general were visibly represented at the dignitaries' front seats by El-Bashir, Taha, Nimeiri, and Suwar El-Dahab, the SPLM/A and the Southern Sudan only visible personality on that podium was Dr John Garang de Mabior. While the SPLM/A leadership and Southern Sudan was represented in the general audience, as they should be, it would have been right thing to do if the top leadership of the SPLM/A, in addition to Rebecca Nyandeng de Mabior, were seated behind Dr John Garang on the dignitaries' podium, so as to send a clear signal to the North that the South is united. At least the SPLM/A number two in the command, Salva Kiir Mayardit should have been seated behind the Chairman. Needless to mention that had it been as originally planed, the agreement would have been signed on behalf of the SPLM/A second man in the Movement, who is in terms of institutional structures of the movement, is the counterpart of Taha. One should add that symbolism in historical events such as the one witnessed by the world in Nairobi is very important. Those images, which were screened live in Kenya will have great impact on the coming generations of the Sudan, and history will be written about Sudan from them.

I also observed that some of the Southern Sudanese leaders, who are either leaders of political parties or organizations in exile, did not attend this historic occasion. While some of them might have been invited either by the government of Sudan or the SPLM, one noticed that the absence of some of them in that historic event, is a sign of concern, which I believe would require that the long awaited South-South dialogue will have to take place as soon as possible before the interim period commences in July 2005. There are already three forums in place through which South-south dialogue could be jointly organized: the SPLM National Liberation Council, South Sudan Democratic Forum and the House of Nationalities Peace Forum.

The SPLM/A leadership must put its priorities right, especially during the period between January and June 2005. By priorities, I mean leadership being positively sensitive and willing to listen to those views, which take advisory form and views that might not necessarily be supportive of the approaches currently in place, but which can build consensus in the South. The SPLM/A leadership must have by now noticed that the question of who will lead the South at least until next elections in 2007/8 has been put on hold, and Dr John Garang will act as the spokesman for the whole Southern Sudan until then. I believe Dr Garang and his colleagues listened carefully to President Thabo Mbeki who told the audience in Naivasha on 31 December 2004 that the people of Sudan expect the SPLM/A and the National Congress Party administrations to build schools, clinics, roads and work for inter-dialogue among Sudanese. Similarly, the sixteen members of the SPLM/A Leadership Council should start behaving and acting as leaders of the Movement. It is only logical that each of them should be assigned a specific duty to perform.

Blaming Dr Garang for controlling everything in the movement through his relatives and personal advisors is a sign of weakness of some, if not all the members of that Council. For what is the use of being a member of a body which suppose to run the Southern Sudan, while one does not have a say in how it works? If this is the case with the SPLM/A Leadership Council and the National Liberation Council (the SPLM Central Committee), the implication is that there are other structures in place within the SPLM/A, apart from these two central organs, which are operating, running the movement affairs and reporting to the Chairman directly without the knowledge of the rest of the councils' members. If this system is not corrected before the commence of the interim period, then the South will continue to be run by two parallel government structures: the Chairman's advisory group and the actual government of the Southern Sudan which will be formed during the pre-interim period.

Thirdly, the huge attendance of international community delegates during the signing of the Sudanese peace agreement, must be taken to mean solidarity of the world with the people of Sudan, a genuine support which the Sudanese, and the South in particular must make use of intelligently. However, this attendance does not oblige these countries beyond expressing their best wishes to the Sudanese peoples and their leaders for deciding to let go the culture of war, which they have adopted during the past five decades, and start to live their lives normally. Whether all the countries, which attended the signing of the peace agreement or some will support the Sudanese financially to implement their hard won peace agreement, remains to be seen. What is important is that the international community, the African continent and the Arab world have shown solidarity, through attendance, to the Sudanese people.

The real challenge will be whether the Sudanese will accept the ownership of the agreement or not. And that is the real challenge. That agreement is not John Garang's agreement, nor is it Ali Osman Taha and Omar Hassan El-Bashir's accord. It is a result of long-bloody struggle by the Sudanese from Southern Sudan and their allies from the marginalized areas, who fought hard to change the status quo of exploitation by the Arabists, Islamists and Northern elites and especially the power-oriented riverine successive leaderships. It is an outcome of a long struggle by Sudanese who have shown that they are ready to pay the utmost price to make changes in every aspects of their country a reality. Reading the contents of the agreement shows that a genuine desire to change the old ways of doing things was expressed. The question is whether the Sudanese will work hard, each in his/her small way, to make sure that this agreement is implemented? Will Sudanese politicians and bureaucrats, whether from the South or North, some of whom might consider this agreement as a long awaited license for self-enrichment and positions acquisition, be truly committed to make this agreement work?

Fourthly, while listening to the statements by the Sudanese and other leaders of the delegations from the rest of the world, I noticed that they all stressed that this agreement should aim at meeting the expectations and the improvement of the lives of the ordinary Sudanese, especially those from South who paid dearly, by supporting their leaders to pioneer and lead the war of liberation. Liberation means, getting rid of all the ills that caused the war. While the SPLA led the war of liberation successfully, the challenge of governmental and institutional building should be one of the key priorities of the SPLM/A during the war of the liberation.

Indeed, one of the important outcomes of the Rumbek emergency leadership conference on 29 November-2 December 2004 was the recognition that the SPLM/A will not be ready structurally to govern the South once the peace is signed, unless it has done something about it before the interim period commences. While there are ad hoc structures already in place in the SPLM/A liberated areas as well as in the government controlled-ten Southern regions, there is a need to restructure the SPLA's army, restructuring of administrative units in the South as well as restructuring the SPLM as political party, if it is to compete with other political parties in the country. For example, the South needs to put in place structures which will govern the political and administrative relationships between the Central Government in Khartoum and the Government of Southern Sudan on the one hand; and the relationship between the latter and the ten regional governments in the South on the other; and finally the relationship between the local governments at provincial (county) level and the former.

This process of restructuring should be carried out during the next six months. If this process is derailed, intentionally or otherwise, whether under pretext of time limitations or because of any possible power struggle within the movement, the institutional capability and the capacity of the Government of Southern Sudan to carry out its mandate to build the badly needed infrastructures in the South will be limited.

First of all, the SPLM/A leadership must learn to delegate powers. They should learn from the National Congress Party, which is now their partner. The leadership of that party managed, despite splits within its ranks, to rule the country for 15 years because its members delegate powers to each other. For example, the agreement stipulates that the leader of the SPLM/A will hold the post of First Vice President as well as President of Government of Southern Sudan. Should this be the case, and sincerely I hope not, it simply means that the power in the South will be centered on one person and all decisions pertaining to the development and service delivery will have to be approved by the SPLM/A leader.

Ideally, as the experience with Abel Alier era during the 1970s has shown, the two positions should be separated, for if they are held by one person, as Abel did, nothing substantial will be achieved during the interim period. Unless the suggestion is that the post of the First Vice President will be symbolic and decorative, because Ali Osman Taha will take with him all his executive powers when he takes up the post of the Second Vice President from Moses Machar when the new constitution comes to force.

Moreover, Southern Sudanese elite must learn to acknowledge their capabilities and stop relying on outside technocrats, except where such external help becomes necessary. The people of the South are expecting a lot from the SPLM/A leadership, and raising false hopes of the people of the South, by using rhetorical and unsubstantiated policy statements can cause unnecessary upheavals in the country in the future.

Finally, regional and international community financial support can be a blessing as well as a curse, especially if the Southern Sudanese elite who are going to run the South opt to busy themselves with financial enrichment, and less with the developmental needs of the people who fought for the achievement of the objectives agreed upon in Kenya.

CHAPTER SEVEN

# Homecoming of a hero to an enemy's den

LIKE MILLIONS OF SUDANESE WHO FOLLOWED ON SUDAN TV AND RADIO, the heroic visit of the SPLM/A leadership to Khartoum on 8 July 2005, I was almost convinced that the North-South's military confrontations have come to their final halt, at least for the next six years and half. The visit itself was historic in many ways, and was interpreted by Sudanese in different ways. Indeed, the reception of Dr John Garang de Mabior and his colleagues seemed to have sent mixed messages to different constituencies in the country.

Sudanese from the marginalized regions of the Sudan including the South, considered Dr John Garang's visit to Khartoum as a new beginning and a true birth of the New Sudan dispensation. On the other hand, those Sudanese who equated the project of the New Sudan with the dismantlement of the Arab-Muslim identity of the Sudan and its replacement with African-secular identity, regarded Dr Garang return to Khartoum as a triumph of the African agenda in the country. Others, especially the leaders of Umma National Party, Popular National Congress, Sudan Communist Party and Democratic Unionist Party understood the return of Dr Garang to the national capital as an inevitable outcome of the Naivasha process, and thus in terms of long term politics of Naivasha peace process, the real change in Sudan will come after four years when general elections, which they hope to win, are conducted.

On the timing and the route of the visit of the SPLM leadership to Khartoum, some argued in the South that it was a wise decision from the SPLM/A leadership to first visit Khartoum, since it is the national capital to send a clear message that the SPLM/A is a national liberation movement, with a national agenda. Other Southern Sudanese contended that Dr Garang should have in fact visited Juba, Malakal and Wau first, during the period between 5 and 8 July, and then arrives in Khartoum on the morning of 9th July, to greet the crowds in the SPLM headquarters and the Green Square and then take the oath as the First Vice President of Sudan and President of Southern Sudan in the afternoon or the evening.

From personal perspective, Dr Garang's visit to Khartoum was an emotional event. After almost 19 years, since I last visited the South, the 9th July 2005 was a special day for me. While following the historic visit, I observed that the visit was marred by some unnecessary, but sensitive logistical challenges, which would have been avoided, had the NCP ruling party and the SPLM advanced team did their homework carefully and shared their notes closely. While the displaced people of Southern Sudan and their brothers and sisters from Nuba Mountains, Southern Blue Nile, Darfur and inhabitants of the capital and other regions of the country, welcomed Dr Garang with the deserving welcome a hero should enjoy, the SPLM and the NC reception teams seemed to have not fared well in their preparations. In fact, for those of us who expected such an occasion to be a message to the Northern elites that the old Sudan ways of doing things must be done away with forever, the logistical hurddles that accompanied the visit, had caused some disappointments.

Yes, the historical reception, which Dr John Garang was privileged with, was first of its kind in the history of Sudan. There was no other political figure or political party leader in the country, was ever received by over two million people since independence. It was indeed hoped by many Southern Sudanese in particular that the visit of Dr Garang to Khartoum was a great opportunity for the SPLM leadership to show to the entire world its organizational efficiency and its readiness to disproved critics, who accuse the movement of lack of organizational capacity and inefficient coordination among its leaders. It was however, a miss opportunity, which although some blamed it on the NCP, it was equally the responsibility of the SPLM leadership, who were the heroes returning to the national capital, and should have double checked every aspect of the welcoming logistics, and not to leave them to NCP and the National Welcoming Committee.

Some of personal observations, which I thought worth sharing include:

Firstly, Dr Garang did not address the two million crowds, which gathered in the Green Square to welcome him. Those crowds, who, despite the burning heat of Khartoum, patiently waited for the arrival of their heroes from sunrise to about five in the evening. The official reasons given for Dr Garang not to address the crowds was that the microphones were smashed by the huge gathering and that the crowd was so huge that it was not possible for him to address them as they were pushing towards the podium. The truth of course was that the microphones were dismantled, not by the crowds, as suggested by the official version of the 8th July events, but apparently by some individuals who were not impressed by the huge turn out. Even if we were to believe that the microphones were dismantled or smashed by the crowds, it would have been natural that the organisers of Dr Garang's reception should have anticipated that a huge crowd would gather in the Green Square, and should have used wireless microphones, which are normally used in huge public gatherings such as the reception of the SPLM/A leadership.

It is to be mentioned that the capital at different times, had witnessed big crowds such as the visit of Pope John Paul II, who was able to address a huge crowd in the same square and used microphones. I think the SPLM/A cadres in Khartoum should have been more sensitive to the reception of the SPLM/A leadership. Unfortunately, they did not seem to have had plan B. Instead of sending away the crowds, they should have sent for wireless microphones, and allowed Dr Garang and colleagues to enjoy that moment; a moment they waited for 23 years to enjoy. In fact, such occasions do not come by easily. One still wonders, how did the SPLM/A advanced teams which were received in the same square three months ago, were able to address about a million people who fluxed the square, were they not using microphones?

Secondly, it seems that the SPLM/A Offices and the SPLM/A security agents in the capital were overwhelmed by the event. Looking at the magnitude of the crowd, it was obvious that the crowds were tired an anxious and some indeed climbed into the podium which was reserved for the dignitaries, and thus the 20 meters distance which crowds are supposed to observe was closed up as the day comes to an end. There were no 20- meter distance steel bars separating the crowds with the podium.

Another logistical loophole was that it seems that the timing of the visit was not well coordinated, because the SPLM/A leadership kept the crowds waiting for the whole day until about five in the evening. Had Dr Garang arrived earlier, may be the crowds would have not pushed itself to the podium and would kept their distance from the podium, and Dr Garang would have addressed them easily. The security police and the army, which were supposed to seal off the people, using blocks seemed to have not been prepared for the job, and so the crowds found themselves dancing on the podium, which was supposed to be used by the dignitaries. Those who saw Dr Garang and Vice President Taha entering the podium would concur that the police, the SPLM/A and NCP reception teams have a lot to explain. It was a security nightmare to say the least.

One of the things that drew my attention, when Dr Garang and Vice President Taha were entering the Green Square was that some of the SPLM/A senior commanders were seen to be pushing people away from Dr Garang's vicinity on the podium. In fact, I was surprised that they would be doing what they were doing at the square, when they should have been busy monitoring and analyzing security reports in their offices somewhere in Khartoum or Rumbek, receiving reports from all over the country relating to the visit.

One would not imagine Generals al-Gosh and Al-Ataa, the heads of the Sudan government security agencies acting as bodyguards to General Al-Bashir in such occasions. I am sure that the SPLM/A has several, if not hundreds, of security personnel who should be responsible for the protection of the SPLM/A leadership, while the top brass of the SPLM/A security agencies should be doing other important things. I think the SPLM/A leadership will need to review the events of 8 July 2005.

Thirdly, those who have watched the Sudan TV on the evenings of 8 and 9 July would have noticed that, despite the historic visit of the SPLM/A leadership to the capital, the national TV programs were not up to the occasion. The usual programs were played as if nothing had happened. Apparently the message that the ruling party was sending to the Sudanese was that the return of the SPLM/A leader and his colleagues was just another return, like other leaders had done before him, namely Sadig al-Mahdi, Jaafar Nimeiri, Zein Abdin al-Hindi, and hopefully in November 2005, when Mohamed al-Mirghani returns home after sixteen years in exile.

In fact, the evening of 8 July was the most ordinary time of the day on the Sudan national TV. For example, those who were interviewed live in the studios, to discuss the importance of the 8 July, were either, cadres of National Congress Party or from the Northern opposition parties. There were no SPLM/A members in the studios; some of the SPLM/A members of the National Interim Constitution Review were interviewed three days earlier, and every now and then, their interviews were aired. While some SPLM/A members were interviewed live at the airport, their images were not shown live. In fact, the regular Friday program "Fi Sahat al-Fida" or "In the Battlefields', in which popular defense force's officers and soldiers are shown in the Southern bushes singing Islamic songs and declaring jihad against the SPLA, was shown on the evening of 8 July. On that evening, late General Zubeir Mohamed Salih, was shown addressing a gathering, in which he was sending a message to the then enemy, the SPLM/A and indeed to Dr Garang asking him to accept the peace path.

I think that that particular TV program was the wrong message to the Sudanese people on the day they were supposed to be celebrating the end of the war in the South. Instead, they were told to take the return of Dr Garang as another ordinary day. I think that the SPLM/A leadership, as partners to the NCP, will need to review the national TV programs.

Fourthly, the organizing committee of the SPLM/A leadership's return visit, and due to its historic importance and political sensitivity, should have carefully scrutinized the SPLM/A leaders' first day itinerary carefully. For example, why would the SPLM/A leader, upon his arrival, visit the NCP headquarters first and not the SPLM offices in the capital? His itinerary should have been to visit upon his arrival the SPLM offices in the capital, the NCP headquarters, and then the Green Square in that logical order. Yes, the visit to the NCP headquarters was an important political gesture, whose reconciliatory significance could not be underrated, but not to visit the SPLM Offices in the national capital was an important symbolic gesture overlooked.

Fifthly, the decision to invite over 3000 SPLM/A members, in addition to over 200 SPLM/A leadership members to attend the inauguration, in terms of security assessment, was one of the decisions that the SPLM/A leadership should have been cautious to take. Although some SPLM/A members might have rightly thought it was important to accompany their leadership to the 'former enemy dent' after 23 years in bushes of the South, to take the entire leadership of the Movement to Khartoum was, to say the least unwarranted step.

In such circumstances, it is always safe to select an official delegation of say, 20 to 25 of leaders, but not 200. Of those who accompanied Dr Garang, including members of the advanced teams, were about 3000 SPLM/A members from the movement's liberated areas and abroad, the fifteen members of the leadership council (Cdr Salva Kiir Mayardit asked to be excused not to take the journey to Khartoum); and almost all the SPLM ministers, Members of the National Liberation Council (Parliament), undersecretaries, and top senior military commanders. On the other hand, for security reasons, senior SPLA commanders such as Oyay Deng, Obote Mamur, Pieng Deng, Gier Chuang, Thomas Cyrillo and other top commanders should have been exempted from visiting Khartoum at that particular time.

What further bothered those of us, who followed the visit closely, was that the SPLM/A visit to Khartoum took place at the time when the (1,500) SPLA troops, which were supposed to protect Dr Garang and his colleagues, were refused entry to Khartoum by the Sudan Government, three days before the scheduled visit. According to one government owned newspaper report, the excuse of the GOS for not allowing the SPLA troops to enter Khartoum was that the SPLA soldiers were 'over armed', with armament equal to that of 10,000 troops! The reality of course is that the SPLA soldiers in question, as part of the Joint Integrated Units (JIUs), were to bring with them between 15 to 30 tanks, plus light weapons. The al-Bashir government insisted that they should only take with them personal guns to Khartoum. Apparently, this situation would not have occurred had the SPLM/A and the NCP leaderships had officially inaugurated the Joint Military Committee (Board), which according to the CPA, is authorized to discuss issues pertaining to the Joint Integrated Units and the logistics of their deployments. Had that been the case, the SPLA team in that committee would have negotiated and advised the leadership on what to do should government react the way it did.

Instead, Taha and Dr Garang continued discussing the issue of the SPLA JIUs until the date of the arrival of Dr Garang in Khartoum. The question then is why the SPLM/A leadership decided to take its whole leadership to Khartoum, while its troops, which were supposed to intervene in case of emergency were stopped in Kassala, and refused entry to Khartoum.

Sixthly, there is no doubt that the bulk of the logistical huddles which took place during the visit of the SPLM/A leadership to the national capital must be partially blamed on the SPLM/A advance team and the SPLM Offices in Khartoum. The advance team of the SPLM/A spent about four months in the capital coordinating contacts between the SPLM and the NCP, as well as coordinating with the other political parties. Part of their brief, jointly with the SPLM/A Offices in Khartoum, was to prepare for the visit of the SPLM/A delegation to Khartoum. By and large, it seems that the two teams did not do a satisfactory work, considering the enough time availed to them.

In terms of peace building process, which the South is currently undergoing there are certain sensitive issues which the SPLM/A leadership must be keen to consider whenever it handles its affairs. One of these issues is taking care of its leadership welfare. A nation that does not take care of its leaders is doomed to chaos. The SPLM/A cadres should learn from the National Congress Party, which whenever there is a national occasion, it invites former presidents, prime ministers and vice presidents and former chief justices. When the SPLM/A delegation arrived in Khartoum between 7 and 8 July, about 80 percent of them were hosted at Soba Military barracks, while the rest were accommodated in hotels in the city.

One of the logistical hassles, which happened on 8th July was that the movement had had some difficulties to accommodate some of its leadership Council members. They had to be accommodated in a building in Arkuwait suburb (which some of them referred to as a dormitory (Dakhiliya), hurriedly furnished for their accommodation. Some of those leaders who were accommodated in the Arkuwait building, together with some of their spouses, included commanders Riek Machar, Wani Igga, Theophilos Ochieng, Lam Akol, Kuol Manyang, Lual Diing, Samuel Abu John and few others. The logistics and the coordination of the visit have therefore revealed that the SPLM/A leadership ought to be more sensitive to security of its senior members.

Seventhly, it was observed that the National Congress Party ideologues, perhaps with consent of some SPLM cadres, made it point that the person who is being welcomed, was not the SPLM/A, but Dr Garang alone. All the posters and photographs at the airport, the Republican Palace and on the streets of the capital were that of Dr Garang. The SPLM/A leadership was by and large omitted, which made Dr Garang to comment "everybody in the capital should know that the SPLM has arrived", hinting that it was not him as a person. The people of Khartoum were made to understand that the man they were waiting for so long is finally in Khartoum, and the rest of the movement's leaders were ignored. It was a deliberate political message, and therefore one was not surprised that the media committee responsible for the reception of Dr Garang and the SPLM/A leadership did not depict the visit as that of the SPLM/A, but the 'return' or 'aw'da' of Dr Garang.

Another message articulated by the media and the NCP leaders was that Dr Garang was 'returning' to Sudan, when every Sudanese and non-Sudanese knew that he was coming from Rumbek in Lakes state, and the Sudanese knew all along that for the whole duration of the liberation struggle that the SPLM/A forces were operating inside Sudan, with only the Movement's foreign relations coordinating offices based in the neighboring countries and abroad.

On a positive note, the inauguration ceremony on the 9th July, with exception of few interruptions, went very well. However, one

## Homecoming of a hero to an enemy's den 153

observed on the faces of Mrs. Rebecca Nyandeng and Dr Garang a sense of exhaustion; partly because of the 8th July busy day events. As the ceremony progressed however, they became relax. There was no doubt that the presence of the African leaders, especially the neighboring countries, the UN Secretary General, representatives of the US, UK, Norway and the Arab League during the swearing in ceremony was a highly welcomed gesture by the Sudanese. Compared to the 8th July reception, the 9th July ceremony was a jolly day for DR. Garang and the netire leadership of the Movement, and no wonder he obliged the UN top man, Kofi Anan and Ali Osman Taha to dance with the youngsters. Mrs. De Mabior did not join the dance though, had she joined Moses Machar and others, the dance would have been an interesting mix! The song, which Mohamed Wardi, Cherhabil Ahmed and other top Sudanese singers sang, was up to the occasion, and moved even those who did not understand the words. It was long one though!

Eighthly, one of the first directives by Dr Garang as a First Vice President was to form a joint eight-man committee with the NCP, whose mandate is to form the government of national unity. The terms of reference include: receiving the names of the candidates for ministerial, constitutional and judicial posts, and discuss it among themselves. The committee also has the mandate to coordinate with other political parties who accepted to participate in the Government of National Unity. The SPLM four members in the committee were Nhial Deng Nhial, Pa'gan Amum Okiech, Edward Lino Abyei and Yasser Said Arman. The SPLM members of the committee were also mandated to supervise the formation and the appointment of the members of the Government of Southern Sudan, the governments of the ten states in the South, in consultation with other Southern Sudanese political groups which will participate, in accordance with the power sharing formula stipulated in the agreement, in the government of Southern Sudan and governments of the Southern states.

The immediate implications of this directive can be interpreted in two ways: that the Chairman of the SPLM/A has decided, as the constitution empowers him, to handle through this four man committee the appointment of the SPLM members to various layers of the governments, including members to the National Assembly in Omdurman, Government of National Unity, Government of Southern Sudan and its Assembly, the Southern states' governments and their assemblies, in addition to other constitutional and judiciary positions, at national, regional and state levels. The second implication of the directive is that the role of the SPLM leadership Council and the National Liberation Council will be minimal in the formation of various levels of governments in the country. It is interesting to note that the membership of the committee did not include SPLA (military) members.

It is to be mentioned that the National Interim Constitution empowers Dr Garang, as the Chairman of the SPLM to appoint whoever he wants to fill in the positions allocated to the SPLM in the Government of National Unity. The National Interim Constitution also gives the President of Government of Southern Sudan the power, in consultation with his Deputy, to form the GOSS and governments of Southern states, which must be approved by the Southern Sudan Legislative Assembly and the assemblies of States. Whether Dr Garang will follow this constitutional route remains to be seen.

One should note though that the concentration of powers on the First Vice President and the President of Government of Southern Sudan by the National Interim Constitution raises immediate political and constitutional issues: For example, will the SPLM four-man committee, be the sole legal body in the South to carry out consultations regarding the formation of various layers of government in the center and in Southern Sudan? What will be the role of the other existing SPLM structures, and those structures that the Rumbek emergency leadership conference of November-December 2004 had established?

Now that Dr Garang will be spending the next few months in and out of Khartoum, working closely with the rest of the Presidency to form the GONU, and considering that constitutionally, Dr Garang is currently the only legal personality in the South until the constitution of Southern Sudan is in place, will the four man committee be the only legal body that would coordinate political affairs of the South with the SPLM/A other structures in Rumbek? What would be the role of the SPLM leadership Council during and after the formation of the Government of Southern Sudan? Who will ratify the Constitution of Southern Sudan: The existing SPLM's National Liberation Council or a new Assembly, which should include members of non-SPLM Southern Sudanese political organizations, will be instituted before the Southern Sudan Constitution is drafted, and which body will appoint its members?

With the signing of the National Interim Constitution and the appointment of Dr Garang, as President of Southern Sudan on 9th July, there are no longer areas under control of the GOS and the SPLM/A. The question then is will the SPLM's shadow government in Rumbek continue to operate, until GOSS is formed, and under whose direction: Dr Garang the leader of SPLM/A or Dr Garang the President of Southern Sudan? What about the dissolved governments of ten Southern states, will they continue to act as care taking governments, or will Dr Garang appoint his cadres to take over until new constitutions for these states are in place? How will the two bureaucracies, the SPLM/A and the old bureaucracy, co-exist, particularly that there has been reports that a whole sale looting of government funds by NCP supporters in the Southern states' has become a phenomenon of a large scale.

Finally, the second directive, which the First Vice President and the President of Southern Sudan issued was dismissal of the staff of the Southern States' Coordinating Council on 10th July. From that date until the GOSS is formed, all the offices of the Coordinating Council in Juba and Khartoum are closed and will be guarded by police. It is to be recalled that the President of Republic issued a degree on 8th July dissolving the Coordinating Council, to pave the way, as the new constitution stipulates for the appointment of Dr Garang as President of Government of Southern Sudan. Thus, as the constitution stipulates, the President of the Coordination Council and his ministers were relieved from their duties on 8 July. There is no doubt that the dismissal of the Coordinating Council's officials, who have been employed in the system for almost three decades, has political and financial implications. For example, if the directives of the President of Southern Sudan are final, who will pay the pensions and compensations and who will be responsible for the upkeep of the Coordinating Council staff until their pensions are paid.

It is to be recalled that the Coordination Council was an old baggage of the Addis Ababa Agreement. It is part and parcel of the old Sudan that Dr Garang went to bush to fight against, which, unfortunately he had to inherit on the 9th July 2005. Between March 1973 and May 1983 the Coordinating Council was called the High Executive Council; its name was changed to an Interim High Executive Council in May 1983, when the South was divided into three regions. In April 1985, following the April Intifada, its name was changed yet again to Southern Council (Majlis Janub) until April 1997, when Khartoum Peace Agreement was signed, its name was changed again to Coordinating Council. The latter name was changed on 9 July 2005 when the Council became the Government of Southern Sudan, which now Col Garang heads. The SPLM/A leadership should think seriously about the future of hundreds of families who will lose their livelihood as a result of the new directive.

If the rationale was that the SPLM/A has inherited the Coordinating Council and would reserve it for its cadres, and to do away with those who were working there before 9th July, I am sure there is other way to go about it. Statistically the entire SPLM/A cadres are not even enough to staff five ministries, which the GOSS will establish in few months time. There are so many positions, as the SPLM/A leader is fond of reminding every Southern Sudanese, in GOSS and in governments of Southern states, which will need manpower, and there is no reason to dismiss those who have experience, which the movement badly need, if it is to start in the right direction.

Yes, most of those who were working under Khartoum government in the Southern states will need political reorientation and capacity building which the SPLM/A should allocate efficient budget for, but certainly there is no justification to dismiss them. It is true that any new dispensation should change old government structures, in terms of ministers and those who occupy political positions; but dismissing the entire bureaucracy, would need thorough study, to say the least. If the SPLM administration's strategy is to dismiss all those who collaborated and worked under Nimeiri, Suwar al-Dhab, Al-Mhadi and Al-Bashir-al-Turabi-Taha administrations, it means that the movement will have to dismiss, not only the staff of the Coordinating Council, but the entire staff of the governments of Southern states.

The Coordination Council was therefore as old as the posts of Vice and First Vice Presidents, which came as the result of Addis Ababa Agreement, that instituted the post of second Vice to be occupied by a Southern Sudanese, while the first Vice President was reserved to a Northerner. Indeed it was hoped by many adherents to the New Sudan project that the Naivasha dispensation, would have done away with the post of Second Vice President (the word second was never constitutionally mentioned, but all Sudanese knew that the post was second) and retained the post of First Vice President as the only hair to the Presidency.

Having said all that, it remains to emphasize that the manner in which the NCP and the SPLM/A organizing teams managed the logistics of the historic visit of the SPLM/A leadership to Khartoum, was to say the least, a bumpy start for the implementation of the Sudan Comprehensive Peace Agreement, and many lessons should be learned from it, especially by the SPLM/A leadership.

CHAPTER EIGHT

# Building the Capacity and Mobilizing Human Resources for Development

Having been briefly overshadowed by Darfur humanitarian crises, efforts are currently exerted by the US, the Inter-Governmental Authority on the Development (IGAD) and the Kenyan mediators to pressurize the Sudanese parties to conclude the long awaited comprehensive peace agreement between the Sudan government and the Sudan People's Liberation Movement (SPLM) in Naivasha, Kenya. There are only four remaining items, regarding security arrangements and implementation modalities on which Ali Osman Taha and Dr John Garang will have to meet and iron out either during the last week of September or early October 2004. It is hoped that the envisaged comprehensive peace agreement will serve as a model for the rest of the country, especially for settlement of Darfur and the Eastern Sudan conflicts.

There is no doubt that some of the immediate challenges which will face Southern Sudanese leaders, as the peace process approaches its last leg, include identifying and quantifying the skilled human resources' potential in that part of the Sudan. The most challenging problem will be the mobilization of the skilled human resources needed for the running of the interim government of Southern Sudan and for developmental purposes of that war torn region of Sudan.

The question is does Southern Sudan have the skilled- human resources for the running of the government affairs during the interim period and beyond? The answer to this question may not be an outright yes; although the potential and the required mechanisms to solicit such a potential are available, as long as the interim government in the South will be keen to make sure that those who have acquired the needed skills, at home and in Diaspora are not, for whatever reason, discriminated against.

Although there is no proper official study has been carried out yet, my preliminary research estimates of the professionals in Southern Sudan have revealed that there are about 150 PhD holders from different fields. Infact, the list that I compiled contains 85 PhD holders, their ages ranging between 35 and 70; about 500 masters and post graduate advanced diploma graduates and over 4500 first degree and diploma graduates. The rest are high school certificate graduates, most of who are located in refuge and displaced camps inside the country and in the neighboring countries, as well as in various government institutions in the ten regional governments in the government-controlled areas and in the SPLA/M controlled areas.

The majority of college and university graduates obtained their first degrees during the 1970s, 80s, and 1990s. Most of them graduated from Sudanese technical colleges and universities; the rest obtained their degrees abroad, especially after 1995, following the resettlement of thousands of Southern Sudanese to North American, European and Pacific countries.

While the above figures and estimates may suggest positive picture of the state of trained and skilled human resources in Southern Sudan, there is no doubt that the war in that part of Sudan has affected the educational system in the country as well as aggravated mass movement of over three million out of the estimated ten million, from the

South into Northern Sudan and to the neighboring countries and beyond. School age children and high school graduates during the period between 1983 and 2003, depending on their locality of refuge and displacement, were introduced to different educational systems. The lucky ones among them managed to enroll into high schools in the main cities of the South, Juba, Malakal and Wau.

As for those whose parents moved to Khartoum or to other urban centers in the South and the North, some of them made it to universities of Khartoum, Nieleen, Al-Ghazira, Umdurman al-Ahalia, Al-Ahfad, or to Juba, Bahr el Ghazal and Upper Nile universities, whose majority of their faculties are located in Khartoum.

In the Neighboring countries, some children of the exiles managed to join colleges and universities in Kenya, Ethiopia, Eritrea, and Uganda and in some Southern African countries, such Zimbabwe and Namibia. In North Africa, Egyptian, Libyan, Lebanese and Syrian universities, enrolled a small number of Southern Sudanese students, most of who were financially supported by Southern regional governments. The financial support for these students were stopped in 1990, when the National Islamic Front government decided to call back all the Southern Sudanese students abroad to go back home. The reason given for that move was that the government decided to open two new universities in Bahr el Ghazal and Upper Nile.

In North America, Pacific and in some European countries, Southern Sudanese college and first degree university graduates, especially among the refugees who went for resettlement in Canada, USA (especially in Mid-west states) and Australia, increased, and a good number of Southern Sudan graduates, especially in social sciences has built up since then.

What these figures entails is that, apart from those employed in the civil service, which is running government institutions in the areas under the SPLM and those working under the government of Sudan in the 10 Southern States, there are Southern Sudanese professionals and technocrats who are scattered throughout the world. It is through these professionals and skilled technocrats that the SPLM interim government should build its news institutions of its administration.

It is always argued that a nation whose leaders have no regard to its human resources is doomed to fail in every developmental program it works to implement. In all fields of human development, there can never be substitute to the human resources. Few years ago I was involved in discussions with a group of Sudanese that believes in human resource development as the best tool for the empowerment of urban and rural societies in Sudan. The essence of the discussions of that group was how can Southern Sudan human resources, particularly the educated and the skilled young men and women be enhanced through building a solid base of quality education so that they could become self-confident in facing challenges of the post war Southern Sudan. Development is an interesting term, because it could mean so many things to different people.

There have been lots of promises from different countries and organizations, pledging to finance the rebuilding of post-war Southern Sudan. The Arab league has put its ideas on a well-written document, pledging to persuade Arab countries and companies to invest in the South once the war comes to an end. The Organisation of Islamic states conference has already established a fund for this purpose.

The EU and USAID have already published impressive documents detailing what the people of Southern Sudan will need during the interim period. The government of Sudan has already published a document containing what it identified as the main developmental projects for the post war Southern Sudan. A development fund for the above purpose is already in place.

On the other hand, the SPLM leadership has already entered into some negotiations with developmental agencies and governments, which put forward these developmental projects. The SPLM initiative apparently aims at finding some role for its agencies, which suppose to handle post war development affairs during the interim period in the South. While there is no harm in these countries and organizations to formulate developmental programs which they are willing to finance in the South during the post war Sudan, one wonders how did these groups and nations come to their conclusions that what the people of Southern Sudan need are roads, schools and buildings.

The question should have been what is the main Southern Sudanese economic capital? Some would rush to answer that it is the oil, and may be second to it would be agriculture and water. While this is true, the missing link is that what the South has in abundance is its human resources, which will definitely need capacity building and empowerment as soon as the war is over. Ironically, so far very few countries have openly pledged to develop and enhance the capacity of the Southern Sudanese human resources.

Among other things, the nature of my academic career, had afforded me during the past fifteen years the opportunity to follow up closely the dynamics of political and economic development of some Middle East countries, especially with regard to these countries' reliance on their human resources.

The first country I took sometime to observe is Lebanon. This country does not have natural resources, and like Hashimite Kingdom of Jordan, it does not have sufficient water for its population, thus it solely relies on its skilled and educated human resource to generate its financial capital. Most of the Lebanese skilled labor migrated to West Africa and to the Gulf region where they helped build those countries. And in the case of West Africa the experience of the Lebanese merchants' presence there has proven to be too expensive for the local population in that region.

Another nation, which I also observed is Palestine. This tiny troubled nation, is known world wide to be the first country in the world with the highest professionals, and tops the list of those underdeveloped countries that have the highest number of PhD holders from different disciplines. Its capital is human resources.

The economic basis of Lebanon, Jordan and Palestine is built in the encouragement of the citizens of these countries to value human resources. The Jordanian slogan "our capital is human being' captures the deep meaning of what government can achieve by building its confidence and the hopes of its people on the capability of its people.

Lebanon have the best banking system in the Arab world, and adopted its own brand of capitalism, which guaranteed that despite the difficulties that the world market has been undergoing during the past decade, and the difficulties of the internal strives which continued from 1975 to 1992, it remained the only county in that part of the world with solid economic structures.

Palestine on the other hand, despite the desperate security situation caused by 50 years of conflict with Israel and despite the fact that the Israeli government have withheld the money which it remits to the Palestinian Authority since 2001, the remittances that the Palestinian Diasporas in the Gulf, North America, Africa and Europe have been sending back home, have kept the Palestinian economy going.

The economic crisis in Jordan, which came as the result of the first and the second Gulf wars, have had great impact on the growth of the country's economy, however, the Jordanian leadership reliance on its human resources have kept that small Kingdom confident that it can proudly admit that its slogan will always pay off, especially in the times of need.

Human resources development in any country should stress the quality rather quantity. Most ruling elites in Africa, Southern Sudan not excepted, see their educated human resource as political threat to their power and economic interest and thus the ruling elites would do everything they could to frustrate the skilled manpower to leave the country or remain in exile.

In Jordan for example, medical services have been incorporated as part of what is known as 'medical tourism' policy. The best Jordanian medical doctors are invited world over to go to Jordan and take along with them the latest modern technology in their fields of specialization, and are exempted from custom fees, and encouraged to open private clinics and private hospitals, using regulated prices. At the same time they are encouraged to work in the government owned public hospitals. What you have is a package that would make it possible to give excellent medical services to those who can afford it and those who cannot.

As early as 1993, Jordan became the medical Mecca for all the Sudanese middle class members as well as military elite who go for medical check ups or treatment. And for political purposes, Southern Sudanese military and political leaders inside the country were allowed only to go to Jordan to seek medical services, because the medical services infrastructure in Sudan have been destroyed by the negligence and lack of responsibility. Needless to mention that in Southern Sudan, between 1983 and 2003, medical services are only provided as privileges and not services, and only in three towns, namely Wau, Malakal and Juba and unless a member of the family is a military personnel or married to one, it is impossible to get essential medicines.

Palestinians professionals abroad have opened banks and multilateral companies overseas in partnership with other Arab partners, with the aim of creating huge investment opportunities to the Palestinian refugees' world-wide, as well as facilitating the economic potential of their emerging state. Unlike its Southern Sudan counter part, a Palestinian exile who lives in the US or Australia would do everything he could to help a fellow Palestinian to get a job and becomes self-sufficient.

Lebanese overseas, especially in Africa (Liberia, Sierra Leone, The Gambia, Nigeria, South Africa, Congo, Central African Republic, Benin and Senegal) are known to have the control of mining industry, tourism sectors and private sector as a whole. The key is close cooperation among themselves and reliance on the human resources to back their national government economy back home

The so-called Southern Sudanese middle class in exile, especially those who have business interests in the neighboring countries, have adopted an attitude where either they do not openly show their financial resources, even for business purposes or they choose not to involve in serious economic ventures which may benefit the national struggle in the long run. And those who have openly embarked into business sector tend not to help those who have shown interest, and have the required qualifications to join investment opportunities. The SPLM for example, although it has modest financial capability, and had received some financial assistance from its many friends on the continent and elsewhere, it has not invested in property nor in industrial business ventures let alone in human resource development. In any event, before mid 1994, investment in the field of education has not been a priority to the movement.

The real challenge for the Sudanese leaders and Southern Sudanese leaders in particular, is whether they are willing to invest in human resources and whether they have collected the data of the skilled manpower in Southern Sudan, both from inside Sudan or in Diaspora.

Are there plans to make this important issue the top priority of the Southern Sudan interim government or will it be just an option among many competing projects, and as a result, building false hopes on oil industry, whose current beneficiary are the NIF financiers, the Chinese, Indonesians, Malaysians and Indians, plus the old and new comers: American and European companies.

Should the SPLM decide to sideline its skilled human resources, and not to empower and enhance their capacity for whatever reason, the result will be that the interim government of Southern Sudan will be run by expatriates from the neighboring countries and from US, Asian, Middle Eastern and European countries. The long run consequences of such policies are well known to everybody.

CHAPTER NINE

# What Lessons the SPLM Leadership must Learn from the Formation of Governments?

The formation of the Government of National Unity (GONU) on 20 September 2005 after several weeks of heated debates between National Congress Party (NCP) and the Sudan People's Liberation Movement (SPLM) have revealed four important lessons which the SPLM leadership must carefully study and take some actions on:

Firstly, the debate over who should take the ministry of energy and mining has sidelined the central role of the SPLM as the guardian of the Sudan's transformation and the guarantor of the Southern Sudanese rights in a united transformed Sudan. The SPLM's ideological and philosophical tenants of change and transformation, from decadent corrupt old Sudan, where leadership's main objective is to accumulate wealth, manipulate poor people's sentiments in the name of religion and Arab chauvinism, using political Islam as a means to rule the country, to a Sudan where the ordinary Sudanese is the main focus of the government, these important tenants were blurred by the Energy and Mining politics.

The NCP leadership was and is aware that the oil is in the South and knew that the SPLM has the right to be allocated the ministry. What the NCP had in it side was time. It knew that the SPLM needs to gain time, and that was what the NCP used against it. Throughout the negotiations over the Energy Ministry, the SPLM was made to concentrate on the South, so that its real potential as the main political catalyst for the transformation of the Sudan in the country could be watered down.

The SPLM is seen by Sudanese to be the vehicle for change and the instrument of change in the country. The fact that the NCP managed to make the SPLM looked during the negotiation as a local Southern party, was a big blow to the SPLM as a national progressive movement. The SPLM must take immediate remedial actions to correct that situation. One way to do so would be to become directly involved in peace negotiations with Darfurians and Easterners and make sure that their shares in power are secured.

The New Sudan ideology was never about distribution of positions or power, it was about equality and just distribution of these positions, but most importantly about bringing change to the whole country where each Sudanese feels that truly he/she is a Sudanese who deserves a government, for which she/he will be proud of.

The SPLM as the guardian of change in the country, there is no doubt that it was hard hit by the death of Dr John Garang. However, the unity and the collective approach which the new SPLM leadership had shown during the past month and half, was so strong that, had its leadership concentrated on its national agenda, by not only negotiating on the behalf of the South, but of all the progressive political forces in the country, it would have won more substantial positions, not only for the South, but even for the Darfurians, the Easterners and the NDA as its natural allies.

What Al-Beshir-Taha alliance did, was to show the SPLM that the NCP is the main power broker in the country, and that it is the NCP that offer positions, and therefore, any talk of power and wealth sharing, should be determined, not by the provisions of the Comprehensive Peace Agreement (CPA), but by new negotiations with the NCP. The SPLM has therefore committed itself to an open ended path to continuous negotiations over government positions, commissions and financial rows that will certainly follow. It therefore does not make sense that the SPLM allowed the NCP to take ministries of defence, interior, finance, energy and mining and Justice, because it's simply means that the provisions of power and wealth sharing in the CPA have been trashed. It also means that the provision that unity should be made attractive to Southerners during the interim period, will no longer have meaning, not only to Southerners, but also to other political groups in the country who feel that the CPA is a good document that could be applied to their situations.

Even if the SPLM leadership was convinced that the NCP was playing with time, knowing that it is the SPLM that will bring back hundred of thousands of returnees and displaced persons into the South and that it is the SPLM that will need to deliver to the people of the South essential services, and therefore the SPLM should have not have wasted time negotiating positions with people who have no respect to agreements, even if the above factors are genuine as they were, there is no reason why the SPLM should have given up all the most important economic and political positions to the NCP, thus creating the impression that every time a new round of negotiations comes, and there will be many of them, the SPLM will give in because the NCP is not interested in implementing the CPA..

Secondly, the formation of the government of national unity has also revealed that while the decision making process within the SPLM leadership has improved compared to what it used to be, where very few were the core of the decision making process, the manner in which positions were announced, without the knowledge of 80% of those who were appointed, has revealed that something seriously needs to be revised in that process. Some members of the movement were allocated positions, which, if they were informed, might not have accepted, or if given the choice, would have declined them, because those positions did not fit well with their experiences. While the SPLM line up is by and large representative, regionally and ethnically, the nature of the line up, especially its technical aspects, have lots to be desired.

The SPLM leadership should make it very clear that those of its members, who are appointed in Government of National Unity, are given assignments to represent the movement not themselves. This could be done in two ways: recalling all those who are appointed in GONU to Juba, for a week of political briefing, where the whole leadership, plus the Southern Assembly give the SPLM ministers in GONU a code of conduct, advise them to work as a team, rather than as individuals. The SPLM leadership may as well ask its representatives in GONU to report every two months to Juba for a briefing. If this is not done, then it will be like sending these men and women to exile, where each of them within the next year or so, will find himself, or herself alone, cornered by NCP petrodollar politics, and who knows what next.

Some of the SPLM members in GONU have protested, because they felt that they deserve higher positions than the ones they have been appointed to. Others strongly felt that the communities and the nationalities they come from were allocated very junior positions, compared to their real political and numerical sizes. Others complained that some individual members of the Movement were allocated senior positions in GONU, which should have been allocated to more senior members, who joined the Movement earlier.

One of the explanations given by some members of the SPLM leadership to answer some of these complains, was that some of these senior SPLM members do not want to work in the north. The question then is, if these members have already informed the leadership, directly or indirectly, of their intention not to work in the north, then why allocate to them positions in the north? These issues should be carefully studied by the leadership, and if the SPLM leadership has not already allocated positions in the government of Southern Sudan and in governments of states, it has to widen its consultations, inform those it intends to deploy.

Most importantly, those who are currently advising the SPLM leadership should open their eyes and ears widely, because the SPLM-NCP partnership suppose to avoid focus on distribution of positions, and concentrate on creating a true change in the lives of the people of Sudan and the South in particular. Giving the impression that the sole aim of the SPLM-NCP partnership is to buy people loyalty with positions, will definitely defeat the purpose of the SPLM/A struggle, for which millions have died, and other millions waiting to go home and find real changes there, when they go back. This is the real challenge for the SPLM leadership.

Thirdly, the lesson which the SPLM should learn from the politics of the formation of the GONU is that whenever a leadership of an organisation preoccupies itself with procedures and take longer times negotiating political issues, the other parts of the organisation, tend to paralyze. This is always the case in centralised system, where members of the movement are waiting in anticipation of getting orders and do not participate in decision making. The SPLM leadership should start to divide roles among its members. And it has lots of qualified people to take up such roles, only if the leadership and its advisors look around them and spread the nets wider beyond their immediate surroundings.

Indeed, it was impressive that once it became clear that the NCP was buying time, the SPLM leadership correctly decided to speed up the process of formation of constitutional structures in the South. It could have been done faster and better. When the SPLM and NCP where busy negotiating positions, the NCP was busy emptying the treasuries of national economy and enriching its cronies and potential allies. The SPLM should have appointed a shadow caretaking government of its own, during the pre-interim period to work with the NCP. The SPLM did appoint one person to deal with NCP as a contact person; it should have appointed a representative in every ministry in central government to monitor the activities there.

In fact, the NCP care-taking government had done so many things during the past six months that it would have not done, even when it was still a government. During the negotiations, the NCP was busy signing contracts, cementing its international relations and indeed was busy emptying the Ministry of Foreign affairs from its staff, deploying them to all corners of the world, in anticipation that the SPLM will find all the embassies and consulates full with manpower, hence leaving no room for the new minister to employ Southerners and members from the other marginalised areas.

The SPLM leadership should therefore come up with a new mechanism, through which a selected dedicated group of its members are allocated responsibilities, to monitor every aspects of the CPA. Each of these members should be assigned specific tasks, which relates to the implementation of the peace agreement, so that when any new round of negotiations with the NCP commences, that group will have worked out all the modalities, so that time is not spent on small and minor things which should be delegated to technocrats within the movement.

Fourthly, the formation of the National government has revealed that the SPLM needs to strengthen its information and international affairs units. The SPLM should inform on daily basis the international community and African countries that guaranteed and witnessed the peace agreement about the process of implementation of the peace agreement. The SPLM diplomats should be assigned specific tasks to keep the world informed about the delays the NCP creates on daily basis. The Sudan TV and Radio were definitely supportive of the NCP position on the negotiations over the positions of GONU and the printed media was bias, to the extent of disinformation. International community representatives in Khartoum were daily given the impression that the Energy and Mining fiasco was under control and that it was going to be allocated to the SPLM.

The disinformation campaign was so well organised that each senior member of the NCP has played his role very well. Only Al-Beshir and Taha were not allowed to give any statements over the issue, except when they were cornered by the independent media, otherwise they avoided to give interviews. The impression was given in the media that the chief negotiators from NCP were Nafie and Khalifa, the reality was that Taha was the main reference point from the government side. Everybody else who is who in NCP was asked to play its role in the disinformation campaign.

As a result, important issues such as peace in Darfur, the frozen negotiations in the East and the drafting of the constitution of Southern Sudan were sidelined in the media for almost a month and half. The SPLM has always been very weak in its information system.

For the time being, the SPLM will need to collaborate with the existing Southern private news papers and to start efforts towards the establishment of a national TV and Radio in Juba. Such a project would not need lots of thinking since the South is endowed with experienced and well trained journalists and technicians. Engineers could be recruited from aboard to run the stations, until such time the Southern technicians are trained. A call from President Salva Kiir and his Deputy Dr Riek Machar to the talented Southern journalists to assemble in Juba to plan for the establishment of TV and Radio stations that would cover the whole Sudan, will be sufficient.

These are serious lessons to be learned by the SPLM leadership, but also are warnings for difficult times ahead. But what are the real political challenges for Post-John Garang SPLM leadership?

CHAPTER TEN

# The CPA: Five Years to go to the Referendum

Despite the tragic death of late Dr John Garang in July 2005 and the slowness of the implementation of the CPA that followed, some progress has been made in putting in place the institutional frameworks that are needed to implement the agreement. Since July 2005, the following frameworks, institutions and commissions were instituted: the Interim National Assembly (the two houses), the Interim Assembly of Southern Sudan, National Interim Constitution, the Interim Constitution of Southern Sudan, the Interim Government of National Unity, the Interim Government of Southern Sudan, Governments of ten Southern States, except for Abyei Administration, the States' Assemblies in the ten Southern states, eight out of ten commissions as stipulated in the CPA were also established.

Irrespective of the modalities and the criteria used in forming these frameworks, governments, assemblies and commissions, the progress so far has been impressive. However, the question of how much is the 50% of the oil net revenue which the South should get, and whether the money comes from Dr Awad Al-Jaz Ministry or from the ministry of finance is one of the mysteries that only the NCP can answer.

So far they seem to be hesitant to say whether the oil money records are kept in the national treasury or in the party treasury. Till that mystery is resolved, the GOSS will have to use the hand outs that it occasionally gets from the central bank governor, who every now and then feeds the press and media with contradictory figures of the GOSS share of oil money.

Regardless of these positive developments however, there are many challenges, that are facing and will definitely face the implementation of the Sudan peace agreement, and the leaders of the SPLM and the NCP will all the good will require in such critical situations. In the same way there are some important actions that the SPLM and the leaders of GOSS should take to fulfill the promises they have made to the people of Southern Sudan and the marginalized areas during the struggle:

Firstly, the peace agreement which was signed in Nairobi on 9 January 2005 will enter its first anniversary on 9 January 2006, at the time when the war in Darfur is continuing and many more hundreds of people are loosing their lives. The reality on the ground in Drafur seems to suggest that the peace in the country will not be comprehensive nor complete until the wars in Darfur and in the eastern Sudan are stopped. As a mass and national movement that is championing change in the whole country and a key partner in the Government of National Unity (GNU), the SPLM should have a written and well thought policy on problems of Darfur and Eastern Sudan. Scenarios for solutions to these problems should be made known to public.

The SPLM position on the status of the Janjawid and the continued armament of tribes in Kordufan and Darfur by the NCP structures in these regions should be made clear. The SPLM relationship with the Darfurian liberation Movements, should take a systematic and a policy oriented approach, where sensitivities expressed by some Darfurian liberation movements about the SPLM current policy towards them or reservations expressed by the Darfurian movements about some individuals who are mandated by the SPLM to liaise with these movements, should be reviewed and actions taken to rectify any misunderstandings.

Secondly, the main architect and leading founder of the SPLM/A, Dr John Garang died in a mysterious plane crash in July 2005. His death has somewhat slowed down the implementation process of the CPA and shifted the balance of power within the NCP, which resulted in sidelining of Taha faction's active participation in the implementation of the CPA and the strengthening of El-Beshir-Nafie faction's grip in power within the ruling party and the government. Although there is no doubt that the smooth transition of power within the SPLM structures was a vital boost for the new leadership, the SPLM leadership and the leaders of GOSS, will have to sit down and think about their proper priorities.

As things are, there seems to be developing within the GOSS factional politics, with some suggesting that late Garang's widow is leading a faction, while the incumbent SPLM/A leader is leading the other. Such a situation if it is true or made to develop into reality will definitely reduce the status of the SPLM, which is supposed to be the ruling party in the South into a job seeking agency, each faction using positions to recruit supporters to its fold. One hopes that this is not the case, because it is simply against all the principles for which the people of the South and the New Sudan fought for during the struggle. In any event the war is not yet over, until the interim period comes to successful conclusion.

Thirdly, the number one SPLM/A priority is to implement the CPA and provide within its limited financial resources the infrastructure require to resettle those who have been uprooted from their homes, provide them with essential needs and to mobilise them politically and socially to participate in the three most important phases of the CPA: census, general elections and referendum. For the GOSS to carry out such important activities, it has to build strong institutions. Ministers and governors must have blue prints of programs for development. A minister or a governor, who has no clue as to what the people of his region or the population of the South want, should be forced to resign, because as we speak, six months have lapsed from the six year interim period. The President and Vice President of Government of Southern should therefore start seriously to scrutinise the capabilities of their ministers and governors. This is because the GOSS is an interim period government that will be judged according to its achievements when the elections come. It is not a normal government. Moreover, some of the ministers and governors were appointed to ministerial positions or governorship as a means of accommodating other Southern political groups and communities.

For example, while I do not question the national credentials of those who have been appointed from other Southern political parties into the GOSS, one wonders why service delivery ministries such as industry and mining, education, science and technology, agriculture and forestry, water resources and trade and supplies, be offered to other political parties by the ruling party. These are key service delivery positions, which the SPLM could have kept and trade them with other key, but not service delivery ministries. The SPLM as a main signatory to the CPA is obliged to implement the peace agreement, and certainly, when it comes to services delivery, it will be the SPLM to blame and not the ministers from the other Southern Sudanese parties that will take the blame should anything go wrong or services promised to the people of the South during the twenty two years of struggle are not delivered.

Fourthly, it seems that the SPLM leadership is dragging its feet to restructure the SPLM and transform it into a political party, especially that all the governance institutions throughout the South have now been established. One of the critical accusations which were levelled against late Dr John Garang was that he made it a point throughout the struggle that the SPLM is dormant and weak so that he could control the movement. So far, it seems that the current SPLM leadership is following late Garang's foot step on the status of the SPLM. The grave mistake that any SPLM member could make is to believe that the GOSS can substitute the SPLM. There is no where in the world where a government can become both a policy maker and an implementer. Governments (ministers and governors etc.) are bureaucrats who implement policies of political parties and national parliaments. The SPLM cannot be replaced by GOSS. Ministers in Government of Southern Sudan or in states can not formulate policies.

It is the SPLM, as the party responsible for the implementation of the agreement, in consultation with other Southern political parties that is responsible for formulating policies, present them to GOSS, which in turn will table them to the Southern Sudan interim Assembly for deliberations and ratification. The SPLM Chairman and his Deputy and the entire leadership of the movement should start preparing for the national convention, while at the same time identifying committed cadres at payam, county, state and national levels to train them on issues relating to organising and transforming a liberation movement into political party. The SPLM leadership should find money to prepare the movement for its transformation into political party. The longer the current status quo continuous, the more likely that the SPLM will not be ready, when time comes to handle the organisation of census, the general elections and the crucial referendum.

The SPLM cannot and should not make the mistake of taking for granted the people of Southern Sudan. The National Congress Party is stronger and has been in power for the past 16 years, despite its split, because it has a vision, and despite internal differences within its leadership, organisationally, it is cohesive. One does not need to emphasise that it will be in the NCP interest to see the SPLM, its main partner in the GNU, dormant and ineffective. It will also be a political suicide for the SPLM Chairman and his deputy to think that the people of South will vote for them, simply because the SPLM brought peace.

Fifthly, relating to the above point is harmonisation of the SPLM policies on national issues and on issues relating to the implementation of the peace agreement. For example, there are currently two designate

SPLM executives, one heading the SPLM Southern sector while the other heading the Northern sector. These senior officials are supposed to act, in consultation with the Chairman of the movement, as the official voices of the Movement rather than each minister or senior SPLM member expresses his/her view without coordination.

In fact, the nature of the agreement warrants that there should be designated official spokespersons specifically for the SPLM, GOSS and for the SPLM caucus in the National and Southern parliaments. This is because the implementation of the agreement requires that there should be clear SPLM positions and policies on Darfur, clear channels of communication between the SPLM and northern oppositions, designated officials to coordinate relations with other Southern political parties and armed groups. The SPLM through its structures should have policies every national issue, especially on national media, particularly on TV and Radio.

Sixthly, the question of Abyei is a potential timing bomb that might force the SPLA to go back to war. An indication of the CPA architects' wisdom was their insistence that the first commission to be formed was the Abyei Border Commission (ABC). In fact, the Abyei commission report was the first item on the agenda of the first meeting of the Presidency on 10 July 2005, which then composed of El-Beshir-Garang-Taha. The dynamics of mechanical majority within the Presidency (2+1) led to the Abyei Commission Report to be frozen. Senior NCP officials and senior Northern opposition leaders have already expressed their reservations about the ruling of the report. Missiriyya technocrats and politicians were given free access to the public media to condemn the international experts' report on Abyei, while any move from the part of Ngok Dinka citizens to urge the Presidency to approve the report, which according to the CPA is non negotiable, is deemed by the NCP ideologues a breach of institutional framework.

This was the case when in early December 2005 Ali Ismail Atabani, one of the owners of Rai Al-Aam daily in Khartoum wrote an opinion page attacking Deng Alor Kuol, Minister of Cabinet Affairs in GNU, for pointing out that the failure of the Presidency to approve the Abyei border commission report may force the SPLM to seek IGAD and IGAD partners' intervention.

In the same article Ali Ismail Attabani attacked Dr Francis Deng for raising the Abyei issue in USA, and indeed suggested that both Deng Alor and Francis Deng were undermining the leadership of Salva Kiir Mayardit and Bona Malwal in Southern Sudan, two of whom happened to be in the Republic Palace and hailed from the vicinity of Abyei, Gogrial County. Of course Attabani's attack on Francis Deng in particular was absurd because he suggested that Dr Francis Deng might have been unhappy that he did not take over the leadership of the SPLM after the death of Dr Garang.

Such alterations from prominent NCP ideologues such Ismail Attabani, are symptoms of a wider policy, not only to use the old tactic of divide and rule among Southerners, but to give an impression that there are serious differences between the Twic Dinka of Gogrial, from where both Mayardit and Malwal hails, and the Ngok Dinka of Abyei. The mishandling of Abyei border report by NCP is a recipe to a serious setback for the implementation of the CPA.

Needless to say, there will be no use for the border commission between the north and South which El-Beshir has established, as long as the Abyei border commission report is not approved by the Presidency. The two commissions were established by the provisions of the same agreement, and unless the NCP and other northern Sudanese political groups act and respect the CPA stipulations, the whole agreement may collapse before the elections of 2009. It was the same Abyei problem that almost led to the collapse of the Naivasha peace process. Southern Sudanese are not ready to leave the Abyei border unresolved; they are not ready for another Kashmir.

Seventhly, the issue of the national capital is one of those issues which, if not handled with care, may in the long run prove to be a real nightmare for the National Congress. For El-Beshir and associates, the question of establishing a joint government for national capital is a matter of offering positions to the SPLM members as they did in the GNU; whereas to the SPLM the power sharing in the Capital falls within the strategic policy of creating a new image of Sudan.

What a capital means to NCP is not the same to the SPLM nor to the Darfurians for that matter. The rest of Sudanese are interested in a capital that represents them and reflect their aspirations. No one would be interested in a capital that discriminates against its citizens, applying discriminatory laws and imposes cultural practices that divides people rather than unite them. Sudanese are not interested in a capital where a minority is living expensive life, while the majority lives in a dreadful poverty. What a capital where the ruling elites proud themselves of ruling the richest country in East Africa, thanks to oil boom, while within the centre of the capital thousands of street children and beggars share the main roads with the luxuries cars that the NCP petrodollar millionaires are using.

Eighthly, the SPLM leaders should start to travel to the villages and towns of Southern Sudan to familiarise themselves with realities on the grounds. After completing the institutionalisation of the CPA, the SPLM leaders, should start to visit villages, towns, refugee camps, the displaced camps, the Southern Sudanese in diaspora, the communities in their areas, so as to explain to them the SPLM priorities as well as to listen to the needs and priorities of the people after the liberation.

In fact, one expect starting from mid January 2006 the new SPLM leadership to visit the SPLA garrisons in Nuba Mountains, Abyei, Southern Blue Nile, Upper Nile, Equatoria and in Bahr El Ghazal, to share with the SPLA officers and soldiers the new leadership's plans for the future. Interacting with local leaders, traditional and religious leaders will definitely help the new SPLM leadership to acquaint itself with the expectations of the people. Managing people's expectations during post war era is the most difficult task that a leadership of liberation movement should take keen interest in. This is because the states and counties are very crucial in the implementation of the peace agreement. In fact, the role of governors and the counties' commissioners during the interim period is more crucial than the role of ministers at GNU and GOSS levels.

While the SPLM and parliaments conceptualise and formulate the development policies, with the help of the GNU and GOSS, the states and counties' authorities are the implementers of the policies. It is therefore crucial that the SPLM, GOSS ministers, governors and especially the President and Vice President of GOSS, should travel intensively throughout the New Sudan territories, interacting with local population and learn from them.

Ninthly, interacting with local population, especially those near to the regional and international borders, require better understanding of what is happening in the neighbouring countries and beyond. The South cannot survive, as a land lock territory without interacting and benefiting from what the neighbouring countries can offer. The visits by the President of GOSS to Egypt, USA, Ethiopia, and Eritrea were very crucial courtesy calls. Similar visits should take place as soon as time permits to other neighbouring and friendly countries, so that a systematic approach to regional cooperation is established between the South and these countries.

The GOSS should continue to encourage friendly countries and organisations to open consulates and trade missions in Juba, Malakal and Wau. The importance of East African Community (EAC) to the economic prosperity of Sudan, and South in particular is very important aspect to observe closely. The GOSS should therefore establish units within its ministry of regional cooperation to monitor the activities of EAC, IGAD, AU, COMESA and other inter-governmental international agencies such as the UN, the League of Arab States and EU. The importance of such units lies in that for the CPA to be implemented, regional and international organisations, and key states which witnessed the signing of the CPA must be kept informed, and that is why, it is important for the ministry of regional cooperation in Juba to seriously begin to institutionalise its activities.

The crucial role played by the US in pressurising NCP to implement the CPA during November 2005, led to the El-Beshir to speed up the formation of the commissions and other important bodies stipulated in the agreement. The GOSS' ministry of regional cooperation should therefore keep the friendly countries and the UN system informed about the progress of the implementation of the CPA.

Finally, the economic boom which the South is said to be undergoing may end up as a curse rather than a blessing if it is not supervised through appropriate institutions and with vigilant parliamentary overseeing.

First of all, most of the 'investors' who are daily travelling to the South are 'brokers' or 'go between' and are not the owners of the companies they are speaking on behalf. The implication of this is that the GOSS of Southern Sudan will find itself dealing with very junior officials who have no final say in the terms of the deals or contracts they are negotiating.

The result is that many ministers of GOSS of Southern Sudan will find themselves negotiating more than once with different agents of the same company, wasting valuable time that they should spend providing the people of South with the badly needed services. Secondly, several investors are travelling to Southern Sudan with the perception that they should meet with the highest authorities of the GOSS, paying little respect to any senior official who is designated to deal with such issues.

The President, the Vice President and ministers of Government of Southern Sudan have found themselves spending many hours daily meeting with various delegations of 'investors', most of who are only interested in striking deals and signing contracts without proper negotiations, as if the South is another Banana republic to exploit. Instead of wasting valuable time of the President, his Vice and ministers in endless meetings, one would suggest that the Council of Ministers of GOSS appoints in each ministry two senior officials (male and a female) to negotiate and scrutinise the offers of investors, and refer to the relevant minister or to the Council of Ministers the cases of those investors who have been deemed to have fulfilled the requirements to be awarded contracts, including successful bidding process.

The President, his Deputy and ministers can only meet with those investors who are coming in to invest in multi-million sectors that fall directly under the jurisdiction of the Council of Ministers or well known personalities in the business world. The way things are currently, it seems that each minister is left to negotiate with investors, without help from professional teams, who should scrutinise the profiles and the financial capabilities of those companies fluxing to the South, before awarding them contracts.

The principle that each company should partner with local company will be the only safeguard for the future of the South. It is important to point out that whatever route that the GOSS will take regarding investment policies in Southern Sudan from 2006 onward, will definitely shape the future of the wealth sharing among southern Sudanese in the post-Naivasha Southern Sudan. Unless the investment sector is handled with care and integrity, the South may end up another Nigeria or Iraq.

CHAPTER ELEVEN

# Prospects of Sustaining the Naivasha Consensus in Sudan

The peace agreement which was signed between the government of Sudan and the Sudan People's Liberation Movement (SPLM) on 9 January 2005 in the Kenyan capital, Nairobi, came as a result of internal and external developments within the Sudan, Africa and in the world politics. Various actors in the country and beyond had shown interest in seeing to it that a peace agreement is achieved. The January 2005 peace agreement have therefore opened the way for the remaining conflicts in the country, namely the conflict in Darfur and eastern Sudan to be resolved using the Naivasha agreements as a model.

The Machakos and Nairvasha road maps have explicitly spelled out a number of the issues, while its drafters have chosen to be vague on others. This vagueness has introduced, unintentionally perhaps, contradictory methods for the resolution of the Sudanese conflict, especially on the following issues:

The first issue is whether the Sudan People's Liberation Movement (SPLM) and the National Congress (NC) will be committed to democracy and the secularism of national politics as viable options for the post-interim period's political, economic and judiciary permanent arrangements between the South and the North.

The second contentious issue is that of the unity of the country, and what this means, in terms of post-interim period permanent arrangements, especially in relation to power and wealth sharing between the centre and regions, including the South. The SPLM is in favour of a new dispensation altogether.

Then there is the issue of self-determination, and the impact it will have on national politics, especially during the post-interim period permanent arrangements (constitutionally and politically) should the South opt to secede from the rest of the country.

The political map of Northern Sudan, like that of the South is very complex and diverse. Unlike the South, however, the political forces of the North, while they differ on the 'type' and the levels of reforms to be introduced in post-war Sudan, are in total agreement on the necessity to maintain the unity of the country. They would do everything in their power to ensure that the country remains united. They include NDA alliance, Umma Party, the splinter groups of Umma and DUP, Baathists, Islamists, and other progressive forces in the North, etc..

When addressing post Machakos and Naivasha peace process dynamics in Southern Sudan, and the manner in which the peace agreement will be implemented, the following questions may be posed:

Will the SPLM leadership try to isolate the other Southern political forces, or will it opt to appease some and antagonise others? What will be the nature of the current alliances between the SPLA and Northern Sudanese opposition parties, especially those in the NDA, during the interim period? Will the Southern Sudanese political and military organisations, opposition parties that are currently involved in love-hate relationships with the SPLM, opt to unite against SPLM leadership during post-war Southern Sudan administration?

On the other hand, two parallel, opposing ideological trends exist within the SPLM – those who prefer a united secular democratic Sudan, in alliance with the marginalised areas (Darfurians (Zegawa, Fur, Masalit, Beja, Nuba, and Ingasana in Blue Nile), and those who envisage the path of self-determination as leading to secession of the South, as the best manner in which to solve the Sudanese conflict. What will happen during the interim period if the SPLM leader, Dr John Garang, decides to ally with one particular trend, thereby sidelining the other?

When discussing external actors and alliances, the neighbouring countries to Sudan come to mind. The current IGAD member states (Ethiopia, Eritrea, Kenya, Djibouti and Uganda) have their own interests and internal problems. Some of them, such as Uganda and Ethiopia, have signed security and economic cooperation agreements with the National Congress government, while maintaining good relations with the SPLM.

Eritrea is not in a good relationship with both Khartoum and Addis Ababa, although it has close ties with the SPLM.

Uganda perceives the prospect of peace in Sudan, as an opportunity for it to uproot the Acholi led Lord's Resistance Army (LRA) from Southern Sudan.

Egypt and Libya have signed controversial integration pacts with the Sudanese government, which may lead to serious misunderstandings with the SPLM during the interim period. For example, the NC and the Egyptian governments singed an integration agreement in January 2004, dubbed the 'four freedoms' pact.

On the other hand, a considerable number of Southern Sudanese seem to feel that the Troika that brokered the Machakos Consensus (USA, UK, Norway, plus Italy), have little interest in bringing about a lasting and just peace in the country. Rather, they seem to be interested in an open-ended and long-term ceasefire agreement, whose fate or success will be left to circumstances during the interim period.

There are other countries, whose economic interests and political sympathy with either side of the Sudanese conflict, during the interim period, will inevitably determine the course, which the implementation of the peace agreement will take. These countries and organisations include China, Russia, South Africa, Nigeria, India, Canada, Indonesia, Malaysia, the UN, the EU, the AU, the Arab League countries (Saudi Arabia, Kuwait, Jordan, Yemen etc.) , the World Bank, and the IMF.

CHAPTER TWELVE

# Challenges and Opportunities for the Implementation of the CPA: Personal Reflections

I would like to thank each and every one of the leaders, friends and relatives who were kind enough to see me, talked to me and shared ideas regarding the future of Sudan and Southern Sudan in particular. I would like to thank those friends and relatives who have written messages to me during the visit asking about my whereabouts. It was indeed very rewarding to meet with my sister, my nieces, nephews and other relatives in Juba, Malakal and Khartoum after twenty years. It was, I must add, a self-fulfilling homecoming, although I am still to take the second homecoming visit to my county and village, which I have not visited since April 1983.

I started my visit to Southern Sudan on 22 July to Juba, the capital of the South. I stayed there for three days, and proceeded to Malakal on 25 July where I spent three days and proceeded to Khartoum on 28 July. I spent four days in Khartoum, and returned to Juba on 1 August. I spent in Juba another four days, and left for Nairobi on Saturday 5 August. It was while in Nairobi that I was told about the change of the date for the transportation of the body of late Prof. Gabriel Giet Jal to Malakal from Sunday 6 to Wednesday 9 August.

## Challenges and Opportunities for the CPA 189

While in Nairobi, Juba, Malakal, and Khartoum, I met many people, some in high positions in SPLA, SPLM, GOSS, and GONU and in some important positions in civil society organisations. I learned a lot from them about the state and politics of the CPA, GOSS, SPLM, NCP and GONU. I have listened to so many of them and discussed so many topics that I am not sure if I will have the time to write about, and even if I have the time, the likelihood is that the piece will be too long. I hope not. Indeed, while in Sudan, I have noticed positive constitutional developments that have taken place in the country since the signing of the CPA:

The South for the first time has its own President who is not answerable to Khartoum. He heads a Council of Ministers that is only answerable to him and Southern Legislative Assembly in Juba.

Although it is facing organisational challenges due to the transformation difficulties from a Liberation Movement into a governing party, the SPLM as the vanguard of the revolution is recognised and structurally spread all over the Sudan. The Movement is now the first political organisation led by Southerners to open offices in every corner of the Sudan.

The SPLA, as the power base of the CPA is being structurally organised and has been recognised, not only by the Sudan armed forces leadership as the main military force in the New Sudan, but also by the whole continent and the rest of the world community. The SPLA is in the process of organising itself, have already made available its units in the Joint Integrated Units (JIUs) and is carrying out a voluntary disarmament of the civilian society in the South, which though has serious political and logistical problems, is progressing.

The CPA has established two houses in Khartoum: the house of representatives (National Assembly) and the Council of the States. The two houses are operational.

A Government of National Unity, which is though not cohesive, is in place in Khartoum, running the daily affairs of the country.

Opposition parties in the South and the North have been directly or indirectly involved, either as part of the GONU or opposition, in the CPA process, particularly that the CPA provides for general elections sometime in 2009. The fact that some opposition parties have decided to accept in principle participation in an election provided for by the CPA and given that the main northern opposition parties have either joined the GONU or decided to talk with it, shows that the CPA is indeed accepted by the northern and southern opposition groups as a framework for resolution of the Sudanese conflicts.

States and counties' assemblies and councils are in place in the south, although a lot needs to be done to build the human resource capacity of the personnel that is running these important legislative and executive bodies in states and counties.

The states and counties governments are in place, although they need operationalisation and close supervision from the Southern Sudan Assembly, SPLM, other Southern opposition parties and the President of GOSS.

The majority of independent commissions that were created by the CPA to opertionalise, supervise and evaluate the CPA are formed, although the NCP has intentionally decided not to operationalise them by either starving these commissions financially or delaying the legal processes to operationalise them.

Independent Commissions that are supposed to supervise and evaluate the performances of GOSS governance institutions are in place, all they need is effective supervision mechanisms and financial support.

While the positive constitutional developments in Sudan and in the South in particular have introduced new understanding among some leaders in the SPLM and other political forces in the South and the North on how to manage the Sudanese chronic political and socio-economic challenges, there are also some acute challenges that I have observed. In fact, some of these challenges, if not carefully handled, may derail the whole process of transforming the Sudan from an old anti-developmental state into a new development oriented state in Sudan.

During the visit to Sudan, I discussed with a considerable number of concerned Sudanese the dynamics and challenges that are facing the operationalisation of the CPA:

There were sensitive questions that kept coming into mind while chatting with Southern Sudanese leaders, students, soldiers and ordinary citizens regarding what next after the interim period. Young people in particular are worried about the future, given that what is at hand seems to be discouraging and blurring the prospects for future. Young people are worried that the CPA is silent about crucial issues regarding constitutional arrangements of post-Naivasha period. For example, some concerned individuals are asking whether the south is ready to secede or not, and whether this readiness or lack of it will affect the future prospects of the region and its people. Some further wonder whether the SPLM and other Southern Sudanese political organisations have alternatives and plans in place for any eventualities during the interim period. What about the future of the oil revenues? Will the current CPA arrangements be adopted as they are after the interim period or will new arrangements (administrative and constitutional) be adopted? Will the ratios of 50-50 remains the same even after the interim period, or will new arrangements be made and who will supervise the discussions over them, the Sudanese, IGAD and its partners or the UN Security Council which is the de fecto guardian of the CPA following the issuance of it famous supportive resolution to the CPA in Nairobi in November 2004. What if the war breaks out again before the interim period comes to an end, and given that the oil is the main source of revenue to both south and north, what will be the new source of revenue for the South in the event of renewed war? Should GOSS introduce investors to other natural resources in the South other than oil, or should these natural resources be kept aside for the time being? These are some of the questions that I heard young people in the south pondering about.

I also discussed issues relating to the implementation of CPA and the challenges (institutional and in terms of human capacity) that the GOSS leaders are facing. Why the IGAD leadership and member states, plus their partners did not meet since the CPA was signed to evaluate its implementation process? Did the SPLM leadership ask the Chair of IGAD to convene an emergency summit to discuss the challenges facing the implementation of the CPA, and if so, what was the response of the IGAD leadership? Other challenges include the ineffectiveness of the modalities for operationalisation of the CPA, the inefficiency and ineffectiveness of the independent commissions, especially the Oil and the Border commissions, allegations of mismanagement of the oil revenues and other resources (many Southerners are wondering why up to this time, the money allocated to the SPLA are still kept in Omdurman Bank in Khartoum, and who decided that arrangement, the GOSS Ministry of Finance or the Bank of Southern Sudan (BOSS)); slow institutional building process (there are widely circulated news of ineffectiveness of administration in states and counties under governors and commissioners). There is a concern that some people around the President of GOSS and the Chairman of the SPLM do not allow some senior SPLM and senior government officials' access to him. The fact the SPLM Chairman is also the First Vice President of Sudan, also means that his national duties require him to pay attention to his duties as the Chairman of the SPLM as well as the second person in Sudan. In fact, some Northern Sudanese senior members of the SPLM, including some from Nuba Mountains and Southern Blue Nile, are complaining that they are being sidelined within the movement; that they were left out of some sensitive assignments, such as senior government positions, diplomatic assignments and other SPLM sectoral positions. Perhaps President Kiir will need to look into the current structures of his offices in Juba and Khartoum and see if something can be done.

There is also the need for the President of GOSS and the SPLM leadership to support the vital envisaged role of the newly established Auditor General in seeing to it that public funds are spent according to the budget items; the infrastructural challenges (particularly in the four priority areas: roads, health, education and water sanitation, plus security), allegations of inefficiency of coordination of government activities (GOSS-states-counties) and lack of harmonisation of policies and priorities (SPLM-GOSS-Parliament). These are some of many other challenges that relate to the implementation of the CPA, which need special attention from the SPLM and southern opposition parties' leaderships. Of particular interest to many Southern Sudanese and observers is how to deal swiftly with the issue of alleged corruption from the top of GOSS and lack of accountability among senior government officials. These are, I believe, serious challenges that call for the reconstituting of GOSS and its priorities, as the CPA enters its second year. These challenges can be addressed, and from looks of things, it seems that President Kiir is slowly, but sure moving towards that direction.

Other issues of concern to some youngsters and ordinary citizens in the south are related to the SPLA organisation, restructuring, strengthening of the DDR Commission, and the empowerment of the Demining Commissions, whose mandates are vital to the restructuring of the SPLA, harmonisation of military ranks; challenges of the integration of the SSDF forces into the SPLA; harmonisation of the SPLA salaries; implementation of the Abyei Boundary Commission Report, which has everything to do with the demarcation of the South-North boundary; the strengthening of Joint Integrated Units (JIUs), challenges of how to deal with those armed groups that have not yet joined the SPLA ranks, Mbororo Arab militia, and the future of LRA in Southern Sudan, given that there are two LRA groups operating in the South: the Sudan-LRA forces which were recruited by the NCP and the Uganda LRA forces. These are security challenges to the GOSS, and unless clear and well defined policies are mapped out, they could become serious obstacles to GOSS President and his colleagues.

Another issue which caught my attention during my visit was connected to the future development of the SPLM as the guardian for the CPA and a senior partner in GNU, its role as the majority party in the South, the future and the current state of the "New Sudan Vision", after the untimely death of Dr John Garang; the role of the 'New Sudan' vision as a catalyst for change and its potential role as an ideology for all the Sudanese who are for the transformation of Sudan into a new political and economic giant. I heard people asking about the future status of the Nuba Mountains and the people of Southern Blue Nile after the referendum in the South? Will the Nuba and Angessena people join the South? What are the guarantees that they will not be mistreated by the rest of the North, if they are left with the north, once the south secedes? Another issue of concern which was raised by a number of concerned SPLM supporters was the challenges of the current interim structures of the SPLM and their viability and whether the SPLM leadership is cohesive enough to guard away rumours of internal differences. The challenges of funding of the SPLM activities, the role of its two main branches in the South and North in mobilisation of masses and what policies required to elevate the status of the SPLM as a potential majority party in the whole country during the upcoming elections in 2009. Is the SPLM leadership cohesive, and is the SPLM vision is intact? I noticed during my brief discussions with some leaders of the movement including the Secretary General and some of his colleagues that the recent Rumbek SPLM leadership meeting and its aftermath is regarded to be a right step towards close cooperation among SPLM leadership members. Other 'what ifs' questions also dominated my discussions, for example what if the South opt to secede, what will be the future of the remaining parts of Sudan, what will be the future of alliance between the marginalised areas and the south and what will be the future of the

SPLM-northern sector? Is the current SPLM Northern Sector capable of sustaining the movement in the north after 2011?

Another disturbing reality I observed in Khartoum is that the NCP is adamant to continue monopolising national wealth, power and dominates national security organs. It continuous to enrich its cadres, while it starves financially supporters of other political groups in the country. The idea of power and wealth sharing as stipulated in the CPA, from developmental perspective, is not reflected in practical terms. All political shades within political north see themselves as victims of NCP domination of the Petro-dollar national economy. Certainly, economically weakened and fragmented opposition parties would not serve as effective and credible alternative, unless they have all united and embraced wholeheartedly the ideals of the New Sudan as laid out in the CPA. The sad news in the north is that the opposition is divided; some splinter political parties are allied to NCP, while others are confronting it militarily. Although the CPA had emphasised the need for the democratisation of the political atmosphere of Naivasha Sudan, the nature of the existing NCP's security oriented policies, suggests and directs to the opposite direction, namely continued one-party monopoly.

Throughout my journeys, I heard people complaining, while others politely tried to caution the prophets of doom to wait and give both the GOSS and GONU a chance to proof them wrong or right. In terms of challenges, the following were the most prominent in my discussions:

The issue of service delivery is regarded in the South as a sacred number one priority. The GOSS 2006 budget has prioritised the provision of essential infra-structural needs such as schools, clinics, clean water and roads as number prioty. The main question remains: have GOSS and States authorities shared these priorities with the local population, given that the financing of such projects requires lots money, which GOSS do not have enough of. GOSS President, the SPLM Secretariat and other Southern Sudanese leadership have not been on the ground on regular basis in the South; hence do not seem to appreciate why Southerners are pushing for urgent delivery of services. This is because, in the view of the ordinary Southern Sudanese, GOSS President, his ministers, Governors are not regularly on the ground. The oil industry in Sudan, the main source of money, is dominated by the NCP and its Asian allies. Pipelines are built to carry crude oil from the South to north, and the same is with refineries, which are scattered all over the northern part of the country. The SPLM government has the obligation to quickly negotiate and start immediately to construct pipelines to the neighbouring countries (Kenya and Eritrea via Ethiopia), and to asked friendly countries to help it built refineries in the south. There is no way the South can survive economically, during the remaining few years of interim period, if its oil is being transported, stored and marketed in the north. There will be no proper time to build refineries and pipelines, because this is an interim period where everything must be done quickly and efficiently. The proper and the right time is now. Chinese, South African or Japanese companies can build pipe lines and refineries in the South within a year and two as China did in northern Sudan.

The issue of the Darfur and Eastern Sudan conflicts and their impact on the implementation of the CPA also dominated my discussions with various friends and leaders. There was a concern that the incompleteness of the Darfur Peace Agreement (DPA) and its negative repercussions for inter-Darfur relations and its side effects on derailing the transformation momentum that the CPA had availed was seen by some to be a serious potential setback to arriving at a comprehensive peace agreement in Sudan. The issue of factionalism in Darfur and Eastern Sudan politics, the role of the NCP in it, the role of Petrodollar in dividing Darfurians is regarded as another negative aspect that will keep Sudan unstable. Will peace ever come to Darfur and Eastern Sudan given the factional character of politics that is emerging in these regions? What should be the role of the SPLM in bringing a comprehensive peace agreement in these regions and in the whole country?

The CPA had three pillars as a transforming peace agreement: Making unity attractive to Southerners, guaranteeing Self-determination for Southerners and the restoration of democracy through general elections in the whole country. My discussions with some influential members of the SPLM suggest that other political groups in the South and north are not sure whether the unity will be made attractive, nor do they foresee any hope that self-determination will be exercised by Southerners, let alone the conduction of general elections. This gloomy picture seems to have originated from the fact that Northern political parties such as the UMMA, DUP, Sudan Communist Party, National Popular Congress and others are disillusioned by the fact that what was supposed to be the GNU is not functioning as such. The CPA is implementation not moving, and the possibilities for elections are getting slimmer and so, the likelihood that these parties may opt to adopt other strategies is most likely. What are these desperate strattegies, God knows. What seems to be clear is that neither of them trusts NCP and they seem to regard SPLM as a mass movement that has temporarily lost its vision. And that is not a good picture for a country that is supposed to be living in a new dispensation.

I was surprised to learn that the World Bank seems to have underestimated that Southern Sudanese have a clear knowledge of its historical role in under-developing Africa. At some stage it seems that the Bank officials in the South were ready to run the Ministry of Finance and Economic Planning of Government of Southern Sudan through its "experts". I was stunned to learn that the Bank officials, at one point had tried to blackmail, as they often do in many countries, local officials, by suggesting that unless the GOSS implements their 'suggestions' they may not cooperate. For example, the World Bank was asked officially by the GOSS to manage the funds that the donors will be granting GOSS under the Multi-Trust Fund. That was a fair deal because GOSS/SPLM leaders did not want to be responsible for funds that are donated and opted to manage the GOSS' own money. The surprising element is that some of the so-called emergency projects that the Bank has asked the GOSS officials (Ministers) to submit for funding since January 2005, have not been implemented and the money in question were not released, with exception of some funds for the construction of regional roads, which are partially funded through WFP by the GOSS. The highly talked about Joint Assessment Mission (JAM) Report, which was supposed to be the World Bank's developmental interim program in war affected areas in Sudan, especially in the South, is not heard about these days, and remember that hundreds of thousands of dollars were spent to produce that famous JAM report. Senior government officials in GOSS and states are complaining that the Bank officials and some UN agencies' staff are discouraging other friendly agencies and individuals from helping in transferring directly their experiences to the GOSS officials. Based on my discussions, two things stood out: GOSS officials are not in favour of the Bank to be responsible for drawing up of GOSS and States budgets. Two, the Bank officials must be aware by now that GOSS is in favour of cooperation and not competition with its officials. The fact that some donor money are spent by the bank officials on expensive accommodation, undertaking unnecessary project proposals, which are not applicable or suitable to the developmental needs of the South, and spending donors money on expensive air tickets are not definitely things that the GOSS and the SPLM should be happy about. The relationship between the Bank and GOSS will have to be re-defined before it reaches unaccepted stages.

The role of the UN peacekeeping forces is highly appreciated in the South, at least by those with whom I talked to. What seems to be a potential problem is the behaviour of individual peace keepers and their relations with the local populations. I noticed that all the UN peacekeeping units are located in the main towns in Southern Sudan; in other words in the seats of the state and county headquarters throughout the New Sudan, Khartoum and Kassala. It is easy to notice that tens of new 4X4 cars, which are not in use, packed in the UN compounds (at least that was the case in Juba, Malakal, and Khartoum)! The new role of other UN agencies in the South, which suppose to change from relief oriented activities to developmental ones, definitely has a lot to be desired. There is also a need for the faith- based local and international organisations which are operating in the South and from Lokichioko to be more people centred and developmental oriented.

The role of investors was another hot issue I spent quality time discussing with some concerned people in the South and in Khartoum. It seems that the would be 'investors' visiting Juba are reluctant to acknowledge that the government of Southern Sudan and its people vividly and clearly understand the principles and objectives of their long struggle, which inform their new priorities. Investors are moving to Juba with fixed ideas on what they perceived to be 'what exactly the South need'. There is no doubt that the booming nature of an emerging market often comes with its own challenges. For example, the erecting of tents as means for badly needed accommodation in Juba has opened opportunities, not only to foreign investors, who want to make quick money without paying taxes, but also to local officials who, thanks to lack of accommodation and high prices for rent in Juba, to join the business of tent hotels. Booming tent hotels business is discouraging investors to build concrete structures in the capital. Most of the newly employed officials in GOSS, some ministers and others who are in government pay rolls pay daily at least $120 for accommodation in those tents. The amount of money that is spent weekly in this business is enormous. It seems to me that some very influential people in GOSS and SPLM are involved in this lucrative business. The sad news is that this tent business is likely to interfere with government budget system, as I am sure these huge amounts were not budgeted for in 2005 and 2006 budgets, which means that ministries and departments may temper with chapter one (salaries) as well as with developmental budgets of GOSS and states.

There is no doubt that, given the nature of the new dispensation in the country, challenges and opportunities are abound for the authorities in Sudan. How does one make use or address them depends on how the leadership evaluates and prioritises its activities. There were several concerns that were raised:

Huge spending for the up keep of Ministers and senior officials, who travel to and from the neighbouring countries and beyond. Given that 90% of Southern Sudanese ministers, members of various commissions, members of parliaments and senior officials have their families in neighbouring countries and further abroad, it means that each has to maintain a family house abroad, most of them spent their holidays in abroad, and have to maintain a house in Juba, Malakal, Torit or Wau, plus Khartoum, where he/she permanently lives and works. This is a serious financial burden that requires urgent attention and solution.

One of the issues that I thought was positively acknowledged by the GOSS/SPLM leadership is the need for human resource capacity development for all the GOSS and states officials. While this has been acknowledged, what seems to be lacking is institutional framework through which this important task could be carried out and coordinated. For example, since the CPA was signed, hundreds of senior officials were sent to Kenya, Uganda and so far over a couple of hundred of senior officials, including President Kiir, his deputy and others were sent to South Africa for orientation and training. Two things seem to be apparent regarding human capacity building in the South: First, the need to appreciate and making use of the skills acquired during these trainings. Ministers and various states' senior officials should show their appreciation for the new skills as well as giving clear job descriptions to the trained officials. In fact, I understand that since they were appointed, very few ministers called for meetings to introduce themselves to their staff, let alone introducing their programmes to them. Secondly, once officials are sent to acquired news skills, the role of the so-called "experts consultants" should be minimised, because what is a use of spending thousands of dollars to train officials, while giving their assignments to old friends, who guise themselves as expatriate 'experts'. There are hundreds of Southern Sudanese professionals scattered all over the world, and all they need is a clear, well-defined project that would help them go to the South and put into use their expertise in various fields. In fact, the Ministry of Regional Cooperation should be tasked to establish a desk whose sole assignment would be to attract and facilitate the return of Southern Sudanese professionals back home. Moreover, there is also a need for an institutional framework through which all the capacity building could be carried out, a department or directorate under GOSS' Ministry of Regional Cooperation or the Ministry of Public Service, Labour and Human Resource Development that would deal with Special programmes and capacity building.

One of the biggest concerns expressed bitterly by the majority of young people I met in Juba, Malakal and Khartoum was the state of higher education, especially the continued exile of the three Southern Sudan universities in Khartoum, namely: Bahr El Ghazal University, University of Juba, and Upper Nile University. The main challenges facing the reallocation of these universities are: Lack of clear policies regarding the status of these three universities vis a vis other higher education institutions in the country. The CPA in Power Sharing Protocol (Part V, Schedule D (3), the Interim National Constitution of Sudan (Schedule D (3) and the Interim Constitution of Southern Sudan in the Schedules section (Schedule D (3) give the GONU, GOSS and States legislative and executive competencies on Tertiary education institutions during the interim period, but it is not clear exactly how these powers should be exercised by these three spheres of the government, especially with regard to the status of those universities that are supposed to be physically located in the South. One of the immediate concerns is the shortage of funding for rehabilitation and construction of new campuses for the three universities, coupled with the ambiguity over who should appoint the Vice Chancellors of the three universities. There are some indications, however that the GOSS' Ministry of Education, Science and Technology and its counterparts in Southern ten states may have some say in the construction and rehabilitation of the campuses of the three universities, using GOSS funding. A question however remains: should the Bhar El-Ghazal and Upper Nile Universities be merged as one university and evenly distribute their colleges or should the two universities be demoted into colleges' status so that they take their natural growth until such time it becomes ready to transform them into university status? Finally, who should take the final decision to transfer these institutions to the South as their role is very crucial during the interim period in helping GOSS develop its human resource capacity.

The question of what type of foreign policy GOSS should adopt at regional and international levels was also raised, especially that the GOSS' Ministry of Regional Cooperation remains until recently without a minister since the resignation of Minister Nhial Deng Nhial three months ago. There are concerns that unless the South clearly maps out its foreign policy priorities, its developmental agenda during the interim period may be misunderstood and compromised. Without a clear foreign policy agenda, shared openly with all the countries of the world, especially with friends of Southern Sudan, it is likely that some countries and international agencies will take GOSS for granted. In fact, some countries up to this point in time are not aware that the CPA, especially the Power Sharing Protocol ( Part V, Schedule D (19); the Interim National Constitution of Sudan (Schedule D (19) and the Interim Constitution of Southern Sudan (Part III, Chapter 1, Article 46), clearly permit GOSS to "initiate, negotiate and conclude international and regional agreements on culture, sports, trade, investment, credit, loans, grants and technical assistance with foreign governments and foreign non-governmental organisations". Moreover, some countries seem not to understand why GOSS has allowed some friendly countries to open consulates in Juba. The main reason is that all the three documents mentioned above, permits GOSS to do so, hence GOSS can indeed, as it has already done in several neighbouring and friendly countries, open liaison offices to coordinate its relations with different countries in the fields mentioned above. These are important realities that the Ministry of Regional Cooperation, which is the de fecto ministry of foreign affairs of GOSS, should explain to friends of Southern Sudan abroad. For example, the decision by GOSS to mediate between the Lord Resistance Army (LRA) and the Ugandan government was taken by the GOSS President and his deputy, with the support of the SPLM, while the Ministry of Regional Cooperation was almost left out of the picture. It is true that the custody of the foreign policy formulation remains to be the responsibility of the SPLM, other Southern political parties, GOSS and Southern Sudan Legislative Assembly, but the implementer of such a policy must always be the Ministry of Regional Cooperation throughout the interim period.

What about Dr Garang's Legacy in Sudan? My visit to the tomb of late Dr John Garang in front of Southern Sudan Assembly in Juba, led me to think deeply about many things regarding the possibilities and speculative scenarios that the future of Sudan have taken were he alive on the driving seat both in Juba and Khartoum. For one, I thought of the legacy of John Garang the leader of the SPLM: what is it that the SPLM inherited from his legacy as a political leader apart from the visionary ideals of the 'New Sudan', 'united, democratic, secular and diverse Sudan" What do these phrases mean to the Sudanese today, compared to when he was alive?. What has the current SPLA leadership inherited from Col John Garang the military officer, the commander in Chief, the comrade in arms and the leader of the struggle? To what extent are the Sudanese from the South aware and recognise the late Garang's personal sacrifices and contributions to the struggle? Do they regard the CPA a viable product of Dr Garang's persistence? Would late Garang manage to achieve what he has achieved without close cooperation and support from his colleagues, especially General Kiir and his colleagues in the leadership? What does the ordinary rank and file of the SPLA feel after the departure of the man they looked at as their hope for a bright future? At late Garang tomb, I saw the anguish and uncertainty in the eyes of the three young soldiers who guard his tomb. I asked one of them if he ever thought Dr Garang would depart this soon, he replied, 'I am orphaned at very young age (referring to the CPA), but if this is the price we must pay to preserve CPA, I accept it. As long as Commander Salva is in Saraya (Palace), I am hopeful things will be fine'. I looked into his eyes and could see many unanswered questions such as what about the New Sudan, a dream he was ready to die for. Is the South moving towards secession or there still a hope, which I have not seen in the eyes of the young man at Garang's tomb for creation of a new Sudan? Will the programmes such as 'moving cities to rural areas' ever be implemented? Will the SPLM truly take charge as the vanguard of the Revolution, not only in the South, but especially in the North? Are there tangible plans to strengthen the SPLA as a deterrent force for those who might try to disturb the implementation of the CPA? In the eyes of that young soldier, I noticed lots of questions looking for answers: How would Dr Garang have performed as the First Vice President of Sudan taking up his duties in the Palace (Dr Garang was the first Southern Sudanese to have offices inside the main Palace building. All the former vice Presidents: Abel Alier, Joseph Lagu, George Kongor, Riek Machar and Moses Machar were all hosted outside the main building). What would have been the fate of the 16 former SPLM members of leadership Council, once he appointed new cabinet and governors? What would have been Dr Garang's policy towards multi-party system in the South, war in Darfur and Eastern Sudan? Would he have managed to run the South from Khartoum, or he would have chosen to spend more time in Juba? Would he have negotiated and accepted the integration of General Paulino Matiep Nhial's forces into the SPLA? Would Dr Garang have kicked off developmental projects immediately after the formation of the Cabinet? With whom would he have allied himself in the Palace: Ali or El-Bashir? On the other hand, Dr Garang was also a great lost to his family, colleagues in the struggle, his opponents who considered him as a competent competitor, and especially those individuals, whether Sudanese or regional and international leaders or ordinary people, who met him, interacted with him, and discussed pertinent issues to the Sudanese survival with him. To some of them his untimely death has left the work incomplete, hence it has put a big burden to his long time colleague and number two in the SPLM/A, Salva Kiir. To his family, especially Madam Rebecca, whom I had the opportunity to meet and talked to about the challenges of transition, the untimely departure of Dr Garang has ushered every Sudanese, friends and neighbours of Sudan to face a formidable challenge: how to work together to achieve what Dr Garang believed in and fought for. To her 'the legacy of Dr Garang is alive in every SPLM/A cadre and those who took up and shared his ideas". Dr Garang's legacy in Juba, Malakal and in Khartoum is noticeable; one must add however that, the uncertainty that I saw in the eyes of the young soldier at his tomb in Juba, is a worrisome aspect that the SPLM leadership must work to clear in the minds of those who are not yet ready to move on. That is what I saw in the eyes of thousands who attended the first anniversary of late Garang's memorial in Omdurman stadium on 30 July 2006.

CHAPTER THIRTEEN

# Challenges of Service Delivery and Infrastructure Development in Southern Sudan

Those who visited Southern Sudan capital Juba and elsewhere in the states, especially during the period between January 2006 and March 2007, would notice that Juba and most capitals of the Southern Sudan states, Southern Blue Nile and Nuba Mountains have not changed in terms of development, and instead, there seems to be no interest among the stakeholders that things should move ahead.

There are certainly immediate challenges that are facing the SPLM and GOSS leaders, among which are: challenges of transforming the SPLM into a political party, training of its cadres, preparations for its upcoming 2nd National Convention; the harmonization of old and new laws in Southern Sudan; lack of trained manpower in states and counties; possible difficulties in integrating the former SSDF and other armed groups in the SPLA and possible outbursts should the integration process derail as SSDF commanders negotiate high ranks with the leadership of the SPLA; lack of functioning administration in Abyei; delays in the formation of vital national commissions and other host of administrative and management challenges in various levels of governments in the South.

Indeed the urging questions then are: why is that despite the availability of funds in billions, since the first budget was approved in 2005 roads are not yet paved in the main towns, hospitals are not built, clean water and sewerage systems are not in place, thousands of police and civil servants from the SPLM liberated areas and those from the NCP controlled towns are not yet integrated, and schools are not built?

Who is responsible for these delays?

Is it the GOSS ministers or the lack of capacity of strategists in GOSS ministries or is it the lack of experience of governors and counties' commissioners or should the blame fall on the lack of supervision by the SPLM leadership over these vital projects as the ruling party?

What is the role of the World Bank as the international financial institution responsible for supervising the awarding of contracts in Southern Sudan and the institution which manages donors' funds, and as such is responsible for disbursing these funds in allocated five services areas: education, health, roads, water sanitation and electricity generation in the South?

What about GIBB Africa, the Kenyan consultant company that is responsible for the supervision of construction of roads, renovation of 700 government offices and houses in Juba, and for the installation of power plants in Juba and water sanitation and sewerage system in the town? Has GIBB Africa been up to its mandate, and why is it that it seems the company, as a consultant firm, responsible for supervision of these projects, is not interested in finishing these projects on time, and instead, it is accused of delaying the completion of these projects intentionally?

What about the National Congress Party (NCP), does it have a hand in the delays that the developmental projects in Juba and elsewhere in the South, Southern Kordufan (Nuba Mountains) and Southern Blue Nile states have witnessed since October 2005 when the government of Southern Sudan, governments of Southern Kordufan and Blue Nile were formed? Is it true that the NCP has been intentionally delaying release the oil funds allocated to the south on time? Who are the NCP affiliates in Juba? Does it have influential members in the GOSS and in Southern Sudan Legislative Assembly, who have interest in delaying development in the South?

I was faced with these questions during my last visit to Juba in March 2007, and tried while in town to find some answers to them. My preliminary conversations with some of the actors in Juba have revealed that, leaders of Government of Southern Sudan and the SPLM have the big share in the blame, because as the main beneficiaries, they should take keen interest in seeing to it that these projects are completed on time and that funds are not wasted on unnecessary man-made delays.

One of the pillars of the SPLM ideology is the establishment of a New Sudan, where ordinary Sudanese who have been deprived of all kinds of development opportunities could enjoy equal distribution of resources, equal access to power and live in a country where leaders serve their people with dedication and respect. The CPA and the National Interim Constitution of Sudan have, for the time in Sudan history, provided the framework for the achievement of these rights. Indeed, millions of Sudanese who supported the SPLM policies and slogans during the twenty two years of struggle were convinced that the movement was well-placed, given its commitment to justice, equality and freedom, to provide them with clean water, quality roads, health care and education and access to sources of energy and electrification. The SPLM, soon after the formation of the Government of National Unity and the Government of Southern Sudan was therefore expected to speedily implement a comprehensive developmental programme, particularly in those marginalized areas, where its power based was located.

It is this understanding of the SPLM historical mandate that informed my discussions in Juba regarding the challenges of implementation of developmental projects in the South:

Firstly, it seems that GOSS developmental projects are not coordinated; each ministry seems to concentrate on its projects. The ministry of roads for example does not coordinate its activities with the ministries of housing, education, and health, which means that the same contractor or consultant company that supposes to carry out or supervises these projects, in the same city/town/state, is accountable only to the ministry, which signed contract with it. The fact that the ministry of finance pays these companies regularly, even when they have spent over a year without having completed any of these projects, meant that the ministry of finance does not coordinate with other ministries, which are beneficiaries in these projects.

GOSS as the voice of Southern Sudanese people should work as a one unit, and that is why there is a Council of Ministers, which meets every Wednesday to discuss all aspects of governance and service delivery throughout the South. The question is: what do they talk about whenever they meet, if the resolutions of their meetings do not have effect on the ground. Governors of Southern States up to this time have not started building schools, clinics and other service oriented projects, simply because the majority of them believe that GOSS will take care of these projects. Did GOSS give these governors and commissioners some funds for developmental projects, if not, how do they expect them to carry out their duties, given that they are living among 90% of the Southern Sudanese population, on whose behalf the struggle was waged and are expecting rewards and dividends for their long struggle?

It is difficult to understand for example that without an integrated comprehensive economic and developmental programme for the whole Southern Sudan, which should be supervised and implemented by the Ministry of Finance and Economic Planning, the GOSS, states and counties can not pursue any substantive developmental programme. Each ministry, state and county, can only implement its allocated portion within this comprehensive economic and developmental policy.

That is why it is only natural that organizations such as the World Bank and United Nations Development Programme (UNDP) can come in and become the developmental agents and planners for the economic system of Southern Sudan because there is no comprehensive economic policy for the south. Economic policy of any nation is informed by the ideology, historical and economic realities and capabilities of that nation.

The South for example has fought against marginalisation and underdevelopment in the old Sudan. Its main goal was to address and does away with these evils. If today, after over two decades of struggle, GOSS found itself managing $1.7 billion dollars, as an annual budget, it is only natural that such a budget is spent before the end of the budget year, because the needs of the people in the South are enormous. To hear that hundreds of millions of dollars were returned to the treasury because they were not spent in 2006 meant that GOSS as a government has no unified and central agency responsible for ascertaining what has been spent and what was not. This is the work of the minister of finance and the treasury (Central Bank of Southern Sudan). The Bank of Southern Sudan (BOSS) was a demand by the Sudan People's Liberation Movement (SPLM) during the negotiations in Naivasha, for it to act as the treasurer where the money is kept, while the ministry of finance was supposed to supervise the balance sheets: how much has been spent, on what and how much remains unspent in the treasury.

Instead, what we hear today is that the ministry of finance keeps the money as well as disbursing them. It has taken over the work of BOSS. This explains why, when the financial year came to an end in January 2007, some ministers were surprised to learn that they have not spent 80% to 90% of their budgets, because no one told them that they were under-spending, because they assumed that they committed huge funds to projects which were underway. These are simple realities that the undersecretaries and director generals of ministries and governors can deal with on regular basis. GOSS is therefore responsible for the lack of implementation of projects, which its ministries signed contracts to handle.

Imagine a minister telling his colleagues in a cabinet meeting recently that the ministry of finance has incurred a lost worth of $131 millions US dollars because of fluctuation of exchange rate of dinar and dollar. The question asked was why informing the cabinet only now, and not a year ago, when GOSS could have done something about it. The result of that unnecessary negligence was that every GOSS employee throughout the south will receive his/her salary less of at least %20, unless another alternative solution is found. This is what I meant by the lack of coordination between cabinet ministers.

Secondly, what is the role of the SPLM as the ruling party and the guardian of the Sudanese revolution in the ongoing underdevelopment policy in the South? Developing an economic policy has always been the prerogative of the ruling party, and has never been that of the government. The SPLM as a mass movement fought for a purpose, that objective was concretized and institutionalized in the protocols of the Comprehensive Peace Agreement (CPA). The philosophy and ideology of the SPLM were therefore embodied in the CPA, particularly in power and wealth sharing protocols and in the security arrangements protocol. In fact, the blue prints of the SPLM economic policies were enshrined in the wealth sharing protocol, where service delivery (taking towns to villages) became the point of reference for any government official. The oil revenues were divided fifty-fifty, despite the reservations of Southerners, because the SPLM wanted to have access to funds and to prove to the people of the South and the marginalized areas that underdevelopment policies of the Old Sudan were the enemy that ought to be fought, and more so during post-conflict period.

To achieve that the SPLM had gain access to oil revenues and GOSS and states' governments were to be the custodians of development in the New Sudan. Any contractor, consultant company or international agency, such as the World Bank, would come in as a consultant, but the supervision of the implementation of these projects was to be the sole responsibility of the SPLM, GOSS and other Southern political parties as the guardians of the development in the South.

The above explanation was necessary in order for us to understand, why the SPLM and GOSS should bear the responsibility of managing, supervising and making sure that contractors and consultants are up to their expectations.

Managing people's expectations is the most difficult situation a post conflict government could find itself in. The SPLM and GOSS seem to have relaxed and left the fate of development in the South into the wrong hands. It is a collective responsibility, because the Council of Ministers is a collective, and no single person is expected to take decisions on behalf of the collective. The same applies to the SPLM, it is a collective responsibilty, thus any decision on shortcomings facing the development projects in the South, should be taken by the whole leadership. Therefore, if anything is to be rectified, it is the GOSS' cabinet and the SPLM National Council to ask themselves, have we given up some of our revolutionary duties to non-SPLM members, and what can we do to regain our sense of responsibility? The answer is obvious: SPLM and GOSS must sit down and remember that two years have lapsed and nothing substantial has been done in the rural areas, counties, states and in Juba. Someone or some people must be responsible for this situation and something serious must be done about it urgently, unless the SPLM and GOSS leaders are waiting for public protests in rural areas, payams, counties, and states against the lack of service delivery and development, a probability that may happen if things remain unchanged.

There is a perception that the difference between African elites and their Asian, European and American counterparts is that the latter, in terms of implementing developmental projects, make sure that, once they receive their handsome commissions in full, projects must be completed on time.

On the other hand, African elites receive their commissions in full and in collusion with contractors and consultants, make sure that projects never get completed and these projects become the source of living for them as long as new budgets are allocated for the completion of the same projects each year, even if it means one project is financed for five to ten years.

Is this what has been happening in Southern Sudan since July 2005?

While GOSS and SPLM may appear in the first instance responsible for the delays in the service delivery and developmental projects in Southern Sudan, it seems that other stakeholders carry some blame.

Indeed, during my stay in Juba in March 2007, I was made to believe that, while GOSS and SPLM bear some responsibility for the lack of supervising the developmental projects in the South, particularly in Juba, other stakeholders equally deserve the blame for the delay, they include the World Bank bureaucrats stationed in East Africa and in the South, GIBB Africa consultants and the NCP and its operatives in the South.

From the conversations I have had in Juba, I got the impression that the above mentioned stakeholders somehow had something to do with the ongoing state of stagnation in the development arena and service delivery structures in the South.

Firstly, what about the World Bank, does it bears some blame for the lack of development and service delivery in the South? As may be recalled, during the last lag of the Naivasha negotiations, as part of the wealth sharing modalities, the SPLM, NCP and the United Nations, as represented then by the World Bank, worked out the details of the Joint Assessment Mission (JAM), a programme which was meant to assess the needs of the Southern Sudan and the other war affected areas in Sudan. These needs, most of which were infrastructural and service delivery oriented, were to be implemented within the period of three years from the time of signing of the CPA (2005-2007).

The JAM process was detailed in terms of items to be carried out and time frames. The World Bank became the leading agency to supervise the implementation of the JAM programme. On the other hand, in run up to the Oslo donor conference, which was held in September 2003, the SPLM and the NCP agreed that the developmental funds which were to be received from the donors, as part of the Oslo process, were to be kept and disbursed by the World Bank through Multi-Donor Trust Fund (MDTF). The understanding was that all the developmental projects which were to be financed through the MTDF, including the awarding of contracts, must get the "No Objection Note" from the World Bank representatives in Southern Sudan. The JAM process identified five areas as developmental priorities in Southern Sudan, Nuba Mountains and Southern Blue Nile: education, health, roads, and water sanitation and electricity generation.

Based on the above understanding GOSS started to invite bidders to compete for contracts in the areas specified within JAM process and based on the needs of GOSS. Until early 2007, about ten companies from United Nations (UNDP), Kenya, Italy, China, Germany, Uganda and other countries were awarded contracts, with the blessing of the World Bank. The agreement between the World Bank and GOSS was that every one US dollar that the MTDF contributes to developmental projects in the South, GOSS would contribute two US dollars. Two years since the CPA was initialed in Nyayo Stadium in Nairobi, Kenya in January 2005, the contractors who were awarded contracts did not complete their work to date, and the World Bank, which gave the go ahead to these contracts, has not reacted in a manner that would suggest that it cares.

For example, while acknowledging existence of differences with GOSS over how to go about implementing developmental projects in the South, the World Bank representatives argue that they were given a go ahead by President Salva Kiir to apply their governance guidelines and regulations in Southern Sudan. This is of course an argument that would require qualification: President Kiir, like other leaders in Sudan, is aware of the shortcomings of the World Bank bureaucracy in Africa, and would not give a free hand to an organisation that has been largely responsible for damaging the developing countries' economic systems to run a weak region that is just emerging from the war.

The World Bank might have had cordial relationship with Southern Sudan's Finance Minister, but certainly some of its policies, especially those relating to the funding of service delivery projects in health, housing and road sectors were not definitely welcomed by many SPLM cadres serving in GOSS. The slowness in the implementation of some projects, such as the renovation of houses, roads, and construction of hospitals, despite the availability of hundreds of millions of US dollars, has not been encouraging.

The attempts by the World Bank representatives in the South to encourage privatization of service delivery projects in Southern Sudan and discouragement of GOSS policy of proceeding with human resource capacity development is another controversial policy that GOSS should look into with an open eye. Southern Sudan is emerging from war, and one would not expect an infant government to privatize its health sector. For example, GOSS ministry of health was apparently persuaded by the World Bank representatives to award a contract for the construction of what was referred to as "semi-permanent" hospitals in ten capitals of Southern Sudan states.

The Norwegian company, which got the controversial contract, is nowadays advertising positions for doctors, nurses and lab technicians for these hospitals. In other words, the contractor will be in charge of recruiting, managing and constructing these hospitals. The pretext, which the World Bank representatives gave, was that privatizing these essential services will speed up the delivery because GOSS does not have the capacity, while the people of the South are desperate to get these services. Another thing that irritates regarding the politics of contracts in Southern Sudan is that huge amounts are spent in projects, which could cost less if thorough studies were carried out. For example, the renovation of one office or house of the Addis Agreement era is costing the Ministry of Housing between $150,000 and 200,000 US dollars, an amount, which, some argue, could build at least 2 three-bed new houses.

Another important aspect, which requires immediate attention, is an apparent lack of transparency in the reports of the World Bank operations in Southern Sudan. For example, how much funds has the World Bank committed to projects in Southern Sudan, Nuba Mountains, and Southern Blue during the years 2005 and 2006. The recent World Bank media reports talked about buying 750,000 mosquito nets, medicines, school books, but did not talk about having constructed clinics, schools etc. Another question which requires an answer is to who did KPMG, one of the leading South African accountant firms, submitted its reports on the funds that were spent during the 2005 and 2006 budget years. KPMG was assigned, upon recommendation of the World Bank and donor countries, to handle the accounts for the funds, which the MTDF were spending in Southern Sudan. This was an appropriate decision because the SPLM then, did not have the manpower and the trained accountants to handle such sensitive assignment.

These are serious issues, which GOSS should discuss closely with the World Bank and the United Nations agencies involved in developmental programmes in Southern Sudan. The World Bank is an important financial institution that the South must have cordial relations with, however, this kind of relationship must be informed by mutual interests, which must be managed transparently.

Secondly, GIBB Africa, a Kenyan consultant engineering company, is one of the consultant companies supervising the implementation, among others, of the following projects: pavement of 60 Kilometer road inside Juba, electricity plants in Juba, renovation of 700 government offices and houses in Juba, and installation of water sanitation

## Challenges of Service Delivery and Infrastructure Development 217

and sewerage system in Juba. GIBB Africa came into contact with some SPLM leaders during the negotiations in Naivasha, and had shown interest in helping in developmental projects in post-war Southern Sudan. Two years down the line, GIBB Africa seems to have difficulties carrying out it duties: either it is unable to push the contractors to complete their work, or it has interest in delaying the completion of these projects.

For example, ministers and their employees have been told to evacuate their offices and houses, some since mid 2005, and none of these ministries and houses was renovated. In every house or office, handful workers are assigned to do the work, and in most cases, only work until mid day, especially if they are Chinese complaining about the heat. In fact, most of the GOSS officials are complaining that they are displaced from their houses, where some are forced to spend US$250 daily to get accommodation in the tents and containers' hotels in town, while they could not employ new employees, apart from the displaced directors, because the offices are still under renovation since the government was formed last year.

On the other hand, GIBB Africa seems to have difficulty in urging its engineers to push contractors to finish work in Juba roads: the Italian company which won the contract, with the blessing of the World Bank, has been in Juba since early 2006. The impression everybody has in Juba is that the Italians are not doing their work and are taking their time. On the other hand, the Italians seem to have difficulties in communicating their frustrations to GOSS. According to the World Bank contract regulations, the contractor and the client (GOSS) have no direct communication; they must communicate through the consultant, and in this case the Italians are not allowed to talk to GOSS. GIBB Africa is therefore the link between Italians and GOSS. This is also the case with the installation of Juba electricity, which thank God has partially been installed and functioning and water and sewerage system, which is still not operational. The Ministry of

Housing, Land and Public Utilities can not communicate directly with the contractors, but through GIBB Africa. What does this means in practical terms; it seems that, according to this arrangement, and as the consulting company, GIBB Africa decides when the projects should finish. One wonders indeed, if each consultant engineer is being paid since early 2006 between $14,000 US dollars and 29,000 US dollars every month by GOSS, why would that engineer be in hurry to urge the contractors to complete the renovation of GOSS offices, houses or the roads in Juba!

GOSS and the SPLM are directly responsible for this impasse and should take drastic measures to resolve this problem by calling the consultants, contractors and the World Bank officials to an emergency meeting to explain some of these shortcomings.

Finally, is there any role for the NCP and its operatives in the delay of the implementation of the developmental projects in Southern Sudan, Southern Kordufan and Southern Blue Nile? In Sudan, conspiracy theories abound when talking about whether NCP has a hand in any negative development in Southern Sudan or not, especially things that directly affect the wellbeing of the Southern Sudanese and the marginalized areas.

Since the CPA was signed, NCP has presented itself as partner to the SPLM, however, soon after GOSS was formed, it became clear that the NCP has decided to either penetrate the SPLM through some of its cadres; use local militias to destabilize the region or delay the release of oil revenue funds on time to GOSS. Access to telecommunication system in the South, despite the presence of three national cell phone networks, Sudantel, Mobitel and al-Sudani, is almost non-existence, as Sudan security agencies use sophisticated technology to jam these networks. It is difficult to access these networks in Southern Sudan, thus making communication between and with Southern Sudanese impossible. It is much easier to call any town in northern Sudan, than to call someone within Southern Sudan.

If you happen to be a politician or a senior SPLM member, it is most likely that you will never receive a call through one of the three networks mentioned above and even if you do, it is mostly likely that your phone is bugged. This might explain why the SPLM had opted to permit the Gemtel mobile network to operate in Southern Sudan, to at least assist the GOSS, SPLM leadership and Southern Sudanese to communicate among themselves and with the rest of the world.

In Abyei, Southern Kordufan (Nuba Mountains) and Southern Blue Nile, the situation in the South, in terms of developmental projects is much better, because at least there are developmental projects underway in some towns/cities, while in the three areas mentioned above nothing has been done since the CPA was signed. In Abyei, up to date, the administration, which supposes to run the daily affairs and implement developmental projects and deliver services to the citizens of Abyei during the interim period, is not yet formed.

For two years the NCP has refused even to consider the idea of establishing an interim administration until the two partners come to agreement over the Abyei Boundary Commission Report, which was compiled by the international experts. In recognition of this devastated situation the GOSS cabinet had to approved in March 2007 the release of $10 million US dollars to assist the Abyei people meet some of their immediate needs. Instead of sending health care and educational facilities to the area, Sudan army soldiers and members of popular defense force are sent to Abyei in a sizeable numbers monthly, thus raising tensions and insecurity in the area.

In Nuba Mountains and Southern Blue Nile, the NCP had made it a point to creating internal conflicts among local communities in these two states, while making sure that there are no developmental projects implemented there. Although the CPA has stipulated that 28% of the manpower of public servants in these two states will come from SPLM members, up to date, the whole bureaucracy is still under control of the NCP affiliates. In fact, areas such as Kurmuk and Kauda, which were under the control of the SPLM before the signing of the CPA, are deprived of services or developmental projects, hence making it looks like the SPLM has neglected people of these areas.

The CPA is clear in terms of who will pay the civil servants and develop these areas: the Government of Southern Sudan would pay allowances to and maintain the SPLA soldiers, which are not part of the Joint Integrated Units (JIUs), and that is why, SPLA soldiers from Nuba Mountains and Southern Blue Nile are paid as part of the mother SPLA. As for the civil servants, police, correctional services and wild life soldiers in these two areas, the CPA gave the responsibility of their maintenance to the Government of National Unity.

Moreover, the NCP representatives in the governments and parliaments of the two states have been frustrating their SPLM counterparts, making it difficult for them to initiate developmental projects, let alone implementing them. Imagine the offices of Governor of the Southern Kordufan and the Deputy Governor of Southern Blue Nile, both members of the SPLM have no access to internet, functioning telephone lines, fax machines, and two years down the line, they still use Thuraya satellite phones, which they were using when they were still in the struggle. There is no doubt that as a result of the NCP activities in the marginalised areas an impression developed among some of the local population in Nuba Mountains and Southern Blue Nile that the SPLM has given up some of its responsibilities towards its supporters in these areas.

The leadership of the SPLM will have to take serious steps in order to explain to its supporters in Abyei, Nuba Mountains and Southern Blue Nile that it is aware of the NCP activities in these regions and that it is in practical terms has solutions to some of these challenges.

CHAPTER FOURTEEN

# Culture, Conflict and Reconciliation in Sudan

In most African countries, cultural diversity has been associated with conflict, especially where religious, ethnic, racial and linguistic diversities are in conflict. Culture by its very nature is a complex mixture of society's heritage, history, customs, language and norms. There are however, other virtues and characteristics of humanity that may be transformed into socio-cultural, economic and political mix, some of which can serve as reconciliatory or conflict triggers in a given society.

In Sudan, culture has been at the heart of the conflict in the country for almost five decades since in independence in January 1956. In trying to understand the role of the culture in the Sudanese conflict, both as a source and cause of conflict or an asset for reconciliation, the following questions must be raised:

Can religion be transformed into culture? In Sudan yes, both Islam and Christianity have acquired cultural embodiment to those groups that adhere to them, hence the two religions have become part and parcel of the conflict in the country.

Can race become a cultural point of reference of a people? Yes, in Sudan, actual and perceived racial identity of some segments of Sudanese society, have contributed into a cultural perception, upon which, some Sudanese identify themselves as Arabs or Africans, although in the case of the former, there as many hybrid Sudanese and Africans than Arabs. Being identified as an Arab, denotes a higher social status, hence those who are classified as such, look down on those who contend to be Africans.

Can regionalism or ethnicity become cultural point of reference? Yes, in Sudan, belonging to a political 'north'[1] or to a ruling ethnic group, signifies a sense of belonging to a superior region or ethnic group.

Can a social class become a cultural base of oppression of the rest of the society? Yes, in Sudan belonging to the ruling class and identifying oneself with the ruling elite, is a cultural phenomenon that some Sudanese regard as a privilege and a means to gain a special social status. To be part of the Khartoum ruling class, irrespective of the ethnic and regional origin, is a special reward to many Sudanese elite.

## The problems of the colonial state in Sudan (The Old Sudan)

The colonial state in Sudan did not go through the normal nation building process, where Sudanese should have decided voluntarily on what political system they would like to adopt. It was a construct of a colonial system, which was riddled by deep socio-economic and political weaknesses.

### Identity crisis in Sudan

The Sudan is a multi-religion, multi-ethnic and multi-cultural society. One major problem of the 'Old Sudan' colonial state is that it has been

---

1   By 'political north' we mean the east, west, centre and the north of the country. The inhabitants of these regions espouse Islam and mostly have been culturally Arabiscised.

looking and is still looking for its identity. The country is regarded as Arab country as well as an African state. Meanwhile, a considerable number of Sudanese are hybrid, and in many ways they are fit to be referred to as Afro-Arab. The question of who they Sudanese are has always been part of the identity crisis, where those who consider themselves as Arab, who dominate the government structures in the country, are keen to impose the Arab identity as a form of national cultural affiliation to the rest of the Sudanese society.

*The unity dilemma*

The unity in the 'Old Sudan' has always been rooted in the economic, political and cultural domination of particular cultural groupings, where other groups essential to the formation of the Sudanese society are excluded and isolated from effective participation in political power, from expressing their national and cultural identities, and from an equitable share in national wealth. Such a unity is neither viable nor sustainable, because it is founded on the basis of an uneven development paradigm.

*Imbalances of power distribution*

In order to transform the country from old to new Sudan, there is a need for a radical restructuring of power of the central government in a in such a way that takes into consideration the interests of all peripheral regions and peoples, particularly, those who have expressed their dissent through arms and those who patiently opposed in silence within the country. It is through this radical restructuring of the system that an end could be brought to the monopoly of power by a few in Khartoum, whether they represent political parties, family dynasties, religious sects or army officers. It is equally important to redefine the relationship between Khartoum and the regions and devolving more powers to the regions in form autonomy, where and when necessary, and federalism, a form of regionalism that would enable the ordinary

Sudanese, not the regional elites, to exercise real power for economic and social development and the promotion and development of their respective cultures.

### Participatory governance and human rights

For the democratic New Sudan where equality, freedom, economic and social justice and respect for human rights, to be achieved, a participatory political system has to be established in the country. In the New Sudan, democracy should not be just a sham procedural electoral process of the past, which was an excuse for the perpetuation of vested interests of the Sudanese elites.

### Equitable and sustainable development

The New Sudan vision advocates and calles for the establishment of an economic paradigm that would make rational use of the country's vast natural and human resources to correct unequal development, put an end to all forms of marginalization and deprivation and equitably distribute the fruits of growth. An integral part of even development is the appropriate and fair sharing of wealth among the various peoples of the Sudan.

### The pillars of the Sudan Comprehensive Peace Agreement (CPA)

In an attempt to address the causes of the conflict, particularly socio-economic and cultural weaknesses of the Sudan's old state, the CPA, identified the following as the basis for the resolution of the Sudanese conflict and creation of a new dispensation in the country:

Acknowledged that the power structure of the old Sudanese state is concentrated in the center, and thus needs to be radically restructured in order to accommodate the Sudan's multi-diversity and attend to all forms of exclusion and marginalization of its people.

Recognized that the country's problems should be resolved within the context of a united new Sudan that affords democratic and human rights to all nationalities and guarantees freedom to all religions, beliefs and cultures.

Accepted that unity of the country should and must be an integral part of the New Sudan vision, an objective cherished by wide segments of the Sudanese society in all parts of the country.

Acknowledged that the separation of religion from the state should and must be regarded as a corner stone to the building of a nation-state in Sudan, hence making it part and parcel of the New Sudan.

The adoption of a one-country-two-systems model by the negotiators in Naivasha, following the government's adamant refusal of separating religion from the state, was seen by some Sudanese as a diversion from the New Sudan and a recipe for separation. However, the essence of this model lies in that the voluntary unity in the New Sudan is conditioned on the creation of a political and socio-economic commonality that brings all the Sudanese together as equal citizens in rights and obligations. This would not be possible if the religion of any particular group of country were to become, and not the constitution, the source of legislation.

## The New Sudan Vision

The establishment of the New Sudan by its nature ought to be a transformative process for radical socio-economic transformation and political restructuring that would build on all of the positive elements of the Old Sudan, informed by the Sudanese historical and contemporary experiences and aware of, and equipped for, the formidable challenges of the 21st century.

In order for the Sudanese cultural diversity, which used to be a major cause of conflicts in the country to be transformed into reconciliatory tool in post war Sudan, the CPA and the New Sudan vision, as conceptualized by late John Garang, the leader of the Sudan People's Liberation Movement (SPLM), have introduced the following solution modalities to the socio-cultural, economic and political conflict in post war Sudan:

Model 1: New Sudan: The New Sudan is a transformed, democratic Sudan that belongs to all the Sudanese people. It is a Sudan, where the religion and state are constitutionally separated, and where freedoms, liberty, equality, and human rights are granted and respected.

Model 2: Confederal Minimum New Sudan or a "Two System-One Country": The reason why the CPA had adopted the two system-one country, was that confederal arrangements will attempt to make unity attractive and to provide space for promoting and fostering Sudanese unity during the interim period, at the end of which, Southern Sudanese will vote to either go back to Model 1, a New democratic Sudan, or to Model 5, two separate states.

Model 3: Islamic-Arab Sudan: This is the Old Sudan, which has been the cause of the problems in the country. This Model assumes a character of an Islamic-Arab Sudan dominating the South (the pre-CPA situation), which if remained unchanged, will definitely lead to the separation of the South.

Model 4: Indigenous African secular Sudan: This is purely theoretical model, where an indigenous African secular state would dominate the country and thus, like in the case of Model 3, would lead to the formation of an independent state in the North.

Model 5: Two separate states: This model assumes the split of the country into two or more independent states, one in the south and the other(s) in the north.

The best approach to maintain unity in the country is to move directly from Model 3 (Old Sudan) to Model 1 (A Transformed Democratic Sudan), and this means radical and decisive transformation of the incumbent regime, which espoused the cultural heritage of the Old Sudan.

CHAPTER FIFTEEN

# The Cairo Massacre: A model of neighborhood relations?

The news of the Egyptian Security forces massacre of over fifty Sudanese refugees and injuring over two hundred at one of the public parks at Al-Muahandiseen quarter in Cairo on the New Year eve (30 December 2005) was a sad moment that will definitely determine the next course that the relations between Egypt and the Southern part of Sudan and other marginalized areas of the country will take. It also will require critical evaluation of all the historical and strategic components of the relationships between Sudan and Egypt in general and between Egypt and Southern Sudan in particular. Egypt was a co-colonizer of Sudan with Britain. Egyptian forces occupied Southern Sudan between 1839 and 1881 and colonized the modern Sudan in collaboration with Britain between 1898 and 1956. Egypt was therefore part and parcel of the Sudanese political crisis and civil wars. Those who were killed in Cairo on Friday 30 December 2005 were victims of the latest two rounds of the Sudanese civil wars in the South, West and East that Egypt was historically responsible for.

On 8 April 1994 I wrote a commentary in a London-based Arabic daily Al-Hayat in which among other things, I evaluated the Egyptian relations with Southern Sudan and the historical role of the Egyptian governments in the conflicts between the southern Sudan and successive central governments in Khartoum. In that commentary, entitled "Does the secession of Southern Sudan pose a real threat to Egypt?" I emphasized the need for the Egyptian government to stop relying on the intelligence reports and listening to Northern Sudanese various Governments' disinformation about the situation in Southern Sudan. I was responding to the then Egyptian foreign minister Amr Mousa, who was at that time obsessed with the theory that the Sudan People's Liberation Movement (SPLM) was a secessionist liberation movement and must be treated as such. Minister Mousa made use of every public opportunity to urge that Egypt should do everything it could to keep Sudan united. In my commentary I urged Mousa that instead of dealing with SPLM by proxy, it was impetrative for the Egyptian authorities to invite the SPLM leaders to visit Cairo and discuss with them the fears the Egyptian leaders were expressing on the SPLM policies.

In May 1997, I had an opportunity to meet some Egyptian intellectuals in an international conference in Amman, Jordan, including Dr Milad Hana, Nabil Abdel Fatah and few others. In that conference, I urged them to advise President Hosni Mubarak and his colleagues to open official contacts with the Southern Sudanese leadership, so as to see whether indeed the South as an entity has separate strategic goals and interests that would make it necessary for Egyptian government to identify separate national objectives for northern and southern Sudan. In November 1997, thanks to efforts of Sudanese nationalists such as Dr Mansour Khalid, after a brief visit to Tripoli, Libya, the SPLM leader late Dr John Garang and some of his colleagues visited Cairo upon invitation by President Hosni Mubarak.

Since then, it became incumbent upon the leaders of Egypt and Southern Sudan to work towards a clear understanding of whether Southern Sudanese leaders should aim at forging special relations with Egypt separate from the Northern Sudan led policy of 'historical and brotherly links' between Egypt and Sudan; or the relationship between

Egypt and Sudan should continue to be regulated as it always were by the ministries of foreign affairs in Khartoum and Cairo. Questions such as what Sudan should Egypt opt to support: a New Sudan or the old Sudan? To what extent was Egypt convinced that the New Sudan that the SPLM was calling for, the historical, ancient, biblical and Christian Sudan which included some important parts of Egypt was the best solution to the Sudanese conflict? Was Egypt ready to discuss the identity crisis (the question of whether Sudan was African or Arab) with the SPLM, and if so, did Egypt buy the idea that the identity crisis was at the heart of the conflict in the country? In fact, some Southern Sudanese observers since then raised some vital questions such as the viability of the re-launch of the Jonglei Canal Project which was stopped due to the civil war in early 1980s, considering that it was initiated and implemented without regard to its deadly environmental and economic side effects on the local population in the South? What are the Southern Sudan's national interests in Egypt and why various Egyptian establishments have been repeatedly stating that Southern Sudan falls within its strategic national interests? Why did for example, Egypt opt to support its peace initiative with Libya to resolve the Sudanese conflict, and rejected the Inter-Governmental Authority on Development (IGAD) peace initiative, and had to relent only after the international community has endorsed the IGAD peace process?

It is within this historical context that one should understand why the Egyptian authorities took the action they did against the Sudanese refugees in Cairo, without the fear that the leaders in Khartoum, with rare exception of the Umma National Party, the Sudan Human Rights Organization and some leftist groups, will condemn their security agencies' action.

Firstly, the massacre of over fifty innocent refugees and asylum seekers in Cairo has revealed that such an act cannot be authorized by the Egyptian authorities, without implicit go head from National Congress Party (NCP) officials and from Sudan government. It means that the Egypt security authorities were aware of the danger of refugees refusing to leave the public park and that was why they had to send 5,000 security forces, with the mission to force the refugee by all means to leave the sit-in place. The consequences of that action were therefore studied by the Egyptian authorities before hand.

Secondly, with the exception of the statement by Ali Ahmed Kerti, Sudan's State Minister for Foreign Affairs in Cairo, in which he supported the Egyptian forces action, and condemned and blamed the UNHCR and the refugees for the outcome of the attack, the fact that the President and the majority ruling party in Khartoum did not condemn the massacre, suggests that President Omar Al-Beshir and his colleagues in NCP are not ready to anger Cairo, in return for Cairo's support of the NCP in other issues such as the political implications of war in Darfur and the looming International Criminal Court case against some of the top NCP officials.

Thirdly, the statement that was issued by the Government of Southern Sudan (GOSS), in which it condemned the massacre, has to be viewed within the context of the relationship between the SPLM and the NCP on the one hand, and the relationship between the NCP and the Egyptian government on the other. The statement has revealed that the government of Southern Sudan has shouldered its responsibilities towards its citizens, wherever they happened to be. The statement has also revealed that the GOSS is the legitimate authority in Southern Sudan, recognized by the international community in accordance with the provisions of the Sudan Comprehensive Peace Agreement (CPA), which was witnessed and initialed on 9 January 2005 in Nairobi, Kenya by the representatives of the United Nations, European Union, the League of the Arab Nations, African Union, United States of America, United Kingdom and several other countries and regional and international organizations. It is therefore the task of the GOSS ministries of regional cooperation and ministry of internal security and police to take their responsibilities seriously by organizing a visit to Cairo, Egypt and to other countries, to follow up the situation of Southern Sudanese citizens closely, and learn from the Cairo massacre for future reaction, should similar situation arise.

Fourthly, the statement has also revealed that the GOSS holds the Government of National Unity (GNU) direct responsibility to safeguard the well-being of Sudan citizens, the failure of which renders the GNU illegitimate to claim the legitimacy over the land and the people of Sudan. Analysing the GOSS statement over the Cairo massacre also suggests that the failure of the GNU to condemn the massacre meant that it has implicitly supported the Egyptian government decision to force the refugees out of the sit-in public park, hence the GNU behaved in a discriminatory manner against its own citizens, where its silence suggested that it regarded those victims, who mostly come from the South, west and central Sudan as not part of its responsibility.

Fifthly, by condemning the action of the Egyptian military and police forces, the GOSS is sending a clear message to the Egyptian government that the people of Southern Sudan, in the light of the 30 December 2005 massacre, have the right to question the claims of various Egyptian governments over the past one hundred years that the people of Egypt and Sudan are one nation. By killing over fifty innocent people and injuring hundreds, the Egyptian government has sent a clear message to the people coming from other parts of Sudan other than the northern most of the country and from river Nile state, that they are not Sudanese whose lives worth sparing. Yes, various political and international organizations have tried since 29 September 2005, for three months to persuade the refugees to stop their strike and leave the compound peacefully, including Egyptian officials and some prominent Sudanese political leaders, the question however remains, have all options been exhausted?

Sixthly, through its statement, the GOSS has also sent a clear message to the United Nations and its Secretary General that the manner in which the UNHCR staff in Cairo behaved and handled the

Sudanese refugee problem in Cairo, a crisis which started since June 2004 when the UNHCR office in Cairo revoked and withdrew refugee status of over two thousand Sudanese refugees, has shown the lack of care and sense of responsibility from the part of the UNHCR officials in Cairo. The UN Secretary General should not consider what happened to the Sudanese refugees in Egypt as a mere security incident, because what happened to the Sudanese in Cairo on the New Year eve will have great impact on the future relationship between the UN system and the current and sub-sequent governments of Southern Sudan.

In fact, the Cairo Massacre will require the GOSS to advise the UN Security Council to revisit the deployment of the UN peacekeeping forces in Southern Sudan and other marginalized areas, particularly the forces coming from countries such as Egypt and India. Indeed, if the Egyptian security forces are capable of committing massacres against innocent, unarmed Sudanese civilians in Cairo, what is the guarantee that its peacekeeping forces will not commit the same atrocities in Nuba Mountains in the name of self-defense?

No one would deny that the relationship between Sudan and Egypt, whether under Ismail Al-Azhari, Abdalla Khalil, General Ibrahim Abboud, Sirr El-Khatim Khalifa, Mohamed Mahjoub, Sadig al-Mahdi, Jafar Nimeiri, Suwar EL-Dahab or Omar El-Beshir, was informed by vital historical links and strategic interests between the two countries. While Egypt has every right to protect whatever interests it deems vital to its survival or those that fall within what its regards as its national and strategic interests, the Sudanese government also should protect the rights and interests of its citizens. It is therefore logical to conclude that the GNU has the right to protect its population, irrespective of their status in the country where they live. This is true of course of the Sudanese refugees who flew the country due to the brutality of the National Congress' government during the 1990s.

It would have been logical that following the signing of the CPA and the ongoing negotiations with the Darfurian liberation movements in Abuja, Nigeria that the NCP should have shown a change of the heart, acting as a partner in the GNU, by urging the UNHCR to handle the case with utmost care or by trying to persuade the refugees to return home. In fact, by not acting, directly or behind the scenes, to avoid the severe action that the Egypt security forces have taken, the Sudan government was in fact expressing the obvious: that it sides with Egypt.

The silence of the National Congress Party and its refusal to condemn the massacre in Cairo can also be explained within the NCP's domestic policies. In fact, the massacre has brought into fore the debate which has been triggered in the Sudanese media following the leakage of the former Finance and National Economic Minister Abdel Rahim Hamdi's famous economic policy paper that he presented to NCP economic workshop. In that controversial paper Hamdi recommended to his party that in terms of economic development policies during the interim period, his party should concentrate the economic and developmental projects in the so-called Dungula-Sennar-Kordufan Axis.

These are the regions of Sudan where the so-called 'Arab' Sudanese are living. The fact that the NCP refused to condemn the killings in Cairo seems to suggest that the NCP priorities, in terms of protecting and safeguarding the well-being of the Sudanese, are based on Hamdi's paper which divided Sudan into two racial groups: Arabs and Africans. Those who died in Cairo massacre were, according to Hamdi's classification, Africans.

It must be emphasized that the first country that Dr John Garang visited soon after the peace agreement was signed in January 2005 was Egypt. Similarly, the first country that Lt General Salva Kiir Mayardit visited soon after taking oath as a successor of late Dr John Garang was Egypt.

The only explanation that one could give to the SPLM leadership's interest in keeping Egypt informed about the peace agreement would be that the leaders of the South value Egypt as an important neighbor as well as an important potential spoiler. Now that Egypt has acted the way it did, and in order to send a clear message to the Egyptian government and to the NCP leadership in Khartoum, the GOSS should reconsider its position and reevaluate the historical relationship between Egypt and Southern Sudan and indeed the status of the following Egyptian projects in the South:

Firstly, historically, Egypt has established since the turn of the twentieth century permanent offices along the Nile, particularly in Juba, Malakal and Wau. These offices, manned by senior security officials working for the Egyptian ministry of irrigation, are assigned the work to monitor the Nile water flow as well as the measurement of the Nile flood levels throughout the year. These irrigation offices have influenced the local authorities throughout the South by not allowing the local population to open up streams or small canals or use water for commercial purposes such as gardening etc, without permission from Egyptian irritation department officials based in Southern Sudan.

Although the Egyptian officials deny that they prohibit the local population to open up streams or dig small canals or use water for commercial activities, the practice over the past many years, has shown that local population, especially in urban centers have chosen to be law abiding citizens when its comes to the use of the Nile water. Perhaps the GOSS should begin seriously to investigate the presence of the Egyptian irrigation department's officials in Southern Sudan and the status of the irrigation department's offices in the South in the light of the new Nile Basin Initiative. The GOSS should indeed ask the appropriate authorities for an observer status at the Nile Basin Initiative Secretariat.

Secondly, the Jonglei Canal Project was initiated by the Egyptians, and persuaded General Jafaar Nimeiri to accept its implementation, without any serious scrutiny of the Canal's environmental and economic effects on the population of the Jonglei province. All the efforts which were made by some Southern Sudanese politicians and students during the early 1970s to highlight the negative repercussions of the Canal were countered with violence by Abel Alier Government in the South, who decided unilaterally that the project was good for the people of the area.

To the best of my knowledge, the SPLM did not clearly spell out yet its position regarding the resumption of the Jonglei Canal Project after the CPA was signed. It is time for the GOSS and the SPLM leadership to revisit the Jonglei Canal Project files and perhaps open discussion within the GNU and with the Egyptian government on its future of the Canal.

Thirdly, as part of the compromise embodied in the Nile Basin Initiative, Egypt has been trying to persuade countries such as Uganda, Kenya, Tanzania, Rwanda, Burundi and Democratic Republic of Congo to jointly build a Hydro-electric project which, supposed to be built on the water falls of the Southern Sudan town of Numeli, to generate electricity for the whole region. This is an important project, which Southern Sudanese have been dreaming to implement since the 1970s, but thanks to Egyptian government objections, the central governments in Khartoum did not bother to seek financial support for the implementation of the project from the World Bank, since it knew that the Egyptian powerful officials working in the Bank will block the grant application. Perhaps it is time for the GOSS to investigate different aspects of the Numeli Hydro-electric project, and discuss with the Egyptian officials the merits of the project. The GOSS should also consider, after thorough feasibility studies, building small dams for hydro-electric purposes along the Nile.

Fourthly, for the purposes of bilateral relationship between Egypt and Southern Sudan, it is important that GOSS should start, through its ministry of regional cooperation, the process of discussing the status of the Egyptian consulate in Juba. The Egyptian consulate in Juba should have a status of independent diplomatic mission, to make sure that, during the interim period, issues pertaining to bilateral relations, whether economic interests such as investment or political issues, between the South and Egypt are discussed bilaterally and directly and not by proxy in Cairo and Khartoum. This is in line with the CPA, which granted the GOSS to establish bilateral relations with other nations, until the time of referendum, when new arrangements will have to be worked out as a result of the outcome of the referendum in July 2011.

Finally, there are plans to establish the Egypt-based Alexandria University branch in Juba. While some Southern Sudanese current leadership are proud to be graduates of several Egyptian universities including Alexandria University, the GOSS should reevaluate the value of opening Alexandria University branch at the time when the Southern Sudan's three national universities are still in exile in Khartoum. It is therefore logical, policy-wise that, the GOSS appoint a team to reevaluate the need for foreign higher educational institutions to establish their branches in the South as well as evaluating the need for universities such as the Sudan's University of Quran al-Karim to have branches in Juba and Malakal. This is a policy issue, which need from the part of GOSS a thorough study of its implications before a go ahead is issued by the ministry of higher education in Khartoum to allow the Alexandria University or any other foreign university to establish its branch in Juba or elsewhere in the South.

CHAPTER SIXTEEN

# "Attractive Unity": A minimum goal towards the establishment of the New Sudan?

During the past couple of years, Sudanese and non Sudanese academics, intellectuals and politicians have been engaged in intense debates dealing with different aspects of the Comprehensive Peace agreement (CPA), which was signed in January 2005 between the Sudan People's Liberation Movement (SPLM) and the National Congress Party (NCP), a document, which brought to halt the long running conflict in Africa between north and south Sudan. The main features of the agreement include granting the right of self-determination to the people of Southern Sudan, working to promote and cement an attractive unity for Southern Sudanese during the six-year interim period and to establish a united democratic secular Sudan through a country-wide transparent and inclusive electoral exercise.

The agreement has created 'one state-two systems' in Sudan, a model, which is unique in its features, and can only be compared in part to the Hong Kong-mainland China model. The challenging task of operationalisation and sustaining this system lies in that, it has put the Sudanese elites, as Wathig Kamier put it, into a difficult task of transcending and transforming the 'one country-two systems" model into "one-country-one system", a goal which is a vital condition for maintaining the country's unity. Secondly, the role of the SPLM, in collaboration with other political forces in the country, in bringing about and leading the transformation.

In terms of the Naivasha consensuses, the use of the term "attractive unity" was meant to argue that having failed to convince the Islamists in Sudan during the Naivasha negotiations (2002-2005) to separate state affairs from religious politics, there is a need to create unity on new bases in Sudan.

It is therefore imperative that in order to contextualise the concept of "making unity attractive", its real meaning must transcend the life-span of the CPA, which is six years. It must mean more than the two words- "unity and attractive", which is, indeed much deeper than what it is often believed to be.

In the context of the CPA therefore, understanding the true meaning of "attractive unity" must be informed by the following realities in Sudan:

Firstly, from historical perspective, the type of the socio-economic and political systems that existed in Sudan prior to CPA era was unattractive and not suitable to attract the marginalized and others who did not accept the Islamic-Arabist systems in the country. Because of unattractiveness of that unity, three brutal wars were fought between the centre and the South in particular (1955-1972), (1975-1982) and (1983-2005).

Secondly, the marginalized people who chose to resist the marginalisation politics during the past decades, which was manifested in terms of segregated socio-economic and political underdevelopment and exclusion, did not only include the dissatisfied from Southern Sudan, but also the Beja, Nuba, Angessena, Darfurians, Kordufanians and others from other regions of Sudan who believe that the unity which was created in January 1956 was not attractive to them due to its discriminatory nature. Some therefore argue that, the January 2005 attempt through the Naivasha consensus to make unity attractive on new bases, ought to be looked at as a point of departure to right direction, not only to Southern Sudanese, but also to others who refused to accept the old dispensation, and are not willing to join the old Sudan unity, unless its attractiveness has become tangible and inclusive.

Thirdly, attractive unity is a desire of all the Sudanese who are in tune with inevitability of progressive-sustainable transformation in Sudan. A good example of this desire is expressed in contents of all the agreements which were signed by the National Congress Party (NCP) (imposing itself as the de-facto center of power in the country) with marginalized and opposition groups in Naivasha, Abuja, Cairo and Asmara. In all these agreements, the parties accepted the principle of making unity attractive to or what is referred to by some as 'voluntary unity', between the Sudanese who are dissatisfied with the status quo.

This new way of thinking, one must admit, is a paradigm shift both in content and in spirit from the old Sudan way of thinking, meaning that the progressive forces in Sudan such as the Sudan People's Liberation Movement (SPLM), which pioneered this way of looking at things, are urging every Sudanese to move away from the old Sudan to a new dispensation. In fact, some of the key concepts in these agreements include: decentralized democratic transformation, citizenship, multi-cultural, equitable share of power and wealth between the center and the regions, respect of human rights and the exercise of self-determination.

Fourthly, the Naivasha process, which resulted from Abuja, Cairo and Asmara consensuses has interpreted 'making unity attractive' in short and long term perspectives. For example, for Southern Sudanese who believe that the "political north" have not been willing and successful in making unity attractive for the past five decades, and are not expecting it to do so within six years of the interim period, attractive unity to them would mean a short term kind of 'wait and see' attitude until July 2011 when they will have voted in an internationally supervised referendum to choose whether to remain part of the confederation as it is to day, or opt for an independent state of their own. In other words, they are saying if the "north" (including NCP), failed to provide the incentives and the dividends for making unity attractive during the interim period, such a unity will be unattractive to many of them.

Fifthly, it would be equally unfair to suggest that the Sudanese progressive forces such as the SPLM, the Sudan Liberation Movement (SLM), the Sudan Communist Party (SCP) and other progressive groups in the country, would look at attractive unity from a merely short term perspective and indeed, one would be doing injustice to the CPA which has contextualised the attractive unity as a framework and road map for genuine long term- progressive change and transformation in Sudan. In terms of the CPA interpretation, making unity attractive is a long-term perspective, which means creating a new Sudan on new bases, within, but also beyond the Naivasha consensuses and time frames, to attract all those who have rebelled against the old dispensation.

It is true that some of these frameworks are unrealistic, ambitious, and short-term in out look and require substantive good will from the parties to implement them. In other words, the CPA urges Sudanese to adopt new mind shift, and adopt philosophical and long term ideological process of transforming the Sudan into either new attractive nation for all those who have despised the old constitutional and social contracts; opt for confederal arrangements between the centre and the regions, as the CPA has created or the country will disintegrated into small unstable independent entities, some of which will not be sustainable.

Sixthly, it should be emphasised that even if the South chooses to secede in July 2011, it should not necessarily mean that the rest of the marginalized forces, who advocate the New Sudan ideology would give up the struggle for making unity attractive. This is because it is no longer the South that needs attractive unity, but all those who have been disadvantaged by the old system, who are nowadays the pioneers of the new attractive secular united Sudan.

The New Sudanese are the Sudanese who daily join the ranks of the SPLM in different parts of the north, south, east, west and centre. These are those who are convinced that the backwardness of the Sudanese socio-political consciousness lies in the refusal by the riverine elites and the religious zealots of the Islamic political parties to accept that Sudan is what it is and every citizen must accept its diversity as it is.

However the good news is that, in the long run, even the South, which might choose to secede in 2011, may revise its conditional-secessionist option at later stage, if the attractive unity they have been fighting to achieve since June 1947, become a reality in the remaining parts of the country.

Thus, attractive unity, as espoused by those who believe in it, is regarded as the essence of the progressive forces' revolutionary struggle in Sudan, and means revising and applying new long term perspectives to the manner in which Sudanese have been relating to themselves, their institutional and national socio-economic frameworks.

To the New Sudanese therefore, advocating for an attractive unity is an expression by the marginalized of their rejection of policies of marginalisation, discrimination, religious fanaticism, and all forms of underdevelopment policies. But it also means that the current coalition of anti-change, anti-attractive unity and anti-transformation in the centre (who are guising under the 'jama al-saf al-watani'- 'uniting national ranks', an initiative by former President Sawar Al-Dahab), which has been the beneficiary of the old system, must be held responsible to make unity attractive and it must be forced to have every reason to be worried if it does not take steps to that effect. This is because the rest of the country, the south, far north, east, west,

Kordufan, Nuba Mountains and Blue Nile are saying they do not see any change in the current unity paradigm and are determined to replace it, if the old Sudan ruling elites do not succumb to the ongoing wave of transformation.

On the other hand, making unity attractive has to be understood to mean opening up political space, not only in the federal north through transparent participation of the Sudanese in all aspects of political, social and economic life in the country, but also opening up political space in the South, where the SPLM, the guardian of transformation in the country is in power.

The SPLM elites are currently in power both in the north and in the south, and have instituted, what can be regarded as a transparent political system in the south, where the federal nature of the government, as stipulated in the two interim constitutions in Khartoum and Juba, is reflective of some of the expirations of the people of the New Sudan.

The first burden the SPLM has to carry is to build itself as a formidable political party, with strong political structures, which can withstand socio-economic pressures from the regions (states) and nationalities that form the South. It is imperative therefore that the unity within the South and among the Southern regions and nationalities must be attractive, otherwise, whether the South remains part of the current confederal Sudan or a separate independent state, the type of the unity its leadership will forge must be attractive to all those who live in Southern Sudan, otherwise, new complains about marginalisation will resurface in the South.

This is the burden of being a new Sudanese.

The second burden the SPLM is likely to carry is the burden of protection of the CPA. The northern political parties were all against the Addis Ababa Accord, and did everything to trap Nimeiri into giving up its alliance with Southerners. All the military coups that were staged against Nimeiri's regime during the period between 1974 and 1982 were repelled and quelled down by Southern Sudanese soldiers who were made to believe that they were protecting the Addis Ababa agreement and the unity of the country.

In fact, Numieri May regime's strategists made it a point to blackmail the South in every way they could. Unity of the country was linked to South's acceptance of its guardian role in making the unity attractive. The 3rd March of every year was celebrated as a Unity Day, not in the whole country, but only in the South. When Nimeiri and his lieutenants got convinced that the opposition and pressure against the Addis Ababa Agreement has reached its peak from the Umma National Party of Sadig Al-Mahdi, Democratic Unionist Party of late Sherif Al-Hindi, the National Islamic Front of Dr Hassan Al-Turabi, the Sudan Communist Party of Mohamed Ibrahim Nugud, the Sudan National Party of Father Philip Abbas Ghaboush and other opposition political parties, Nimeiri signed the famous "National Pact" agreement with these parties in 1977, hence turning his back to the South.

As a result, the Islamist parties in Sudan allied themselves with Nimeiri and successfully abrogated the Addis Agreement. Today, we see the same scenario repeating itself, in the name of the "uniting national ranks" an initiative by General Sawar Al-Dahab, a well-known Sudanese elder, who was once a Defense Minister of General Nimeiri's regime. Sawar Al-Dahab and Dr Jazuli Dafalah, both members of the National Islamic Front, led the interim government between 1985 and 1986, which later on paved the way for election of the "National Pact" signatories into power in June 1986.

The burden of the Addis Ababa Agreement was carried by Southern Sudanese leaders, who themselves, as represented then by Joseph Lagu and Abel Alier, became the victims of their attempts to carry the burden of making unity attractive between the north and South and indeed their attempts to force Nimeiri to implement the Agreement also were frustrated. Will the SPLM and its leadership become the victims of the burden of the CPA? The repeat of the 1977 is in the making, and unless the SPLM/A made the price of not implementing the CPA by the NCP and the northern political parties higher than the price of implementing it, the SPLM may find itself confronted by the National Pact coalition in 2009, when general national elections are conducted. This is because El-Bashir, El-Mahdi, El-Mirghani, El-Turabi and Nugud have already bought into Sawar El-Dahab's initiative, and these leaders did actually meet and were paraded on Omdurman TV recently, a typical show of solidarity against the CPA. The question is what is plan B of the SPLM as the "National Pact II" moves on to destroy the CPA?

In the final analysis, moving away from 'one-state-two systems' to "one state-one system" requires that the attractive unity paradigm must be seen as a natural outcome of the Naivsaha consensuses, in which every political force in Sudan, should accept the new dispensation as an irreversible natural course of creating a new united Sudan or a second republic as some would prefer to call it.

Indeed, some argue that the south will secede, if it does, as a result of historical accumulative resistance of change and transformation by the centre and the traditional-religious political forces and not because the NCP or the sectarian parties did not make unity attractive during the interim period (2005-2011) through physical development.

Thus, making unity attractive is a statement of faith by all the progressive forces and acts as a political manifesto for attaining their future goals-namely, creating a united democratic, secular new Sudan, which is voluntarily joined and accepted by all those who believe in it. The role of the SPLM as the pioneer advocate for the creation of new Sudan is imperative, but the ownership of the transformation process, which may take another five decades or more, must transcend the pioneering role of a single political force.

CHAPTER SEVENTEEN

# The Second SPLM National Convention: Looking beyond the 25th Anniversary

The core of the SPLM as a vanguard of liberation struggle in Sudan lies in its vision, which informed its conceptual frameworks (manifesto 1983, and as revised in 1994 and 1998), and programmes of actions such as Peace Through Development Framework (1998) and Rumbek Working Committee Reports (2003), all of which were embodied in part in the Comprehensive Peace Agreement (CPA), January 2005.

The core of the SPLM vision include among other things:

1. The realization of New Sudan vision as a process of transformation of all aspects of the country, without limitation to time frames, given that the process itself is a transitory in nature. In other words, all formations of the SPLM, unionists and secessionists have the opportunities to achieve their visions, without necessarily tampering with the rights of others to enjoy the ownership the New Sudan Nation.

2. The realization of new democratic secular Sudan requires complete adherence to voluntary formula of unity in diversity, as stipulated in the SPLM Manifesto of July 1983/1994/1998 and CPA (January 2005) through the right to self-determination or any other formula that would give each and every Sudanese the right of citizenship.

3. The historical evolution of the SPLM/A since its inception in 1983, had witnessed serious political and military challenges, some of which have shaped the political settlement embodied in the CPA. What these challenges had posed on the character of the Movement can be explained through clear short and long term perspectives. I am sure some of the papers to be presented in the 2nd Convention will tackle them.

## Conceptual and ideological challenges

The 2nd National Convention will have to deal with and try to provide answers to some of the conceptual/ideological questions/challenges especially those issues which are not widely and openly discussed by the members due to lack of public forums. For example, what does it means to create a new 'nation state' for newly converted Sudanese members to the SPLM membership, let alone to the sectarian or Islamic political party members within the context of historical and ideological tenets of the SPLM struggle: what does self-determination or a united democratic secular Sudan means to the sectarian parties' membership against the background of referendum for Southern Sudanese in 2011, and has work been done to explain it to them?

Does the new Sudan 'nation state' mean, building 'New Sudans" as suggested by CPA: one in the north and the other in the South if attractive unity is not realized within the interim period framework or does it mean 'reformed old Sudan' and 'transformed new Sudan'? Can the emergence of the ' New Sudans' formula be postponed, or rather, as the attendants of the 2nd National Convention members prepare themselves, has unity been made attractive enough at least in the eyes of the SPLM leadership, or could it have been made more attractive, and who should have done that?

Would the results of the elections abort any possible tendency to secede among Southerners or indeed, should the SPLM 2nd National Convention concentrate working towards winning elections, and suspend temporarily strategizing for the practical challenges of post-2011 status of South? The SPLM is a national mass movement, whose membership comes from all over the country, and the secession of the South, some argue, would discourage the Movement from working towards achieving its long term objectives. The question then is, given time limitation, will the SPLM delegates be ready to discuss post-2011 scenarios for the rest of the country, without necessarily giving up other options. For example, if it becomes clear that the result of the elections is not in favor of the SPLM and its allies will such results pave the way for the Nuba Mountains and Southern Blue Nile Populations to decide to join the South, should the referendum takes place and the South secedes?

Will the new "Greater South Sudan" accommodate others who might chose to join, and what will be the criteria, i.e being like-minded? Here the question of con-federal arrangements between the "Greater South Sudan" and the rest of Sudan becomes an option that needs discussion by the SPLM affiliates and those progressive Sudanese formulations who feel that short of taking over power in the next general elections, the SPLM should opt to seek a confederation arrangement between the Greater South Sudan (possibly composing of Nuba Mountains, Southern Blue Nile, Darfur, Eastern Sudan, be later joined by Kordufan and the far north), until such time it becomes possible for the SPLM to realize the New Sudan nation.

One wonders if the convention will put this matter on agenda. It is a challenging concept, because it falls within the central politics of Self-determination.

Alternatively, one may still ask: does the "new nation state" to be established depends only on the SPLM winning elections, and indeed, is there enough political will and commitment, based, I presumed on continuous discussions between the Movement and its allies, which will consolidate strategic alliances between the SPLM and the progressive forces and other marginalised areas, a process which will guarantee their success in winning an over all majority in 2009 elections? What if the SPLM does not win the majority, hence could not agree with the winning parties on the modalities of the transformation and peace building in the country: for example on reaching just and lasting peace in Darfur, Eastern Sudan Front might not have made its mind as to which side to ally with, and the majority members of the SPLM from Southern Sector might be preoccupied with local electoral politics rather than with the greater issues of transformation in the country. If it becomes clear that the SPLM will not win the majority votes in the next election, can it opt for the postponement or cancellation of the elections and what would be the implications of such decision on the rest of the road map (CPA) implementation?

## Lessons

The 2nd National Convention will definitely stock check on issues which were discussed during the 1st National Convention 1994. The First National Convention came about as a result of political discontents within the Movement, where, among other things, lack of internal discussions on major issues was noted, lack of clarity of vision of the Movement among ranks and file at that stage: in fact there were two floating ideas- creation of new democratic secular

Sudan versus independent Southern Sudan; there was concerned that the Military-Politico High Command organ (the highest military and political decision making body in the Movement at the time) was not functioning and hardly met, thus there was a need for rationalization of leadership command; there was also the demand for separation of the military from the civilian administration; it was also noted that the traditional leadership, whose vital role in supporting the struggle was paramount, were beginning to feel that their role in administering their areas was declining; the women members of the movement were starting to raise their voices and asking for more role in political as well as administrative spheres in the liberated areas; some friends of the movement were sending signals that the SPLM should instututionalised its foreign policies and relations through regional and international representations in key and friendly countries as Cold war politics reached its peak; some members of the movement were concerned that the status of members of the Movement from other marginalised areas and their role in the revolution needed rationalization and formalization.

The result of the 1st National Convention, among other important undertakings, was that new structures were established (NEC, NLC, and the military organs were rationalized). The vision of the movement was clarified to be the creation of a new united democratic secular Sudan, while at the same time leaving all the other options such as federation, confederation and self-determination opened during the negotiations with Khartoum regime. This affirmation was consolidated by the Asmara Declaration in June 1995, which for the first time, put the SPLM on the center stage as the transformation agent of the Sudan from decadent weak state to a democratic new nation. In fact, like the Chukudum Convention of 1994, where the self-determination was accepted as a natural right for the Sudanese regions who wish to exercise it, the Asmara Declaration affirmed the concept of 'voluntary unity'.

## National Agenda for 2nd National Convention and beyond

The ideas discussed during the 1st National Convention, in my opinion should inform the period leading to the establishment of Naivasha protocols, all of which reaffirmed the unity of the Sudan on new basis, self-determination for the people of Southern Sudan and popular consultations for the people of Nuba Mountains and Blue Nile, and democratic transformation of the country through democratic electoral system. These principles: attractive unity, self-determination and democratic transformation informed and shaped the constitutional framework that established the Government of National Unity, Government of Southern Sudan, judiciary, legal and legislative system including the electoral law, which supposed to govern the general elections in the country.

It is through the lessons learnt from the 1st National Convention resolutions 1994, the Rumbek crisis management conference 2004, and the Naivasha institutional framework 2005, that the SPLM is now preparing itself for the 2nd National Convention. There are certainly realities that should inform the formulation of the 2nd National Convention's slogan and programmes:

- Thorough discussions on reexamining the validity of the Movement's vision as provided for in its Manifesto 1983.
- Re-evaluation of the Movement's performances since 1994 to January 2005.
- Re-evaluation of the Movement's performances since January 2005 to third year of the interim period.

## Consolidation of unity of ranks and file of the Movement

Reorganization of the Movement (structuring of the Movement organs; revitalization of effective roles of youth and women leagues, and consolidation of historical relations with sisterly progressive organizations throughout the world in order to learn from their experiences

Deal with polemics of creation of south-north sectors versus the unity of the party membership: Should SPLM remain a centralized party, and do away with two sectors, a formula which seems to suggest the existence of two parties in one. What are the short and long term repercussions of the current system and those of centralized party system on the future of the SPLM in the north?

Discuss economic policies: the neo-liberal economy which some SPLM leaders seem to favor, versus mixed economy that encourages state interference in redistribution of national resources.

Renewal of party commitment to its ideals namely-unity, freedom and integrity: it is argued by some that ever since the SPLM transformed itself into ruling party in the South and senior partner in GONU, the Movement's ideals and objectives were not pushed hard enough to become the basis of governance in the country: there has been a lot of talk of freedom of press and fight against corruption in the South, but little has been said about the rampant corruption and oppression of press in the GONU, where the SPLM is a partner.

The role of the SPLA as a transforming military factor within the framework of the CPA security arrangements needs to be clarified. Is SPLA an SPLM army, or a Southern Sudanese army or a national army? At GOSS level where the SPLM is the ruling party, funds has not been availed for the SPLA to transform itself, a situation, which raises the question about how the SPLA can be starved financially by an SPLM Ministry of finance.

Activities of political parties are often shaped and strengthened by regular meetings of their executive arms: the Secretariat. There is a need to rationalize the SPLM leadership structures in such a way that the SPLM Secretariat, as the working committee of the Movement regularly meets and issue statements on issues are deemed important, rather than wait for the IPB and INC meetings that take place upon request.

The decision making bodies of the SPLM, even prior to the passing on of the founder late Dr Garang, has shown that the Movement, political wing, the SPLM lacked strong structural organs and as a result avoided internal political discussions on vital issues such as: validation of the revolutionary objectives; political orientation, devising of advanced tactics of mobilisation of the masses and recruitment of membership from areas outside the traditional SPLM areas; convening of regular political rallies and political debates; these issues are pressing at the moment and would require mechanisms through which they could be addressed.

The SPLM should reconsider redeployment of its intellectual reservoir, individuals who have the capacity to think and provide well-informed advises to the movement's leaders, by either recalling them back to party Headquarters, and assign them less time consuming assignments to enable them doing party work or relieve them from their executive/legislative positions.

Strengthening the link between the SPLM ideology and the daily operations of different apparatus of the organization. As a ruling party/senior partner, the SPLM ideology should inform all the policies of GOSS/GONU through its sectorial committees. In the case of the GOSS, one notes that the GOSS runs the government affairs and not the SPLM.

The management and equitable distribution of the resources and delivery of the services is the responsibility of the SPLM. Cadres deployed to carry out tasks on behalf of the Movement are accused of behaving as if they own the portfolios they are deployed to run.

Deployment of cadres needs to be accompanied by clear instructions of what their responsibilities are, job descriptions, monitoring mechanisms and accountability modalities.

Sectorial strategy for the division of labour within the Movement structures and strengthening and channeling of and strengthening of information sector across the board.

From the discussion above, it is important that the 2nd SPLM National Convention Slogan should read as follows: Looking beyond the 25th Anniversary; Towards Building a New Sudanese Nation: Organisational Renewal for Managing the Transition to Transformed and Democratic Polity Guided by Committed Visionary Leadership.

The SPLM leadership should therefore be mindful that the Movment went through bitter periods of internal crises in the 1980s and 90s, and the movement had to convene critical fora to resolve some of these challenges. One of the important results of these debates was the achievement of reunification of the Movement, without which the CPA would have not been concluded. Now that the SPLM is in the middle of the interim period, the 2nd National Convention should take time to reflect on the challenges of past 25 years of struggle, examine the present challenges brought about by the CPA and look beyond the Naivasha consensus, so that it charters the way towards achieving its objectives and goals. There are more challenges after 2011 than they are today, discussing them in the 2nd National convention would pave the way for better understanding of challenges to come.

CHAPTER EIGHTEEN

# Managing daunting agenda of unity and peace in Sudan

As Sudan prepares itself to organise general elections nation wide, it seems that the mood in the country continuous to be divisive. There are over forty political parties in the country ready to join the race. The Comprehensive Peace Agreement (CPA), as a peace agenda, stipulates that general elections must aim at establishing a democratic transformed Sudan, where peace agenda should reign in the whole country. What scenarios are there and what options do the Sudan People's Liberation Movement (SPLM) and its allies as driving forces behind the peace agenda in Sudan have? What options are available for the marginalise forces, in order to realise the unity agenda in the country. The driving forces for the unity agenda in Sudan include the SPLM, which was formed in July 1983, Darfurian political and militant organisations, the Eastern Front organisations, the Nuba Mountains and the Blue Nile regions. A united Sudan can only be realised if and when the peace and unity agenda prevail in the country.

All biases and political-religious extremisms that the country had witnessed during the past fifty years can be attributed to competition between those political forces who espoused the war agenda to keep power abreast and those who espoused peace and unity agenda, through reform and transformation of the country into a nation that accommodates all its citizens and their aspirations.

From historical perspective, Sudan has not been at peace with itself for too long because the elites who were in charge of the evolution of the country political life were uncertain of some of the important ingredients of nation building:

Firstly, even before the independence in January 1956, there was no agreement on the identity of the country, a situation that created a rift among citizens, each perceiving the other as an alien and a potential enemy.

Secondly, religion was regarded by some as a criterion for belonging to the country. To be a Muslim was equal to being a super citizen in Sudan, at least in perception. Those who were not Muslims were looked down as third class citizens.

Thirdly, cultural chauvinism, based on perceived superiority of 'Arab' Sudanese, was used as a tool for legitimisation of power in the country. To accept belonging to the 'Arab' culture and perceive oneself as Arab Sudanese was a tool for ascendancy to power and prestige.

These contradictions and perceptions resulted in long fierce political conflicts in the country. The first region to say no to these divisive ideas was the South in August 1955, a 'no' which resulted in a seventeen year long civil war, brought to an end in February 1972 following the conclusion of the Addis Ababa Peace Agreement. Political ideas, which were advanced to look out for alternative options to deal with the deliberate socio-economic and political marginalisation of some communities and regions due to cultural and identity biases, were ignored and as a result, what was seen as 'Southern problem', became, by 1980s, a contentious problem for the whole country.

In fact, the culture of war and the war agenda became enshrined in Sudanese political life, to the point where by 1960s; it has been institutionalised by the central governments. The politics of marginalisation by the centre, the deliberate use of religion as a vehicle for political manipulation since 1956, manipulation of public opinion in the name of democracy, through elections as a means to ascend to power (1954-1958, 1966-1969, 1986-1989), the use of military coups (1958-1964, 1969-1985, since 1989) by military elites in collusion with their civilian counterparts as a deterrent force against the reformists and the deliberate impoverishment of the peripheries to force them to submit to the centre, all these policies had deepened the rift between the centre and the regions.

Attempts were made by various political and militant groups to identify which agenda worth adopting: peaceful co-existence of cultures or their clash. In the 1960s there were those, in the north who recognised that the identity question was the base of crises in the Sudan. They tried to advance new ideas in an attempt to convince the Sudanese to accept that Sudan is a multi-cultural and multi-religious and a hybrid of Afro-Arab heritage. They tried to marry the desert and the savannah. Those genuine attempts were condemned by Arab- chauvinists' riverines and regarded them as divisive. Even the reformists such as the Republicans, who in early 1980s, tried to provide an alternative view of what Sudan should stand for, were suppressed and persecuted. In 1980s, the SPLM began the mobilisation of the Sudanese to espouse its vision of the New Sudan.

Even though the Movement managed to attract considerable supporters from the peripheries, the Sudanese traditional oligarchy, remain un-amused by the new ideology, and began to play the religious card, declaring the SPLM as anti-Arab and anti-Islam and condemned any northern Sudanese who is a member of the SPLM. Eventually, major aspects of New Sudan vision were enshrined in the CPA, as a result of which, a peace agreement, between the SPLM and the National Congress Party (NCP) was signed in January 2005. One of the cornerstones of the CPA road map was conduction of internationally supervised national elections at all levels in the country in July 2009.

## Possible Challenges to Elections

As the country enters into new phase in its political struggle to transform itself, the SPLM as a guardian for managing the daunting peace and unity agenda in the country, has to explicitly make its electoral agenda clear. Indeed, the next elections, as an integral part of the CPA road map, must be informed by three important aspects of the CPA:

Firstly, the 2009 elections are about transforming the country from a hostage of political manipulation and exploitation by unpatriotic chauvinist religious zealot elites in the centre, into a multi-cultural, multi-religious and a democratic united nation. The SPLM and its allies in the east, west, centre and the north, will have to take seriously their historical role in seeing to it that they work collectively and discuss all aspects of the transformation, including forging alliances to enter the election race. The peace and unity agenda should become the base of their campaigns.

Secondly, the ongoing conflict in Darfur can be a recipe for change and transformation in the country, but also it can transform the country into pieces if not handled with care. In fact, the Darfur conflict can be transformed into a unity agenda by those who would like to see the country united, irrespective whether the South chooses to secede or not. In terms of political heritage, population and historical role in the country, Darfur has characteristics of glue in service of unity of the country. The SPLM should therefore engage the Sudan Liberation Movement (SLM) leaders (Abdel Wahid Al-Nur, Mini Minawi, Ahmed Abdel Shafie, and others) and the JEM leadership on their stand on upcoming elections. The Movement should also interact with its Eastern Front allies, especially now that they are facing internal divisions, their unity will strengthen the SPLM election alliance.

Thirdly, the referendum, which the South is waiting to exercise in 2011 is a challenge to the Sudan unity and peace agenda. Unless the SPLM and its allies, especially the Darfurians, began to deal with issues of unity and peace in the country before the elections, the country may find itself in serious challenges. There are two paradoxes regarding the link between the unity of the country and the referendum in the South: The SPLM as a ruling party in the South, while advocating the unity of the country, cannot ignore or skip the exercise of referendum by Southern Sudanese in 2011, because its power base is there. On the other hand, the SPLM has the responsibility to make sure that its peace and unity agenda for Sudan, if managed correctly through the upcoming elections, may save the country from disintegrating.

Lessons to be considered

The question then is what are the SPLM and its allies' strategies for the upcoming elections? What are the scenarios and options available for the SPLM, its allies and the other political forces in the country who may opt to forge an alliance with the SPLM? What are challenges of the post-2009 elections in Sudan?

Firstly, before entering into general elections, the SPLM leadership must learn from the dynamics of its Second National Convention in May 2008. During the Convention the organisation found itself confronted by three bitter realities: the leadership of the organisation was not prepared enough to manage the congresses' elections at various levels, resulting in senior cadres loosing their seats to individuals who may be considered as new recruits or defactees from the National Congress Party or its allies. The SPLM Convention was convened concurrently with the general census in the country, another milestone in the implementation of the CPA, hence dividing the focus of the organisation's leadership. Therefore, the lack of preparedness for the convening of the Convention was a serious political omission that should not repeat itself. The second reality was that the delegates to the Convention were mot given the opportunity to take time, during the Convention to discuss the SPLM's policies, whether political or socio-economic sector agenda. It was expected that the delegates should have spent enough time to evaluate the SPLM organisational structures, the performances of its cadres since October 2005, revise its policies on national issues such as developmental policies, Darfur conflict, educational, health and infrastructure policies, management of resources, accountability, and deployment policies of its cadres.

Finally, the organisation's leadership devoted a considerable time debating the structure of the organisation, especially the positions of Deputies Chairperson. These matters are always dealt with before the convention convenes to avoid sensitivities and polarisation of the delegates during the convention. In fact, the organization's convention was paralysed for almost a week, where leadership spent time trying to settle the question of who will be number two in the party, almost resulting in factionalisation of the organisation into power centres, where some tried to ethnicise and regionalise their positions.

Secondly, it is very important to appreciate that the chances for the next elections to take place depend very much on three vital factors: the dynamics of the International Criminal Court (ICC) charges against President El-Bashir may impact on the manner in which the internal politics within the NCP expressed itself. The NCP controls the resources of the country; manages brutal security organs; controls sixty per cent of the army and police force in the country, and controls the public and private media. Unless the internal dynamics of the ICC implications within the NCP become clear, the likelihood of some influential cadres within the party disrupting the process and preparations for elections is a possibility. If President El-Bashir is indeed indicted as seems to be the case, who will be the candidate for Presidency from the NCP and will the party agree on one candidate. Secondly, the Darfur conflict may derail the election process all together. The continuous war in Darfur may escalate into large scale war, if the Darfurian factions' leaders feel that they are being ignored, through partial elections process, or if the NCP leadership feels that it will not win the elections, it may opt to escalate the war in Darfur, hence making it impossible to conduct peaceful free, inclusive and fair elections in the country. Will the SPLM be ready to accept conduction of elections before the peaceful settlement of the Darfur conflict?

Thirdly, the Sudan People's Liberation Movement is regarded as the custodian of the CPA and like the NCP, is responsible for its implementation. The three pillars of the CPA are: trying to make unity attractive during the interim period, through establishment of new political, economic, social and legal structures, establishment of a democratic transformed new Sudan through general elections, where all shades of political forces in the country would participate and the right to self determination for the people of Southern Sudan, to decide whether they want to remain part of the Sudan or secede. These principles require the SPLM and its allies who converted to the CPA ideological principles to respect them and implement them. The general elections therefore pose challenges to the SPLM and its allies as a co-ruling party in the country.

## Scenarios

Analysing scenarios for the upcoming elections is a very daunting task for any analyst. There seems to be five different scenarios opened to the SPLM leadership and its allies to consider, if they want to influence the process and the outcome of the 2009 elections:

Firstly, the SPLM may decide to persuade its leader, General Salva Kiir to contest elections on behalf of the marginalised block, on unity, peace and new Sudan agenda. This would mean that all the marginalised groups and other progressive forces in the country will rally behind Chairman Kiir's candidacy and work towards mobilising the voters to elect him as a candidate who would ensure unity, stability and realisation of the new Sudan. The challenge of this scenario lies in that the SPLM will have to convince its allies in Darfur, East, centre and indeed its members in northern Sudan that Chairman Kiir is the right candidate for the alliance.

Moreover, the SPLM must convince Chairman Kiir to accept the candidacy, given that should he decide to accept to contest the elections, and should he fail to win the national Presidency, he would automatically loose his two positions: First Vice President of the Republic and President of the Government of Southern Sudan. Of course he would retain his two other positions, the Chairman of the SPLM and the Commander in Chief of the SPLA. Meanwhile, in the South someone else will have to be elected to fill in the Presidency of the Government of Southern Sudan, as well as First Vice President of the Republic according to Part II, Article 2.3.7 of the Power Sharing Protocol of the CPA and Part Three, Chapter Two, Article 62 (1) of the Sudan National Interim Constitution. However, if Chairman Kiir won the Presidency of the Republic, then the post of First Vice President will automatically be occupied by someone from northern Sudan, who needs not to be from the NCP, because he or she can come from any political party in the north. Another challenge would be that if the President of Government of Southern Sudan is elected from another Southern political party, in case the SPLM candidate did not succeed to win the post, the dynamics of Southern Sudan interim period politics may change, hence creating uncertainty about the implementation of the CPA.

Indeed, in this case, will the SPLA command pay its allegiance to non-SPLM President of the South? And what will happen if the President of Government of Southern Sudan is from another Southern party while the Chairman of the SPLM and the C-In-C of the SPLA is not in power neither in the South nor in the north?

Secondly, in the event that Chairman Kiir decides not to contest, and asked the movement to choose one of its cadres to contest the national Presidential elections, the question then would be: who would be the suitable candidates for the Presidency of the Republic within the

SPLM hierarchy? What would be the criteria for nominating one of the SPLM top brass to join the national Presidential race in 2009? Would any of the top ten of the SPLM's twenty-seven members of its Political Bureau be suitable for candidacy? The challenge with this scenario lies in that if Kiir decides not to contest and asked one of his colleagues to contest the national election for Presidency of the Republic on behalf of the SPLM, and if that candidate wins the race, it will be difficult, constitutionally speaking, for the President of Government of Southern Sudan, who definitely would be another person rather than the one who won the national Presidential election, to become at the same time First Vice President of the Republic. It would mean that the two positions will have to be separated. It would also mean that there would be two centres of powers within the SPLM and in the South. On the other hand, if the SPLM forwarded another candidate other than Chairman Kiir to contest the national Presidential elections, will the other allies accept that candidate? And if the allies express their reservations on that candidate, will the SPLM be willing to present a list of other candidates from whom the allies can choose from?

Thirdly, the SPLM may decide not to forward at all a candidate for the national Presidency, thus implying that Chairman Kiir will be their candidate for the Presidency in Southern Sudan, and who if he wins that position, would automatically becomes the First Vice President of the Republic as stipulated in the National Interim Constitution and the CPA. Such a scenario would suggest that the SPLM would ask its allies to come up with a candidate who would challenge the NCP and other political parties' candidates in the Presidential election. Here, issues such as when and how the Darfur conflict comes to an end will become imperative. The SPLM will have to work hard to see to it that the conflict is resolved peacefully and that peace is restored in Darfur before the elections. Such a situation would imply postponement of the elections until the war in Darfur is brought to an end. Equally, it would mean that the road map of the CPA will be affected and hence may open up undesired possibilities, which may not be acceptable to the SPLM and its supporters.

In the event that this scenario is adopted by the SPLM, the question that begs for an answer would be: who are the SPLM closest allies who would secure the success of the alliance in winning the position of the President of the Republic. There are several options that the SPLM leadership may opt to pursue: One, the SPLM as an organisation has six political centres: the South, Northern Sector, the Nuba Mountains, the Blue Nile, Abyei and the Diaspora. These centres represent the SPLM power house. Two, the SPLM also has historical links with the SLM factions in the West, the Eastern Front and Beja Front, and has political presence in Kordufan. These allies have the potential to form a block with the SPLM to sponsor a candidate for the Presidency of the Republic, and hence secure sizeable votes for their candidates in the parliamentary polls. Other important potential allies to the SPLM from the north include the Sudan Communist Party (SCP), the Umma Reform Party of Mubarak El Fadil Al-Mahdi and other small, but influential progressive forces in the country. The SCP, from historical perspective has been consistently sympathetic with the cause of the marginalise people of Sudan. In fact, a good number of the SPLM leaders from the north, were influential members of the SCP. Making use of this historical and strategic connection, the SPLM may gain the support of the SCP and other progressive forces in the north. Such a broad base coalition would afford the SPLM and its allies, not only to win the Presidency of the Republic, but a possible comfortable majority in both the Senate and the National Assembly.

Fourthly, the SPLM and its allies may opt to widen their alliance to include opposition parties that are against NCP monopoly of politics and governance in the north. These political parties are the Umma National Party of Imam Al Sadig Al-Mahdi, the National Popular Congress of Dr Hassan Abdalla al-Turabi and the Democratic Unionist Party of Moulana Muahmmed Uthman Al-Mirghani. Such a scenario can only be plausible if these traditional Islamic parties have decided to push out of power, once and for all, the NCP and willing to forge an alliance with whoever is willing and able to secure the ousting of the NCP from power. What would be the implications of such a scenario from power politics perspective in the country? Definitely the SPLM would continue to rely on its progressive allies to win votes in the parliamentary national elections, in order to secure enough seats to influence national politics after the elections.

Thus, while the SPLM may opt to create an alliance with the traditional Islamic political parties to sponsor one candidate for Presidency against the NCP candidate, it is not likely that these Islamic political parties would cooperate with the SPLM and its allies in supporting each other parliamentary candidates. This is because, the traditional Islamic parties, would according to this scenario, be interested only in gaining parliamentary votes, rather than win the Presidency. The traditional power base of these Islamic political parties has always been Darfur, Kordufan, Blue Nile, Nuba Mountains, northern and eastern Sudan. These regions are now part of the marginalised progressive political alliance, led by the SPLM. Is such a scenario possible? Probably yes, only if the discussions and debates between the SPLM and these Islamic parties start earlier; because such an alliance would be huge one and the management of various interests would be very hard to handle. Moreover, it would require sophisticated negotiation team from the SPLM and its allies.

Leaders such as Al-Turabi, Al-Mahdi, Al-Mirghani and Nugud are shroud politicians and know very well how to negotiate their interests. They have been around in the Sudanese political scene for a while. Moreover, the 'trio' of Al-Turabi, Al-Mahdi, and Al-Mirghani tend to believe that history of Sudan as a nation has something to do with their families' legacy, and would find it sometimes condescending to negotiate with people they consider to come from the marginalise regions. Perhaps it was only late Dr Garang and the SPLM who skilfully forced these traditional leaders to accept the fact that the fate and the future of Sudan is no longer tied to individuals, whether they come from influential families, middle-upper classes or not.

Fifthly, the SPLM may opt to create an election alliance with the NCP, by supporting an NCP candidate for Presidency, arguing that the two should continue to monopolise the politics of the country until the end of the interim period. The challenges that would face the implementation of such a scenario is that the two partners have been exhausted by continued political bickering over the implementation of the peace agreement. Two, the SPLM, should it chooses to cooperate with the NCP during the elections, will be indirectly expanding and extending the NCP life time in power, hence alienating its allies and other political forces in the country who feel that they were victims of the NCP policies of exclusivity. Three, the SPLM has the moral obligation to support political forces that are willing to promote its policy of establishment of the New Democratic United Sudan. A united democratic Sudan can only be achieved in part or in whole if the SPLM and its allies sponsor a presidential candidate who would secure the unity of the Sudan, or the north, if the South chooses to secede in 2011.

Extending NCP life spand in power would be considered by the other political parties a political expediency from the part of the SPLM. In fact, the SPLM is expected to consolidate its power in the north, so that it inherits the power, through cooperation with its allies in the north, should the south secede. Secession of the South in 2011, if that happens, does not mean, in the opinion of the SPLM Northern Sector's leaders, the end of the SPLM transformation agenda. The SPLM they argue is a national political organisation with a transformation agenda that does not ends up with the secession of any of the regions where the SPLM has supporters. The unity of the Sudan in the opinion of these SPLM leaders is a strategic goal that lives on beyond 2011. If this is the general ideological strategic framework of the SPLM national agenda, it does not matter whether the South secedes or not, and thus it becomes irrelevant, as far as the SPLM transformation agenda is concerned. Thus, allying itself with the NCP during the upcoming elections would not be a desired goal, because the marginalised alliance is perceived to be capable of taking over power and save the country from disintegration during the period leading to 2011.

Finally, what do we make of the scenarios and the analyses presented in this essay? What we have tried to do is to trigger a debate, indeed a serious one, among political forces in the Sudan and beyond, to put on the table the challenges and the complexities before the leadership of the country as they embark on their electoral campaigns. We also emphasized that the next elections seem to be about the unity and peace in the country. By unity we mean, putting in place strategic plans that would make it possible at least for the northern parts of the country to remain united even if the South secedes. The elections are also about the Sudanese political forces of all shades working to achieve and maintain a lasting peace that would bring an end to the misery of the ordinary Sudanese people, wherever they are. Maintaining the balance between managing the unity and the peace agenda in the country is not only the responsibility of the SPLM and its allies, and therefore should be the focus of the leadership of the Sudan during the elections, irrespective of their political ideology, objectives and goals. For what will the Sudanese political parties gain if they win elections but the country is disintegrated into small unviable entities?

CHAPTER NINETEEN

# The CPA: Two years to go to referendum

On January 9th, 2009, the Sudanese partners to peace, the Sudan People's Liberation Movement (SPLM) and the National Congress Party (NCP) and other Sudanese political organisations, gathered in the town of Malakal, the capital of the Upper Nile State, to commemorate the fourth anniversary of the signing of the Comprehensive Peace Agreement, which took place in Kenya on January 9th, 2005. While in Malakal, the Sudanese leaders tried to share their achievements and shortcomings with the Sudanese and looked into the future as they march towards the last two years of the interim period. In January 2006, I wrote a piece entitled "Five Years to go to Referendum". I dealt with different aspects of the transitional politics in Sudan and asked serious questions which I thought should form the basis of management of the transitional period, both at national and Government of Southern Sudan (GOSS) institutional levels.

Yes, time is ticking and although impressive breakthroughs were made in the sustainability of general security in the south and at the borders, implementation of major aspects of the Comprehensive Peace Agreement (CPA), establishment of most institutions at various levels, however, some important aspects of the transition are yet to be realised and the manner in which government institutions were run has lots to be desired.

In transitional situations such as the one of Sudan, what matters is that whatever political culture and institutional systems that the current leadership of the Sudan has introduced during the interim period, whether Sudan remains one or split into more entities, will have far reaching effects for the period after 2011. The current institutional frameworks in Southern Sudan are sometimes levelled by some as inefficient or corrupt, whether it is true or not, the reality is that to reverse the situation will require a lot of hard work. In fact, history has revealed that to be a revolutionary movement, entails that the revolution must be translated into true revolutionary spirit by the revolutionaries, when they take over power. In most cases, the attitude of the revolutionary leadership, their supervision skills of the affairs of government, their commitment to follow up and monitor programs on daily basis to see to it that services delivery is affected in the rural areas, their dedication to the vision of their struggle, and commitment to change, are important aspects for building of any nation. When leaders are seen to have less interest in evaluating their activities and achievements, and concentrate more on obvious things such as maintaining security (of course no government can operate without security), building houses for officials etc, with less interest in visiting villages, interacting with traditional leaderships, such leadership is bound to loose sight of long term repercussions of its mandate.

In fact, leadership of any society, especially a revolutionary one such as the Sudan People's Liberation Movement (SPLM) is often judged and evaluated by the outcomes of its public work and not by the good intentions of its leadership.

The SPLM has been in power for four years now, and its legacy as understood by the general populace of the Sudan is that of revolutionary movement that has the mandate to fulfil its promises/objectives by delivering services in areas such as building schools, training teachers, building the capacity of its cadres, pave roads, provide clean water and sanitation, providing efficient health care, provide decent housing to its population, electrify the rural areas, build river ports, airports, link up the capital with states, and capitals of states with counties and the counties with payams and bomas.

During those years decisive decisions were expected on inter-clans/ethnic conflicts, disarmament of civilians, allegations and rumours that were spread by those who feel disadvantaged by the GOSS such as rumours on "land grabbing" in some towns, accusations of unknown uniformed soldiers and dangerous gangsters attacking citizens and their properties; complains about displaced ethnic groups refusing to return to their original areas; complains about some security organs intimidating and harassing journalists in the South, allegations of uncoordinated and sometimes parallel deployments of security, customs, civil aviation and the SPLA intelligent officers at public places, especially at the airport, and complains about jobs not being advertised in news papers by GOSS and states' ministries and that individuals are employed through acquaintances and relatives.

These allegations have had negative effects on the reputation and activities of GOSS and should have been stopped through proper channels immediately rather than being silent about them or ignored. Of course it would be a daunting task to expect a liberation movement turned into a ruling party to accomplish all that in four years. Nevertheless, the conventional wisdom seems to suggest that the SPLM, as the vanguard of the revolution is expected to take over all aspects of policy and decision making within the institutions of government, given that as a majority and the ruling party, its supervisory role should not be questionable.

During the past four years, hundreds of articles and statements have been written and issued regarding the performances of the Government of Southern Sudan and its institutions, especially the role of the members of the SPLM in these institutions. One must say however, that some of these articles were defamatory, instigative and irresponsible to say the least. From some of these evaluations and criticisms that were levelled against the Government of Southern Sudan and the SPLM, one gets the sense that the remaining two years are very critical and a new approach in dealing with issues pertaining to governance, financial management, institutional building and nation building in general will be vital.

What went wrong and who is to blame for the shortcomings that the Government of Southern Sudan and SPLM were accused of and criticised for? There are five points that one should highlight to answer the above questions: the SPLM as a ruling party had vital role to play to correct things during the past four years; the Government of Southern Sudan should have taken time to answer some of the vital questions that its critics and some of its leaders and members have been asking; the modalities and the manner in which the census were conducted have revealed that both the SPLM and GOSS leaderships need to be careful as they work out the modalities for their participation in the up coming general elections and the referendum during the next two years.

Firstly, the role of the SPLM in governance at different levels during the past four years at best was overshadowed by the role of GOSS and much of what is seen as lack of delivery and accountability, especially by GOSS institutions was by necessity blamed on the SPLM because it is seen as the captain of the ship. By the nature of party politics, the role of the SPLM in governance is not vested on individuals, rather it is a collective responsibility vested on the SPLM institutional frameworks. It is true that during the struggle, the SPLM did not have strong institutional frameworks, and it was only after 1994 Chukudum Convention attempts were made to create institutions that would be responsible for the management of the organisation's activities. This institutionalising process was briefly, but critically interrupted during the first twelve months of the interim period, when the late Chairman of the SPLM dissolved all the institutions of the SPLM in July 2005. It took about a year, for the current Chairman of the Movement to restore them as interim organs, until May 2008, when all the SPLM organs at various levels were eventually elected.

Yes, the President of GOSS, his Vice, ministers, and all the members of commissions, judiciary, and assemblies in Government of National Unity (GNU), GOSS, states, counties and payams are members of the SPLM. Being a member of the SPLM however, void of functional and well established institutional frameworks, would not make the SPLM as an organisation accountable or responsible for the actions of its members unless strong institutional frameworks are put in place to make members accountable. It is when the SPLM is in charge, through its institutions such as Political Bureau, National Liberation councils, Secretariats and sectoral committees that members of the Movement, who are deployed to work in government or legislative or judiciary institutions, could be accountable to the organisation. It is when the SPLM, through its institutions has the authority to call in, any time, its members in the cabinets and its leaders in the assemblies to report regularly on their activities and regularly evaluate their performances that the organisation could be regarded as in full control.

The question is who supposed to impose the constitutional role of the SPLM on the governments and on all other institutions? The SPLM is one of the few liberation Movements in the world with highly qualified cadres, at governmental levels or outside its institutions. Little use has been made; it seems of these cadres during the past four years.

Secondly, it has been argued that the Government of Southern Sudan, despite considerable achievements in various fields during the past four years, has been lacking behind in some critical areas. Perhaps one way to understand or to answer these criticisms lies in finding suitable answers to the following questions, most of which centres around accountability, employment/deployment policies, resources/financial management regulations, service delivery monitoring mechanisms, development programs and policies, operationalisation of decentralisation/federalism system, public security etc. Some of these questions include how consultations are carried out when governments are formed or reshuffles are made whether for the formation of GONU, GOSS or states' governments.

Who consults who whenever a new government is formed and what is the role of the SPLM Political Bureau, National Liberation Council and states' liberation councils? What are the criteria of appointments into a cabinet position or to other levels of governments? How decisions are taken within the SPLM leadership and which organs should implement them? How is the relationship between the SPLM Political Bureau/ National Liberation Council and the SPLM parliamentary caucuses is managed? How major decisions are taken in the GOSS/ states' cabinets? Who supervises the spending of the GOSS annual budget? Who supervises the spending of budgets of the states and to what extent is the funds allocated to the counties are accounted for by the county commissioners? What are the channels of communication between GONU ministries and GOSS ministries? Who monitors the implementation of all contracts that the Government of Southern Sudan and states' governments have entered into with foreign companies?

What are the exact roles of the Ministry of Finance and Economic Planning and the Bank of Southern Sudan (BOSS) in the management of budgets? Who controls the national Reserve of the Southern Sudan and is there funds available for the emergency situations? What is the role of the Auditor General and why is it that it is almost a year since he resigned and there is no replacement to date? It is argued by some parliamentarians that whenever the financial year ends every 31st December, huge amounts are either left unspent or are transferred to the accounts of the relevant ministries at GOSS or states ministries, how are such funds spending supervised and who is responsible for making the ministries accountable for them? A sizeable number of Southern Sudanese have benefited from the quotas and contracts that the Ministry of Finance and other ministries have been distributing during the past four years, as means of economic empowerment of Southern Sudanese emerging business class, and millions US dollars have been spent on these contracts and quotas, to what extent has this important program been monitored and evaluated?

During the past four years, the annual budget of Government of Southern Sudan ranged between $1.3 billion US dollars and $1.7 billion US dollars, mainly from oil revenues. Since 2005 it is estimated that the Ministry of Finance and Economic Planning of Government of National Unity has released to GOSS an amount of $6.5 billion US dollars, an amount which is meant to cover the salaries, services delivery and development expenses for the Government of Southern Sudan in Juba, 10 Southern states, 80 counties, about 400 payams and over 1500 bomas. To what extent has the management of these significant resources been efficient?

Moreover, according to the wealth sharing protocol, the oil producing states were to be allocated 2% of the oil revenues, an amount which ranges between $2.5 and $4.5 million US dollars monthly, depending on the rise and fall of the oil prices. The beneficiary Southern states so far have been the Western Upper Nile and Upper Nile states since 2005 and 2006 respectively. The states of Southern Kordufan, Warrab, and Abyei administrative area's revenues have not been clearly verified and question as to whether the central government have been keeping their percentages or it has been using them or it has given them to the states concerned needs to be answered. Do the producing counties benefit from these resources and what are the criteria for qualification for the counties to benefit in terms of development from these resources?

Another question that begs for an answer is who controls these funds in the states concerned, governors, states' cabinets or the assemblies and how is the accountability carried out, and who report to whom? On the other hand, since in 1994 when it was decided in Chukudum that the SPLM National Executive Council (the SPLM Shadow cabinet) should look for sources of income to deliver services to the population in the liberated areas, levying of taxes from transit goods from the neighbouring countries became a major source of income to the SPLM/A administration. Border posts were instituted, foreign companies were called in to explore minerals and exploit the timber in the Equatoria region.

Taxation became a huge source of income and was regulated so that individuals do not pocket the money. In 2004, when it became clear that an agreement was on sight, the SPLM leadership invested time and resources in seeing to it that taxes at the borders are collected, and by 2005, millions of Sudanese pounds were levied. Unfortunately, taxation/custom system within the Ministry of Finance was not yet operationalised in such a way that funds levied are properly deposited in banks.

It has been reported that hundreds of thousands of Sudanese pounds were carried in bags from the levy stations to the Ministry of Finance, which in turn deposit them in the bank. Now that oil prices are at their lowest, it seems that GOSS cabinet has ordered the Ministry of Finance to find ways to make sure that taxes are levied and proper channels and procedures are followed.

Finding answers to the above questions, would give an idea about the serious challenges that GOSS leadership had found itself in during the past four years. Certainly, it was not an easy task for an infant government like GOSS to deal with all these challenges.

Thirdly, throughout the past four years the National Congress Party (NCP) had tried to corner the SPLM in every stop sign of the CPA road map, and one of the skilful tactics it used was to go ahead preparing for the implementation of these stop signs, without committing itself to seriously negotiate with the SPLM on the modalities of the implementation of the items in question. One such important stop sign was the conduction of census in May 2008. The SPLM had three important reservations regarding the implementation of the census: the census coincided with the rainy season in the South, it coincided with the convening of the SPLM 2nd National Convention, and SPLM also had reservations on omission of the ethnicity and religion items on questionnaire forms.

The NCP, aware that the SPLM has in principle agreed on the conduction of the census as per CPA, went ahead and printed all the forms, formed all the committees and made sure that the census infrastructure is fully operational, while continued to buy time engaging the SPLM. By the time that it is few days left for the census to be carried out throughout the country, the SPLM leadership was put in a catch twenty two situation: if it is to boycott the census, it would be seen as acting irresponsibly because it has given its go ahead in principle, and if it is to accept it, the outcome will have the following repercussions: the census was meant to determine the exact number of Southern Sudanese inhabiting what is referred to in the CPA as "Southern Sudan". Secondly, in order for the border of the South to be determined, the population that are regarded as part of the South inhabiting those areas under the Northern army occupation must be counted, especially in Western Upper Nile, Upper Nile, Warrab and Northern Bahr El Ghazal.

The only way to determine their belonging to the South would be through their ethnic background, which the NCP deliberately refused to include it in the questionnaire forms. Thirdly, the population of Abyei Special Administrative Area, being a disputed area, are supposed to be counted as part of the Warrab state, since the CPA has given them dual citizenship during the interim period, until such time that they decide their fate through the exercise of self-determination. Fourthly, in order for the South to determine the number of its geographical constituencies for the purpose of general elections, it is vital that the population of the South, based on the outcome of the census, must be clearly known. By registering some population of the South in the north, and by depriving them from their identity (ethnicity), it would naturally be difficult to determine the exact number of the Southern

Sudan population, and millions, such as those in the North and in the border areas, will be deprived from participating in elections and in the referendum as Southern Sudanese.

Moreover, by counting some Southern Sudanese who are residing in the oil areas that are forcefully annexed to the north, the question of distribution of oil revenues becomes an issue, because the CPA stipulated that only the revenues of the oil in the south will be divided, thus excluding oil revenues from the areas of the South that are forcefully annexed to the north.

In other words, the consequent of not appointing highly technical and legal experts on the census committees is that the SPLM and GOSS are not sure whether to accept the results of the census or not. The choice of individuals into the committees that are dealing with the modalities of the CPA implementation has proven to be problematic for the SPLM/GOSS.

Technical and negotiation committees do not need to be filled with politicians and ministers; rather committed members of the SPLM and experts in the fields should be appointed and given guidelines to guide them as they carry out the task. The manner, in which the census process was handled, was one of the serious setbacks and shortcomings that the SPLM/GOSS would have avoided had they selected the right people to carry out that work.

Fourthly, elections are won or lost before they are conducted, because through strategic planning and proper preparations and mobilisation it is easier for the party to determine its chances for winning or losing. In fact, elections are not necessarily influenced by revolutionary legacies beyond four to six years. People forget easily especially if their expectations are not met on time.

To win elections a party needs high level of organisation, solid funding, viable and sophisticated media (TV and radio) that would reach every citizen, especially the organised youth. The SPLM grass root institutions need to be organised and prepared. The situation in northern sector is even worrying more, given that so far the membership that has registered has not be cross-checked or screened to determine how many have infiltrated the movement from other parties. In the South there was mass influx of members from NCP and other political parties and so far there is nothing showing that these members are genuine and committed to the SPLM vision and principles. In fact, a sizable number of the new comers occupy about 40% of the SPLM National Liberation Council and states' national liberation councils. The NCP is repeating the same scenario of the census, it is going ahead preparing for elections, while the SPLM leadership is playing along, without necessarily answering the difficult questions such as who will be the candidate of the SPLM for national Presidency, who is the SPLM candidate for the President of Southern Sudan, who are the key candidates that will contest at different levels? Such a debate must start now, because the NCP is far ahead of the SPLM, because once the results of the census are announced, and while the SPLM will be busy denouncing the results, the NCP will be already pushing for the date of the elections, hence creating a another de fecto situation for the SPLM.

The election law has been passed and the electoral committees have been formed. Next is the announcement of the date of the election. It is always relieving to pre-empt the opponents' plans rather than react to them, because the chances are that one will make unnecessary mistakes in reaction to the opponent's action.

I was recently told a story by a young Southern Sudanese activist of an encounter with one of the senior SPLM official, Atem Garang who was asked in a social gathering in Khartoum by young people about why is it that every SPLM senior officials, when asked about whether they fully understand the tricks the NCP is using against the SPLM, their answer always is "we know". The students were implying that they fought with the NCP inside the country for almost twenty years and studied at their schools/universities and know their thinking and ways of doing things. Mr. Atem Garang answered the young people by narrating a story: there was a young man who spent three days without sleeping. His father became restless and asked his son to tell him what is bothering him. The young man refused to tell his father the cause of his sleeplessness. He told his father that "If I tell you what is bothering me, you will not sleep for a long time". His father insisted and the young man told his father what bothered him "I made pregnant a daughter and her mother". His father was so up set that he spent the next few days sleepless.

The SPLM senior official told the young audience that "if we in SPLM tell you what we know about the NCP, you guys will not sleep for a long time." I do not know who was right, the students who spent about twenty years under NCP yoke or the SPLM senior officials who spent twenty one years fighting the NCP in the battle fields and in the negotiation tables.

Finally, there will only be two questions for the people of Southern Sudan and Abyei to answer when they cast their votes in the referendum in January 2011: do they want the south to secede or to remain part of a united Sudan. However, before the people of the South decide on either option, it is very important that they answer two important questions before the end of 2009: where is the border between the north and South and who is qualified to be regarded as a Southern Sudanese? Who are qualified to vote in the referendum?

One of the setbacks that supposed to have been highlighted during the past four years was the work of the National Border Commission, especially composition of its members from the South. According to the CPA the National Border Commission was to compose of equal numbers from the NCP and the SPLM. It is noticed that the SPLM members in the committee composed of three categories: elders who were regarded to have knowledge of the history of the border areas; surveyors or individuals who studied survey and political appointees. On the other hand, the NCP members of the committee composed of specialists in history, economics, demography, Law, consultants and traditional leaders' committee, backed by a sub-political committee that directs and guides them based on the terms of reference that was prepared by the NCP Political Bureau. It seems that the formation of the commission, a vital instrument for the border demarcation was not given serious thought by those who suggested names of Southern Sudanese for membership in the Commission. In fact, from the media statements that some members have given so far, it is clear that some of them lack direction and political vision as to what exactly they are supposed to do or what is expected of them and by whom?

The SPLM is the body that signed the CPA and not GOSS, which means the SPLM, with financial support from GOSS, should direct and supervise the work of the members of SPLM in the Border Commission. The first time that the Southern members of the Commission came to brief GOSS cabinet about their work was in November 2008, when they requested an audience with the cabinet to share their frustrations and challenges. It should be emphasised that boundary demarcation has become a sophisticated field these days, given the socio-economic and strategic-political aspects involved, hence the need to nominate individuals that are well-versed in the relevant fields. The composition of the Abyei Boundary Commission (ABC) should have been a good example for the SPLM, because the five experts of the ABC have different backgrounds of knowledge. What I am trying to say is that the members of the Border Commission from the South have more disadvantages compared to their northern counterparts. And if the outcome of the border demarcation is not up to the expectations of the SPLM/GOSS and the people of the South at large, then it will be difficult to imagine the referendum taking place.

On the other hand, there is no doubt that the results of the census, and the level of readiness of SPLM, Southern/Northern Sudanese opposition parties to participate in elections will affect positively or negatively the readiness of the whole country in conducting the referendum in January 2011. The formation of the Referendum Commission, selection of its members, formulation of its laws, and other procedures are important activities that there should be no compromised on, and unlike the National Electoral Commission where the chairman of the Commission was deliberately nominated by the NCP, it is very important that the membership of the Referendum Commission is thoroughly studied and backgrounds and commitments of each individual would-be member to the spirit of the CPA must be ascertained before his/her name is forwarded.

CHAPTER TWENTY

# The History of the twin objectives: New United Sudan and Self-Determination

The background to this essay is traceable to exchanges of viewpoints that Dr Wathig Kameir, Dr Peter Adwok Nyaba, Dr Biong Kuol Deng, myself and others were involved during and after the Sudan People's Liberation Movement (SPLM) Second National Convention in May 2008, in which Dr Kameir shared with us and the leadership of the Movement that he had noticed during the convention's deliberations that there seemed to have been a drift towards the "South agenda" and less emphasis on the New Sudan as an over all vision for the transformation of the country during the interim period and beyond.

My submission however, was that the leaning towards "South agenda", if this is how it should be described, should not be considered as a new phenomenon in the SPLM political literature, in fact, it could be traced to the origins of the SPLM in July 1983, when the two groups that formed the nuclei of the SPLM/A disagreed, among other power struggle related issues, in Itang as to what vision and goals to be adopted for the struggle: the group led by late Dr John Garang, William Nyuon Bany, Kerubino Kwanyin Bol, Salva Kiir Mayardit and others contended that the struggle must be waged to liberate Sudan from the central governments' hegemonic politics, who were and had been marginalizing all the regions of the country and not only the South. For this group therefore, the problem was not a "Problem of Southern Sudan"; rather it was a "Problem of Sudan".

The other group led by Samuel Gai Tut, Akot Atem de Mayan, and William Chuol Deng argued that the liberation agenda should aimed at waging war against the central governments of Sudan to liberate Southern Sudan, since that has always been the main objective of the Southern Sudan struggle since 1955, whether under Anya Nya One or the Anya Nya two. They further contended that the bulk of the recruits who were in Bilpam were largely from Southern Sudan. To this group the responsibility of the Southern Sudan was to give hand to the recruits from other regions of Sudan who have joined the SPLM/A to liberate their regions or assist them to take over power in Khartoum.

These ideas were communicated to Col Mengisto Haile Mariam and the leadership of the Dergue through the former Governor of Gambela, Thowath Pal Chai and his colleagues, who received and hosted the leaders of the two Sudanese groups upon their arrival from Sudan and later on introduced and arranged for them an audience in Addis Ababa with the Dergue leadership in late June 1983 for them to present their case to the Ethiopian authorities, as a result of which the Ethiopian Government's support to the SPLM was later on based.

The emergence of the SPLM in Two Sectors in July 2005 was thus received with mixed reactions within the Movement and from outside:

The first school of thought argued that the decision by late Dr John Garang to appoint Abdel Aziz Adam El-Hilu and Pa'gan Amum Okiech as caretaker supervisors of the SPLM Northern and Southern Sectors was a breach of the SPLM Manifesto, whose value system presupposes that the SPLM is a national-centralized organization with clear vision of establishing a united democratic secular country, where citizenship is the basis of belonging to the nation of Sudan. According to the adherents of this view within the Movement, the establishment of two sectors in the SPLM was a contradiction to the spirit of the SPLM Manifesto which does not discriminate its members, irrespective of whether they are from the South, north, west or east, nor does it differentiate its members based on religion, region, race or ethnicity. Thus, establishing two sectors, according to this view, entails that the Movement has created two distinct power centers and two separate regional blocks with the potentiality of each creating its own political orientation and ideology.

The second school regarded the decision as a natural course of events and recognition that soon after the signing of the CPA, the SPLM was bound to deal with the issue of its presence in the North so that it consolidates its political presence throughout the country and ready itself to take over power once elections are carried out.

The third school looked at the decision as a reflection of an ideological reality that befell the SPLM since its first convention in April 1994, where the twin objectives of New Sudan and Self-determination were adopted as the basis for any future peace talks between the SPLM and governments in Khartoum. This school of thought contends that it was inevitable that the SPLM would allow the Northern Sudanese in its ranks to run the Movement in the North, as a precaution measure should it become the case that the South decides to secede; this group also argued that after 2011, especially in May 2013 when the SPLM convenes its Third National Convention, the SPLM in the north may emerge an organization of its own. This group further argues, why then excludes the Nuba Mountains and Southern Blue from Northern Sector? Or is it a forgone conclusion that these areas will become part of Southern Sudan after 2011, if South secedes, and when these areas carry out Popular Consultations?

From historical perspective, it seems that the SPLM/A chose the political and military options as means of transforming the old Sudan to the New Sudan out of necessity, having learn from previous attempts to resolve the problems of power relations in the country through peaceful means as were the cases in 1947, 1953, 1956, 1965, and 1972 were difficult processes. To the members of the Movement, as a liberation movement, the SPLM went through very difficult times and paid dearly in terms of material and human loss, to realize the breathing space that the Sudanese are enjoying today. Most observers seem to agree that the struggle, which was waged by the marginalized and progressive forces in the country was sustained by three important elements: The vision of the SPLM to transform the Sudan to create a better life for all and self-determination for those who deserve it; the resilience of the freedom fighters and their commitment to the cause; and the optimism and the support of the rural population and their commitment to the objectives of the struggle.

Moreover, the SPLM was a by-product of different ideas and challenges, most of which were put together and formed the basis of its Manifesto in July 1983. It was enriched by various historical and ideological trends, some of which formed ideological basis for the bulk of the SPLM/A recruits.

Furthermore, the SPLM/A struggle by and large started from the South and given that the majority of the fighters were descendants of the Anya Nya One and Anya Nya Two recruits meant that a new ideology has to be worked out with care: Fighting for unity in diversity or for an independent Southern Sudan.

Indeed, the period between 1984 and 1989 was an important period in the development of the SPLM/A as a liberation Movement. During this period, the ideological dilemmas that the Movement found itself in started to get clearer and the transformation agenda of the Movement began to make sense to a sizable number of its cadres, especially the politicized ones.

Observing from the procedures of the SPLM Second National Convention therefore, it seems that the chance that was availed by the Convention to deal with all the issues of ideological dilemmas inherited from the first convention in 1994, transformation agenda, governmental policies, short and long term strategies, policies on the deployment of cadres, developmental programs etc. was missed out. For example, a sizeable number of delegates were wondering why the leadership of the PLM did not look into the general situation from the perspective that the CPA was in fact a fulfillment of some major objectives of the SPLM, its Manifesto and therefore scrutinizing its implementation and assessment of the SPLM's organs' performances during the first three years of its implementation should have been a top priority?

If we look back to the history of the movement, we would notice that the internal ideological misunderstandings that the Movement had witnessed during the first eight years (1983-1990) of its existence were taken extreme by some members, some ended up in long detentions, the result of which was the split in the Movement in August 1991. That split was the first disturbing sign that the Northern members of the Movement saw as a threat to the unity of the movement, but most importantly a sat back for the realization of a New Socialist United Democratic Secular Sudan.

Unlike Suwar El-Dhab, Koka Dam, Sadig Al-Mahdi and Muhammed Miraghani initiatives of 1985, 1987 and 1988 consecutively, the Abuja rounds of talks 1992/1993 were by all standards the real beginning of internal dialogue within the SPLM as well as with the government in Khartoum regarding its options for the peace agenda. During these talks the SPLM factions entertained various options, but the most visible ones were: United federal/con-federal democratic Sudan versus self-determination for the Southern Sudanese. Before 1991, the debate within the Movement was not opened and most of times informal among colleagues, some being regarded as progressives, while others were seen as conformists. With regard to the main objective of the Movement, the message that the late Dr Garang gave to the recruits was that "for those of you who are interested in liberating the South, after you reached Kosti, you may stay behind and the rest of us will continue the struggle to liberate the rest of the country". What followed was exposure of what turned out to be complex ideological debate:

Firstly, what should the new Sudan look like: Is the New Sudan the old closed districts of the 1920s-black Sudan that includes the Nuba Mountains, Blue Nile and the South? What would the developmental/economic and socio-political/human security agenda of the New Sudan look like? Was the SPLM Manifesto geared towards achieving regime change in Khartoum or it was indeed a liberation struggle that was aiming at transforming the political and socio-economic life of the whole country?

Secondly, did Southern Sudanese accept the concept of 'marginalized' to include the then non-SPLM support basis such as Eastern Sudan and Nubia? Some argued that to a greater extend the answer was yes, as later on proven by the establishment of the Eastern Sudan Brigade, the Darfur Zonal Command under Commanders Abdel Aziz Adam El-Hilu and Dawud Yahya Bulad.

These debates and ideas were taken to Chukudum in April 1994, with clear picture of what took place in Nasir/Kongor and later on in Nairobi, Abuja I and II peace talks. The representatives from all the SPLM support bases went to Chukudum ready to discuss these ideas; as a result of which the twin concepts of the New Sudan and Self-determination were adopted as the basis for any future plan to resolve the conflict. Some of the key ideas that emerged during the First SPLM National Convention in Chukudum were recorded in its resolutions: Issues relating to what economic and political systems to be adopted during the interim period as well as human rights, transparency, socio-religious and cultural aspects of the New Sudan state were also identified. For those who were interested in an independent Southern Sudan, self-determination was offered.

These important debates were in fact reinforced by June 1995 resolutions of Asmara Declaration. In fact, the Asmara meeting of the leaders of National Democratic Alliance (NDA) gave the SPLM the opportunity to share its ideas regarding the transformation of Sudan, not only with like minded progressive forces in exile and in the country, but also with Islamic political parties and regional/international stakeholders. Issues relating to governance, wealth distribution, security and marginalization/self-determination were reaffirmed, and elections as the basis for transformation and participation of all shades of political organizations in the would-be new dispensation were also affirmed.

Yet, it was not clear cut in Asmara Declaration 1995 whether the transformation agenda of the SPLM was to be driven solely on the basis of the New united Sudan (voluntary unity) or it was also subject to readjustments and whether the apparent contradiction of accepting in principle the secession of the South, while continuing to advocate for a united democratic Sudan were the best options. It became therefore apparent that there were doubts, especially from the northern members of the SPLM, as far back as 1985, 1987, 1988, 1991, 1992, 1993, 1994, 1995 and 1998 about marrying voluntary unity and secession as twin objectives of the Movement.

Several efforts were made to reunite the SPLM-a unity that was based on the resolutions of the reconciliation talks in Nairobi between the two SPLM/A factions, Abuja rounds of talks, Chukudum Convention and Asmara Declaration: self-determination in conjunction with a united New Sudan became the agenda. Ironically, these efforts culminated in part in Khartoum Peace Agreement (KPA) in April 1997, which Dr Hassan Al Turabi and his party never meant to implement, and yet enshrined it in 1998 Constitution and the January 2001 Nairobi Declaration between the SPLM and Sudan People's Democratic Front (SPDF). These efforts were perceived to aim only at bringing about the unity of the Movement, but in terms of ideological manifestation of the movement's objectives and goals, these efforts resulted in contradictory direction of goals compared to those of the SPLM Manifesto of July 1983.

In August 1998 in Addis Ababa round of talks, it became clear that the SPLM had to face these internal ideological contradictions: what about the future of the 'northern Sudanese" freedom fighters who are members of the SPLM; questions relating to the status of Nuba Mountains, Blue Nile and Abyei, which were/are regarded as part of "political North"; the status of the south vis a vis self-determination-New Sudan paradigms, became points of contentions.

The reality in my opinion was that the SPLM leadership knew all along that there were bound to be contradictions in its agenda of calling for the establishment of a New Democratic United Secular Sudan and its attempts to solicit support outside Southern Sudan. The establishment of zonal commands in Darfur, under Cde Abdel Aziz and Late Bulad, the Blue Nile Command, and the Nuba Mountains Command, were attempts to persuade all those who doubted the political and ideological commitment of Movement to the liberation of the marginalized Sudanese from the grip of centralized-cultural domination of the centre to join the Movement. Did this approach work? Yes, the mobilization of these regions to adopt the new vision did work. However, in many ways, it was only in June 1995 in Asmara when it became clear that the price for the transformation of Sudan was bound to be too high, and must be paid for. Some argued ironically that the Self-determination, which was offered to Southern Sudan, which was supported by some northern political parties, was a price to keep the rest of the country intact.

The establishment of the Eastern Sudan or New Sudan Brigade in 1996/97 and the subsequent creation of alliance forces were seen by some as the emergence of what would be the SPLM Northern sector military wing. Late Dr John Garang was convinced that the New Sudan agenda was a reality within the social and political fabric of Sudan. Religion, race, and culture can be interpreted in different ways by different people, so according to late Dr Garang, a good Muslim can still fight for the freedom and good life of others, who even if they do not share one ideology or religion can still regard him/her as a comrade. This explains why Muslim and Christian Sudanese were fighting side by side to free themselves from tyranny and marginalization.

The realpolitic, however, has shown that region, ethnicity and culture are important aspects of identity in Sudan. The Declaration of Principles (DOP) in 1994 and later on the Machakos Protocol in July 2002 have revealed that the debates mentioned above did in fact influence the eventual separation of negotiation tracts between what was regarded as "Problem of Southern Sudan" and "Problem of Sudan" as represented by the Nuba Mountains, Abyei and Blue Nile.

Following SPLM decision to negotiate with the National Congress Party (NCP) for a peaceful settlement to the conflict, the National Democratic Alliance (NDA), which was a strategic ally of the SPLM/A was excluded from the negotiations, and new tract had to be created for the NDA in Cairo. Even the Eastern Front, also a strategic an ally of the SPLM/A, had to negotiate separately with the NCP in Asmara.

The concept of 'Marginalization", as the basis for the new understanding of Sudan's problems, was therefore fragmented into several pieces by the NCP ideologues.

The CPA was therefore an outcome of long debates, which sometimes were structured in formal meetings and conventions such as First National Convention and Asmara Conference, but quite often took the shape of informal discussions among cadres of different political formations.

What is witnessed today within the SPLM structures is a result of a contradiction that was destined to succeed if the leadership took note of the complexities earlier on before the CPA. It therefore came as no surprise that the Movement had to be divided into two sectors with each sector specifically tasked to cater for specific objectives.

What seems to be a dilemma is that all the marginalized shades of opinion understood and accepted the vision of New Sudan as articulated in the SPLM Manifesto. Each became part of it and fought for its realization.

The problem is that the vision seems to be so complicated in its formulations, especially at organizational levels of sectors and the difficulty of each sector to domesticate it in order to fit with its specific environment so as to concretize it without looking into those aspects that may be contradictory.

# References

Abuja Declarations, Abuja, Nigeria, May 1992/May 1993.
Adare Declaration, Adare, Scotland, September 1991.
Chand, David de. South Sudan: Claims for Self-Determination. Nairobi: August 1995.
Danorth, John. Report on the Sudanese peace process to President George W. Bush, April 2002.
Frankfurt Declaration, Franfurt, Germany, February 1992.
Koka Dam Declaration, Kokadam, Ethiopia, 24 March 1986.
Mabior, John Garang de. The Vision of New Sudan: Questions of Unity and Identity. Edited by Ghamer Wathig. Cairo: Consortium for Policy and Analysis and Development Strategies (COPADES), 1998.
"Machakos peace process: Southern Sudanese and the option of secession" Rayaam (Khartoum), 20 February 2004.
Machar, Riek. South Sudan: A History of Political Domination, a Case for Self-Determination. Nairobi: November, 1995.
Nasir Declaration, Nasir, Southern Sudan, 28 August 1991.
Ruay, Deng Akol. The Politics of Two Sudans. Uppsala: Nordiska Afrikainstitute, 1994.
Torit Declaration, Torit, Southern Sudan, September 1991.
Washington Declaration, Washington, DC, USA, 21 October 1993.
Asmara Declaration, Asmara, Eritrea, 23 June 1993.
Political Charter, Khartoum, Sudan, 10 April 1996.
Khartoum Peace Agreement, Khartoum, Sudan, 21 April 1997.
Nuba Mountains Peace Agreement, Nairobi, Kenya, 16 April 1997.
Fashoda Peace Agreement, Fashoda, Southern Sudan, September 1997.
Wunlit Covenant, Wunlit, Bhar El-Ghazal, Southern Sudan, 10 March 1999.
Blue Nile Agreement, Khartoum, Sudan, 1999.
Liliir Covenant, Liliir, Jonglei Region, November 1999.

Kisumu Declaration, Kisumu, Kenya, June 2001.
Dinka-Nuer Washington Declaration, Washington, DC, USA, October 2001.
Nairobi Declaration, Nairobi, Kenya, 6 January 2002.
Cease Fire Agreement in Nuba Mountains, Austria, 19 January 2002.
Machakos Protocol Framework, Mackakos, Kenya, 20 July 2002.
Memorandum of Understanding on Government Structure and Wealth Sharing, Nairobi, Kenya, November 2002
Ceasure of hostilities Agreement, Nairobi, Kenya, October 2002
Security Arrangements agreement, Naivasha, Kenya, September 2003
Wealth Sharing Agreement, Nairvasha, Kenya, January 2004.
Sudan Comprehensive Peace Agreement, Nairobi, Kenya, 9 January 2005.
Kameir, Elwathig. New Sudan: Towards building the Sudanese Nation-State. A paper presented at the General Congress of the Sudanese Writers' Union, 19 September 2006, Khartoum, Sudan.
Mahjoub, Husam Osman. Summary: Dr John Garang in the Carter Center, Atlanta, Georgia, USA, Wednesday, 20 March 2002.
Manifesto: Sudan People's Liberation Movement, Bilpam, 31st July 1983.
Sudan Interim National Constitution. Khartoum, Sudan, July 2005.
Vision and Programme of the Sudan People's Liberation Movement (SPLM). SPLM Political Secretariat, Yei and New Cush, New Sudan, March 1998.
Yoh, John G. N. Southern Sudan: Prospects and Challenges. Amman: Al-Ahalia Press, 2000.
_____, "Southern Sudanese dialogue and its impact on the implementation process of the Machakos consensus" Conflict Trends No. 4 (2002)
_____, Isolation, Unity and Secession: The evolution of political thought in Southern Sudan. Amman: Al-Ahalia Press, 2003a.

_____, "The Sudan: Long Road to Peace: Machakos Consensus during the Interim Periond: Part Two" Al-Neshra (Amman) 16 (2003b): 26-37.

_____. New Sudan' /'Two Sudans' Paradigms: Southern Sudan Contributions to Conflict Resolution in Sudan. Paper presented to a seminar in Max Planck Institute of Anthropology, Halle, Germany, 23 September 2003.

**John Gai Yoh** holds BA in Political Science and MA in political history from the American University of Beirut (AUB) and PhD in International Politics from University of South Africa in Pretoria. His assignments included Presidential Advisor on Education, Minister of Education, Science & Technology, Head of Government of Southern Sudan (GOSS) Southern African Liaison Office, Pretoria. He also served as South Sudan Ambassador to the Republic of Turkey. Was Resident Research Associate at the Royal Institute for Inter-Faith Studies, Amman, Jordan between July 1996 and May 2003 as well as lecturer at University of South Africa in Pretoria between June 2003-June 2007. He authored several works on Africa, East Africa, Sudan, international politics, conflict management and resolution, regional and international organizations, security and strategic studies.